CHRISTIAN THEOLOGY
BY
MILTON VALENTINE, D. D., LL. D.
Late Professor of Systematic Theology in the Lutheran
Theological Seminary, Gettysburg, Pa.

CHRISTIAN THEOLOGY BY MILTON VALENTINE

Copyright 2014 Just and Sinner. All rights reserved. The original text is in public domain, but regarding this updated edition, besides brief quotations, none of this book shall be reproduced without permission.
Permission inquiries may be sent to JustandSinner@yahoo.com

Just & Sinner
1467 Walnut Ave.
Brighton, IA 52540

www.JustandSinner.com

ISBN 10: 0692250336
ISBN 13: 9780692250334

Original publishing info:
COPYRIGHT, 1906,
BY THE LUTHERAN PUBLICATION SOCIETY
Rev. Milton Valentine, D.D. LL.D.

CONTENTS

PART II
REDEMPTION: OR THE MANIFESTATION OF GOD IN CHRIST FOR HUMAN SALVATION...7

DIVISION I
THE SOURCE OF SALVATION...7

DIVISION II
THE PERSON OF THE SAVIOR...21

CHAPTER I
THE INCARNATION...21

CHAPTER II
THE DIVINE-HUMAN CONSTITUTION OF CHRIST...43

DIVISION III
THE STATES OF CHRIST...65

DIVISION IV
THE WORK OF CHRIST...71

CHAPTER I
THE WORK OF CHRIST AS PROPHET...73

CHAPTER II
THE WORK OF CHRIST AS PRIEST...74

CHAPTER III
THE WORK OF CHRIST AS KING...119

PART III
THE APPLICATION OF REDEMPTION...131

DIVISION I
THE HOLY SPIRIT AS APPLYING REDEMPTION...131

DIVISION II
MOVEMENTS OR STEPS IN THE SPIRIT'S APPLICATION...135

CHAPTER I
THE CALL OR VOCATION...135

CHAPTER II
REPENTANCE AND FAITH...143

CHAPTER III
JUSTIFICATION...149

CHAPTER IV
REGENERATION AND CONVERSION...169

CHAPTER V
SANCTIFICATION...189

DIVISION III
THE MEANS OF APPLYING REDEMPTION...193

CHAPTER I
THE WORD...197

CHAPTER II
THE SACRAMENTS...205

CHAPTER III
THE CHURCH (*Ecclesiology*)...251

DIVISION IV
THE LAST THINGS (*Eschatology*)...269

PART II
REDEMPTION: OR THE MANIFESTATION OF GOD IN CHRIST FOR HUMAN SALVATION

THIS brings us to the central reality in Christian theology. It is that which determines its entire view. Its consideration must include, I. *The Source of Salvation;* II. *The Person of Christ;* III. *The States of Christ;* IV. *The Work of Christ.* The discussion of these topics, together with that which comes in Part III., viz.: the *Application of Redemption,* will take us through what is known as Soteriology, *i. e.,* the entire doctrine of salvation. Soteriology, it will thus be seen, presents two sides of saving work, one objective and the other subjective: the objective being the work of Christ in His offices of redemptive atonement and provision; the subjective, the inner work of the Holy Spirit, awakening faith, renewing the heart, and sanctifying the life of men. Both together issue in a divine recovery of men from sin and their restoration to eternal life.

DIVISION I
THE SOURCE OF SALVATION

This must be viewed in connection with the great truth of the Trinity of God—the adorable Three in One and One in Three. For it includes the relation of the Father, the Son, and the Holy Spirit to the grace which furnishes salvation and makes it real. It is well to observe and fix in mind how this doctrine of the Trinity supplies the very *basis* on which the whole movement of salvation comes into view. We cannot understand the gospel of redemption unless we keep in mind this divine mystery of the Trinity of God, and adjust our conception to it.

    i. What then does the source of salvation include?

    (*a*) *The free love, good-will or grace of the Father in giving and sending the Son to be the Savior of the world.* The Son Himself states it: "God so loved the world that He gave His only begotten Son, that whosoever believeth on Him should not perish, but have everlasting life" (John 3:16; also 1 John 4:9, 10, 14). The fountain of grace flows from the Eternal Father's heart. This grace of the Father is not, however, to be thought of as excluding the equal gracious love of the Son, but as involving it, according to the Savior's own words: "I and My Father are one." "Verily, verily, I say unto you, The Son can do nothing of Himself, but what He seeth the Father do; for what things soever He doeth, these the Son also doeth in like manner" (John 10:30; 5:19).

This union of the Father and the Son in the fountainhead of salvation has been made, by some theologians, the ground for inserting in their theology the idea of a special "covenant of redemption" between the Father and the Son. The representation is connected with the Augustinian or Calvinistic conception of an eternal election and predestination of a portion of the race to eternal life. It teaches that these elect were covenantly given by the Father to the Son, that He should, in human nature, obey and suffer redemptively for them and bring them all to eternal life. The Scriptures quoted for it are chiefly John 17:2-12; Isa. 53:10-11; Ps. 89:3. For this concurring *love* of the Son for the sin-ruined race, the Scriptures are clear, but for the intrusion of a limitation of that love to an elect few, in any such specific covenant, the passages are no adequate proof.

(*b*) *The voluntary incarnation and work of the Son for the redemption of mankind* (John 1:14; 10:17-18; 1 Tim. 3:16; Heb. 1:3; Phil. 2:5-11). Though Christ appeared only nineteen centuries ago, His relation to salvation is not so late a thing, but was before the foundations of the world (Eph. 1:4; 1 Pet 1:18-20; Rev. 13:8). His coming was promised, from the lapse of man into sin, as the "seed of the woman" who should bruise the serpent's head (Gen. 3:15), and became the determining truth for all the revelatory movement, guiding the whole providential plan and progress of sacred history (Matt 8:11; Luke 15:4-6; 19:10).

(*c*) *The free gracious work of the Holy Spirit*, carrying Christ's work into effect (John 14:15-17; 15:26; 16:7-14; Rom. 8:4; Eph. 4:30). This inclusion of the Holy Spirit's coming and work in the source of salvation needs always to be borne in mind. That source is the love of the whole Godhead.

2. This love or good-will of God as the source of salvation *is properly distinguished as both general and special.* Such distinction is required by the whole tenor of the Scripture statements on the subject, and is clearly brought to view in 1 Tim. 4:10: "We trust in the living God, who is the Savior of all men, specially of them that believe." It rests in the fundamental fact that men, as the subjects of

salvation, are free-agents and may thwart the actualizing of the full aim of that love.

(*a*) God's *general* love or benevolence is, thus, the action of His goodness in which, moved by compassion for the whole race, *He has made provision* for forgiveness and recovery to true life. This provision is for all, and is the basis for a universal, unrestricted gospel call and offer of grace. Its characteristics, as represented in the Scriptures, are:

First, it rests on no merit in those for whom it acts. It is self-moved in its own compassion, in view of the need—not deserts—of the race as fallen under the dominion and curse of sin.

Secondly, it provides for *all* men a free, full salvation, and offers it, not in appearance only, but in reality of saving aim or purpose, without respect to the number or individuals that may accept it. "God so loved the world," etc. (John 3:16).

Thirdly, inasmuch as this general love actually forms and executes a scheme of provision to save all who accept it, Christ becoming the "propitiation for the sins of the whole world," and "tasting death for every man," it is rightly called also the "*general will*" of God, in the sense of a real desire, *i. e.*, it is His "will" that *all* should be saved. Ezek. 33:11, "As I live I have no pleasure in the death of the wicked," etc. 1 Tim. 2:4, "Who will have all men to be saved, and come unto the knowledge of the truth."

Fourthly, it is *conditionate*, *i. e.*, it wills salvation only as men in their personal freedom shall consent to or comply with the conditions on which it is possible and is offered. It is not an absolute force or compulsion, but a relative provision and persuasion. The salvation is founded in *Christ*, with issue dependent on securing, on the human side, the needful conditions or relations for the provisions passing into saving effect. It means the putting of all men into a "salvable," though not necessarily a "saved," state.

Fifthly, it is rightly called antecedent love or will, as it goes before the application of its provisions to men, and is irrespective of the number or particular persons who may accept them.

(*b*) The *special* love or will of God appears in the grace which *actually bestows* salvation upon those who in faith accept the provided forgiveness and reconciliation. While the divine love, in earnestly desiring the salvation of all men, has prepared the way to it for all without exception, yet that same love accomplishes a further special work in and for those who yield assent to its offered grace and submit themselves to its saving aim. God's universal love provides salvation for all; His special love confers it on those that do not reject or neglect it. "For this is the will of My Father, that every one that beholdeth the Son and believeth on Him should have eternal life" (John 6:40). "God so loved the world that He gave His only begotten Son, that *whosoever believeth* on Him should not perish but have everlasting life" (John 3:16). "He that believeth on the Son hath everlasting life, and he that believeth not the Son shall not see life" (John 3:36). This special or particular love or will of God is, therefore, the same as His electing or predestinating love or will. Like the general benevolence, it is marked by distinct characteristics.

First, it is, as usually and rightly described, *consequent* will, as based on the divine foreknowledge of the faith which accepts the proffered salvation. "Elect according to the foreknowledge (πρόγνωσιν) of God" (1 Pet. 1:2). "Whom He did foreknow (προέγνω) He also did predestinate to be conformed to the image of His Son" (Rom. 8:29). This characteristic harmonizes the action of His loving will with the essential constitution and nature of man, whose faculty of self-determination is an indestructible element of the "image of God" incorporated in his being. The divine action does not set aside the intrinsic nature of men in ethically saving it.

Secondly, it is *limited*, because the number foreseen as believing is smaller than the whole number of those for whose salvation provision has been made. This limitation is proved by the various Scriptures which assure, on the one side, the universality of the redeeming provision, and, on the other, the condition of its passing into effect, as John 3:16; 2 Thess. 2:12; 2 Pet. 2:1.

Thirdly, it is an *approving* or *complacent* love or will, in contradistinction from God's general love, which is primarily compassionate. While compassion continues in this special love, there is in it a divine complacency in the believer's faith, an approval of his new relation to right and duty. It is the love of the Father that clothes and jewels the recovered son. This approval, as over against the condemnation of the sinner's previous state, is implied in John 14:22–23; Rom. 8:33, 38, 39; John 16:27.

Fourthly. This special love is *fixed, immutable, eternal.* The theology of absolute predestinarian teaching claims advantage for its view in that it excludes all the uncertainty, the possible change or failure of salvation thought to be involved in its being made contingent on men's faith and perseverance. It assumes that the *absoluteness* of the eternal election or fore-ordination, its entire separation from the contingency of human free-will, is necessary to the believer's proper assurance of hope. But there is no need to break with the Scripture truth that conditions salvation upon its free acceptance by the human will that is at the same time able to neglect or refuse. For the salvation of all believers is eternally and immutably sure apart from that kind of fore-ordination. It is easy to see this by keeping in view the twofold truth in the relation between the general or universal and special will of God. (1) God's purpose, which expresses the plan and end of the redemptory provision, viz.: to *save* every one that believeth, is *fixed and immutable*. This is set forth in all the Scriptures that explain the scope and terms or way of salvation. The "purpose" is that which in Eph. 3:11 is declared to be "eternal." When "the called according to His purpose" are spoken of (Rom. 8:28) we are not warranted in interpreting the phrase as referring to a certain number of individual persons arbitrarily appointed to be saved, but to such as accept salvation according to the only rule or order in which the whole Gospel conditions its possible realization. The "eternal purpose," as we have seen, has the breadth of a "propitiation for the sins of the whole world," a Savior 'tasting death for every man,' opening a way to "have mercy on all," expressing the divine "will that all should be saved," but nevertheless moving in an orderly way (κατὰ τάξιν) to its consummation, according to the essential law of faith and submission. (2) The persons chosen in this special love are *unchangeably certain*, in that God's knowledge or foreknowledge which sees in advance who will believe, is *infallible*. To suppose that election or predestination on the basis of foreseen faith and perseverance in faith might leave the salvation of believers uncertain or insecure, would imply that God did not correctly foresee their faith. But since it is His eternal and immutable purpose to save every believer, and His foreknowledge of those who believe is infallible, His special love to all of them is eternally and immutably certain and fixed.

This *certainty* is, thus, not to be viewed as something grounded in an arbitrary appointment, from eternity, of the individual to salvation, irrespective of the use or exercise of his personal will under the call and working of provided grace. It is to be viewed as the foreseen result of the gracious provision and offer as the issue turns upon human acceptance or rejection. The foreknowledge is intuitional, *not causative*. To know, or foreknow, is one thing—to cause is quite another. This is a psychology of even human experience every day. Prescience and causation are not identical.

Christian Theology

This special love or will, which becomes identical with the changeless certainty of the believer's salvation, rests—so it is meant—in foreknowledge, not in an arbitrary absolute fore-ordination.

It is true that Calvinistic theology has maintained that "foreknowledge is not mere vision, but includes a purpose which is the ground of what is foreseen." It is said that "the divine decree is the necessary condition of the divine foreknowledge. If God does not first decide what shall come to pass He cannot know what will come to pass."

But we are here face to face with the whole subject of *Predestination*, about which earnest controversy has been carried on in almost all periods of the Church, and the different interpretations of which have largely influenced the type of theological systems. Considered in itself, or without regard to other features of doctrine which tend to associate themselves with the differing views, there are but two great systems of teaching on this point in the theology of Christendom. The two systems are distinguished by the answer they give to the question: Are the divine decrees or ordinations by which certain individuals are elected to eternal life and others doomed to eternal misery, *respective* or *irrespective, conditional* or *unconditional*, based on *foreknowledge* or *not*? The systems separate as they answer affirmatively or negatively. Prior to Augustine, although the subject had not yet specially come into speculative theology, the Church Fathers were wont to view election as based on the divine prescience. Augustine, in the fifth century, contrary to his own earlier view, developed an unconditional predestination. It was a distinct innovation in the Church's teaching and his own. His ability and eminence secured a large following, and his innovation has had a wide sway in theology ever since, especially as reorganized by Calvin and incorporated in various Protestant Confessions. The Lutheran Church, however, while adopting the characterizing features of Augustine's exposition of original sin and of anthropology in general, declined to accept his doctrine of absolute predestination, and followed the consensus of the earlier Church writers—fore-ordination based on foreknowledge of faith. From the midst of Calvinism, though not without contact with the already developed Lutheran position and influence, there subsequently arose a reaction, known as Arminianism, against the system of irrespective predestination. In itself this is not, indeed, entitled to the rank of a third view; yet because of its prominent place in modern theology, and of its having, by peculiar doctrinal alliances and developments, become a somewhat distinctive designation, it seems proper to give it a separate consideration. We must, therefore, look at these three forms of presentation.

THE CALVINISTIC VIEW OF PREDESTINATION

Those who hold the view thus designated frame it with some variations in elemental features. Calvin himself went beyond the definitions of Augustine, and formulated the theory in a fullness and rigor of specifications that make his presentation a guide to the extremest forms of the system. It will be enough to see the system, irrespective of modifying variations. It sweeps away the whole distinction we have traced between the general benevolent will of God and His special or particular will, as involved in the source of salvation. It disallows a twofold conception and relation of His will. It includes these points:

1. Predestination means the absolute decree of God, from eternity, by which, of His own will He freely and unchangeably ordained whatsoever comes to pass.

2. Election is part of predestination, another part being preterition or reprobation.

3. The true and only source of salvation is the predestinating election of certain particular individuals of the race to eternal life. Everything that comes after this, *i.e.*, the incarnation and work of the Son and the work of the Holy Spirit, justification by faith, sanctification, etc., is but the eternally and immutably fixed steps of progress through which the divine decrees pass into accomplishment.

4. This election and predestination are not in view of any foreseen faith or anything else in the elect person, but solely and purely out of God's good pleasure and free grace.

5. These particular persons so elected or chosen are then redeemed by Christ, effectually or irresistibly called or brought to Him, and preserved in Him to final salvation. These are the *only* ones redeemed by Christ or effectually acted on by the Spirit.

6. The rest of mankind are passed by or reprobated in God's sovereign plan and choice, and ordained to wrath for their sins.

In this system, therefore, the relation and destiny of each and every man is fixed and settled from eternity to eternity by the secret, sovereign, immutable predestinating will of God—a predestinating will not based on any foreknowledge of either faith or unbelief, but becoming itself the reason and reality of foreknowledge. The reason why some are not saved is that it is not God's will to save them.

THE ARMINIAN VIEW

This is best exhibited in the five articles of the *Remonstrance*, prepared and presented by the followers of James Arminius to the Synod of Dort (1618–1619). It came as a natural reaction against the one-sided and excessive development of Augustinianism by Calvin and his adherents—a development that denied the gracious aim of redemption with respect to all men. The points of Arminian teaching may be condensed thus:

1. God, by an eternal purpose in Jesus Christ, has determined to save every one who, by grace, shall believe in Him, and to condemn the unbelieving or incorrigible.

2. Agreeably to this, Christ died for all men, obtaining for them, if they so believe, forgiveness and redemption.

3. Man is, in and of himself, utterly helpless to save himself, and needs to be born again of God in Jesus Christ, by the Holy Spirit, in order to think, will, and work what is truly good.

4. While, for the beginning, continuance and accomplishment of the regenerating and saving work, prevenient, assisting, awakening, and co-operating grace is indispensably necessary, yet such divine grace is not irresistible.

5. To those who are, by true faith, incorporated in Christ is given power to continue in the Christian life, overcoming sin and Satan and all temptations to the end. The question whether they are capable of neglecting grace so as to become again void of grace and perish, is left for further consideration in the light of Holy Scripture.

This is the view of primitive Arminianism as it shaped itself in revolt against the Calvinistic formulation of predestination, and began to mark the doctrinal position of churches on this question. In large measure the primitive form continues to express the faith of the churches classed as Arminian. But at times, in some countries, churches and organizations assuming the Arminian profession have impaired its integrity by questionable or malforming adjuncts. It is not from these occasional and exceptional depravations from its true and pure self, that the *system* is to be conceived or judged. In its early form it allied itself closely to the conception prevalent in Lutheran theology.

THE LUTHERAN VIEW

Milton Valentine

The Augsburg Confession is silent on this subject. It is, however, presented at length in the Form of Concord, and elaborated by our dogmaticians from the Reformation to the present. The Lutheran view involves essentially the following distinct points, which are held to express fundamental and explicitly revealed truths of the Gospel.

1. On the basis of the numerous passages of Scripture which state the substance and offer of the Gospel, it distinguishes between the *general or universal benevolent will of God* toward all men, and His *special will* toward all the individual persons who yield to the offered grace. The general or universal will, which is understood to be the "eternal purpose" of Eph. 3:11 (πρόθεσιν τῶν αἰώνιων), provides salvation for the whole world in and through Christ's mission and work, opening it to the free acceptance of all and assuring it to every one that believes. This "purpose which He purposed in Christ" includes the entire system of means for offering it to men without distinction and making it effectual in those that accept—an eternal purpose formed out of God's own pure, free grace in view of no merit in man. This, at the very beginning makes salvation *wholly* "of grace." The word "predestination" is sometimes used in the wide scope of this full purpose. That is, His "eternal purpose," as purposed in Christ, *includes* the action of *His universal* benevolence, making redemptive provision for all men, truly desiring and seeking the salvation of all who will yield to the divine love and permit the renewal of grace—as taught by Christ Himself, and in many emphatic Scriptures: "God so loved the world that He gave," etc. (John 6:51; 12:27; Ezek. 33:11; Rom. 11:32; 5:18–21; 2 Cor. 5:14, 15, 19; 1 Tim. 2:4–6; 4:10; Heb. 2:9; 1 John 2:2). The bearing of these and other passages will be traced specifically hereafter in another connection. In a narrower sense the word predestination is applied to God's *special* will, *i.e.*, the ordination of each and every "believer" to salvation. In this use it becomes equivalent to "election" or "fore-ordination" (Rom. 8:29; 1 Pet 1:2).

2. The Lutheran view maintains the essential and necessary distinction between God's *foreknowledge* and *fore-ordination* or *predestination*. It accepts the statement in Rom. 8:29: "Whom He did foreknow He also did predestinate to be conformed to the image of His Son," and 1 Pet. 1:2, "Elect according to the foreknowledge of God," in their plain and necessary sense. This foreknowledge is not causal, but purely prescient, knowing beforehand what will come to pass in the free action of moral and responsible agents. It neither

necessitates the things it foresees, nor rests on any predestination of them. For the apostles, in the words recited from Rom. 8:29, and 1 Pet. 1:2, clearly distinguish between 'foreknowledge' and 'predestination,' and set the one in relation to the other. And they both base the predestination or election on the foreknowledge. Prescience and fore-ordination are thus discriminated as distinct and definite parts of the divine action, and their relation to each other is clearly revealed.

3. God's electing predestination is in foreview of *faith* and obedience of faith, or the sinner's yielding to the call and provided grace of redemption. The Scriptures already quoted distinctly affirm predestination in foreview of *something*. When we ask the Word of God *what* it is that thus underlies election or predestination, the answer comes from a thousand passages, '*Faith*'. "He that believeth shall be saved." Everywhere throughout the Gospel, this is emphatically declared to be the thing on which the sinner's salvation hinges. The doctrine of predestination is thus seen to be in clear and complete harmony with the gospel message and the responsibility of men with respect to acceptance of it and obedience to it. Predestination according to foreseen faith (*intuitu fidei*) is vital in the Lutheran view, being organically involved in the determinative principle of justification by faith. The "*eternal purpose*" (πρόθεσις) to provide and give salvation, and the '*foreknowledge*' (πρόγνωσις) of those who would believe, and the *predestination* (προορίσμος) are all related. The predestination is based on and in the purpose, through foreknowledge. That is, the "purpose" expresses the plan in its provisions and necessary requirements, the "foreknowledge" the prescience of its acceptance, and the "predestination" the election as based on that foreknowledge. The divine predestination, in this its specific and true sense in relation to personal salvation, is thus no "*secret decree*," but the open declaration of the Gospel, that "whosoever believeth shall be saved." The Form of Concord simply reiterates the Scripture truth when it says: "Predestination is not to be sought out in God's secret counsel, but in the word of God in which it is revealed."

4. Predestination has respect only to *believers*. This is according to "Whom He did foreknow," *i. e.*, as believing, "He did predestinate," etc., and "elect according to foreknowledge." "For God hath not appointed us to wrath" (1 Thess. 5:9).

5. The whole of man's salvation is truly and purely "*of grace.*" Not only in this that the entire scheme and all its parts are of God's

pure mercy and unmerited love, but that faith itself, in which the believer fulfills the conditions of salvation, is God's "gift," *i. e.*, as the result of all the provisions and movement of God in His saving work and action. Man is naturally and truly helpless. The faith becomes possible only by enabling grace.

6. *Condemnation* comes only as a result of refusal or neglect of men to *exercise* the faith for which God affords the needed grace. "The reason is that they either do not at all hear God's word, but willfully despise it, close their ears and harden their hearts, and in this manner foreclose the ordinary way to the Holy Spirit so that He cannot effect His work in them, or when it is heard, they consider it of no account, and do not heed it. For this [that they perish], not God or His election, but their wickedness is responsible." "The cause of this contempt of the word is not God's knowledge, but the perverse will of man, who rejects or perverts the means and instrument of the Holy Ghost, which God offers him through the call, and resists the Holy Ghost, who wishes to be efficacious, and who works through the word, as Christ says: 'How often would I have gathered thee together and ye would not.'" Grace labors in vain upon a resisting material. The human will, in and of itself, helpless to believe and obey, is mighty enough to resist or neglect.

COMPARISON OF THE LUTHERAN AND CALVINISTIC VIEWS
A comparison of the Lutheran and Calvinistic views shows them strongly antithetic, in the following features:

(1) The Lutheran makes predestination *relative, respective,* or *conditional;* the Calvinistic, *absolute or unconditional.* (2) The Lutheran distinguishes between *foreknowledge* and *predestination;* the Calvinistic either identifies them, or makes predestination conditional for foreknowledge. (3) The Lutheran makes "God's eternal purpose" *causal for salvation only;* the Calvinistic makes it the cause of both *election and reprobation, or preterition,* finding the sole explanation of the different destinies of the saved and the unsaved in the absolute causality of God's sovereign will or good pleasure. (4) The Lutheran holds grace to be provided, free and open for all, but not irresistible; the Calvinistic, that it is a real provision only for the elect, and as to these the grace is irresistible. (5) The Lutheran view makes the certainty of the believer's salvation unchangeably sure through God's foreknowledge; the Calvinistic, through the absolute decree of predestination or fore-ordination.

Christian Theology

The exegetical principle under which Lutheran theology determines the Scriptural conception of predestination is that the great fundamental explicit provision and message of the Gospel should decide for us the sense in which the terms fore-ordination and election are in various places used. The emphatically declared provision, with the terms of proclamation, as the "revealed" Gospel, must be held as both *basal and true*, as over against any conception of "secret decrees" that would limit it and make it something less. To interpret the comparatively obscure Scripture statements about election or predestination into conceptions that qualify and diminish the literal and ever-resonant offer and promise is arbitrary and illegitimate. The actual truth of the Gospel on this question cannot be approached and reached by any interpretation assuming that God has a secret will in conflict with the revealed message and promise. And what do we find this message and promise to be? Clearly and unequivocally: "God so loved the world that He gave His only begotten Son, that whosoever believeth on Him should not perish, but have everlasting life" (John 3:16); "He sent His Son to be the propitiation for our sins," and "He is the propitiation for our sins, and not for ours only, but also for the sins of the whole world" (1 John 4:10; 2:2); "God was in Christ reconciling the world to Himself," etc. (2 Cor. 5:19–21); "Come unto me, all ye that labor and are heavy laden, and I will give you rest" (Matt. 11:28); "him that cometh to me I will in no wise cast out" (John 6:37); "God hath concluded them all in unbelief that He might have mercy upon all" (Rom. 11:32); "The Lord is not willing that any should perish, but that all should come to repentance" (2 Peter 3:9); "Jesus ... should taste death for every man" (Heb. 2:9). And in view of His own sufferings and death, Christ's direction is "that repentance and remission of sins should be preached among all nations" (Luke 24:47). In view of this explicit Gospel, the Form of Concord is fully justified in saying that the Scripture, " 'Many are called, but few chosen' cannot be rightly interpreted as if it meant God were saying: 'Outwardly, through the word, I indeed call to my kingdom all of you to whom I give my word, yet in my heart I intend it not for all, but only for a few; for it is my will that the greatest part of those whom I call through the word should not be enlightened or converted, but be and remain lost, although through the word in the call I declare to them otherwise.' For this would be to assign to God contradictory wills. That is, in such a manner it would be taught that God, who is, however, Eternal Truth, would be contrary to Himself." The analogy of faith must guide where questionable interpretation of some passage would set the meaning of God's message so untrue to the required form of delivery.

As specific reasons for clinging to the teaching of our Church on this subject, as against the Calvinistic contention, we may justly fix these chief points in memory:

1. It is most thoroughly and consistently Scriptural, as the few passages quoted indicate. During the first four centuries of the church the interpretation of the Scriptures did not discover the doctrine of an absolute predestination, with its limitation of the aims of grace. Augustine's teaching of it was an innovation in theology. Though given large currency through his pre-eminent leadership and influence, and put into favor in connection with his great service of overthrowing the unscriptural anthropology of Pelagius, this absolute predestination has never been part of the Church's œcumenic interpretation or doctrine, but, on the contrary, has been largely dissented from even in the times of its greatest sway; was increasingly rejected through the scholastic period; never recognized in the Greek Church; has been almost eliminated in the Roman Catholic; rejected in the Lutheran from its organization at the Reformation; and in the Reformed Churches of Protestantism, whose theology, mainly through the constructive and dogmatic force of Calvin, it has specially dominated, the reaction expressed by Arminianism has come with widening prevalence, and has demanded and secured revision and softening modifications. We are sustained by the immense preponderance of the Church's Biblical exegesis.

2. It magnifies the *grace of God* in the redemptory work and message when we understand the scope of His "eternal purpose," according to which men are called, as a "purpose" that has made full and real provision for the salvation of all men and desires its acceptance by all on equal conditions of assent or faith, instead of a dwarf-purpose to save only a favored few through a provision made for them alone. Without doubt, it is "of grace," the unmerited goodness of God, that He opens the way to salvation and rescues even a part of mankind or a single soul from guilt and sin. But the grace of God is enlarged and exalted to its supreme richness, fullness, and glory, when, as the Scriptures represent it, the Gospel is viewed as a divine call to a free, full provision for all who do not refuse that call and the Holy Spirit's illumination and persuasion through it.

Christian Theology

3. It enables us to preach a *free* Gospel, to offer and urge a really provided salvation, a redemptive preparation and opportunity intended for the acceptance of every one.

4. It throws the *responsibility of failure* of salvation clearly and wholly on the rejecting and neglecting sinner. Through the remaining power of "will" in corrupt human nature for "*resisting*" the gracious call and its enabling grace, the tremendous reality of responsibility becomes a fact. The responsibility connected with "neglect" of so great salvation needs to be pressed upon men. The sin of unbelief is one against "light" meant for personal guidance. This is the condemnation, that light is come into the world, and men do not respond. But it is difficult for men to appreciate their responsibility upon a point that is unchangeably settled by the eternal decree of God—the guilt of failing to accept what has never been provided or meant for them.

5. In the Lutheran view is seen the best and fullest vindication of both the goodness and the justice of God: His goodness in a love that desires the salvation of all men and has made redemptory provision for forgiveness and eternal life for all; His justice or righteousness in the ruin that results from the rejection or neglect of the grace to which men are called by Christ and the enabling work of the Holy Spirit in the Gospel (John 3:16-19; 15:22-24; Heb. 10:28-29). Man having his essential being in free moral agency, his return from sin cannot be reached except through the consent of his will. God has done all that Love can do to secure that consent.

DIVISION II
THE PERSON OF THE SAVIOR

From the Source of salvation in the Triune God, the "eternal purpose" has moved into realization through the manifestation and work of the Son. The movement of God's love, in answer to the need of man in sin, appears in the coming and person of the Christ, as shadowed forth and assured through the divine self-revelation recorded in the Old Testament and completed in the New. Our examination of this brings us to the study of what is distinctly designated *Christology*. It seeks to understand the truth or reality as to Christ's being and attributes.

Christology will be found to present the pivotal reality that determines the whole nature, authority, and power of Christianity. It may well be said, as it has often been, that "Christ *is* Christianity," in the sense that what He is decides and assures the very essence of what it is. The turning point, as between Christianity and all other or variant religions, comes into view in the correct answer to the question: "What think ye of Christ? Whose Son is He?" (Matt. 22:42). About this, its enemies, seeing the place of its mysterious power, have gathered their persistent assaulting force. But, happily, while the truth here is indeed the innermost citadel of Christian theology, it is, of all its truths, the strongest and most invincible. The subject opens to view, in a consideration of that wonderful event in which Christ's Person was constituted, the "Word made flesh." "When the fullness of time was come, God sent forth His Son."

CHAPTER I
THE INCARNATION

This is to be viewed as the miracle of miracles, the greatest of all, central to all, carrying all others with it. It puts into time and the world, in a sovereign and unique way and for a specific and "eternal purpose," the Presence and action of the Supernatural—all preceding miracles and theophanies being its anticipatory and preparing action, all succeeding miracles and powers its continuance and reverberating movement. As warranted by the Scriptures, and as held in the faith of the Church, this incarnation of the Son of God

Christian Theology

was the superlative event in the world's history, all earlier providential movement being in view of it and adjusted to its significance, and all after ages receiving its sublime increment of divine self-manifestation and saving goodness, as concerned with the realization of its intention and destined to exhibit its issues. It was, and forever is, God's supreme thought and act of love for the world.

1. As we approach the subject, it is important that we fix in mind some essential presuppositions involved in the incarnation. These are conditional truths. There are at least three of them.

(*a*) The first is such a constitution or reality of the Godhead as to make an incarnation possible. Christian theism universally maintains that God can make Himself known in His power and doing. A God unable to manifest Himself would not be God. This generic self-revelation is properly understood as implied in the designation "Logos" or Word, applied to the only begotten Son. Compare John 3:16; 1:1–4; Heb. 1:1–2. It is thus placed in close connection with the entire doctrine of the Trinity, and belongs indeed to its profoundest import. Evidently the incarnation, as a specific act of self-manifestation, must be viewed as resting back upon the same interior reality in the Godhead. The supreme unity consists with distinctions. The truth of the Trinity is thus a logical presupposition of the incarnation. This mystery in the interior of the being of God holds the possibility and power of the divine self-manifestation according to His will. And in thinking of the "second Person" of the Trinity as representing to us the Divine Being or nature as self-disclosing or self-imparting, we must bear in mind that this is equally true, whether the self-expression be in creative action or in redemptory sacrifice of love. For by "the Word all things were made," before human need was answered by the grace of the incarnation. The doctrine of the Trinity is no mere speculative truth, without practical import, but a vital reality, underlying the whole creational and providential economy of the world.

So practical is it, that wherever it has been denied or obscured nearly all the great truths in the order of the divine love and grace, emphasized in the Scriptures, have fallen away with it, especially those pertaining to the way of salvation, such as the true Deity of Christ, the incarnation, the atonement, regeneration, etc. We do not say that without the Trinity an incarnation would have been absolutely impossible; for Sabellianism is not metaphysically inconceivable. But we say, first, that the Scriptures clearly link the incarnation with the tripersonality of God (John 1:1–4, 14, 16, 27; 17:5, 24, 25; Rom. 8:32; Heb. 1:6); and secondly, that the truth of the Trinity furnishes what may be termed a natural basis for it, in the mysterious being of the one absolute eternal God, opening to us an intelligible view of the distinctly declared economy of salvation.

(*b*) A second presupposition is such a constitution of *humanity* as to make the incarnation possible. It is especially proper that this precondition should be looked at fairly. For plausible difficulties may be suggested. The incarnation of God in a human being is so strange an event, so foreign to the regular order of life, as to justify a raising of the question of its credibility. It is not necessary that it should be relieved of mystery, since mystery meets us everywhere in the immense realm of reality. But impediments to faith may be removed, if the mystery can be shown to be not essentially an impossibility nor incredible. And this can be done.

The asserted possibility may, indeed, be made to seem doubtful if the confessedly great difference between God and man be allowed to hide from view the truth of likeness, as taught by revelation and sustained by reason. If, through theories of man's origin, or discrediting appearances in his actual condition, he is reduced to classification with mere animal existence, with no given life or endowment constituting him in any attributes kindred with his Creator, with nothing but positive antithesis to the Divine Nature, then, indeed, we could not conceive of an incarnation as possible. There would be nothing in common, no elements of the same kind of being which could coalesce in conceivable union. But in proportion as consideration is given to the unique place of man in relation to all other created existences on earth, confessedly marked by essential characteristics exalting him far above all other species of living beings, unquestionably constituting him alone an intelligent, rational, free moral personality, after God's own "image," capacitated to "think His thoughts after Him," to understand Him through His works, and to enter reverently into fellowship with His will and purposes, in love, obedience, and worship, the difficulty diminishes. God is absolute, eternal *mind*. As God formed human personality essentially in *created mind*, finite, indeed, but with powers in the likeness of His own nature, it would seem that immeasurable possibilities of kindredship, affinity, and communion may have been provided for. If God is the Absolute, perfect Spirit or Mind, man is created finite spirit or mind. Revelation declares the human mental or spiritual faculties to be after the mold of the

Christian Theology

divine, and the deepest scientific thought of the ages sustains this conception. We are fully entitled to believe that God has made thought, love, and volition essentially the same in man as they are in Himself. Though infinite in Himself, and only finite in humanity, they are correspondent realities, creatively adjusted in man for true knowledge, obedience, and fellowship. The "religious nature" of the race, to which philosophy and science are giving special emphasis, is but an expression and witness of this. It is heard in the forever repeated cry of Augustine: "O God, my heart was made for Thee, and cannot rest till it finds Thee." This revelation of *likeness* of capacities, not equality of them, is the point specifically involved in the possibility of the incarnational union.

The evidence of features in common between the Divine Nature and the human, as thus established, is supported by further truths integral in the teaching of revelation. The reality of "image and likeness" carries us to the truth of *sonship* in man's nature and position. And this human sonship is most wonderfully found resting back on the Trinitarian reality of an "Eternal Sonship" in the being of God Himself. We find that the work of creating humanity in features of filial likeness to God, is by the same Son who comes to redeem. Sonship, constitutional and ethical, appears to be the ultimate principle that underlies the creation. The principle of sonship is in God Himself. The physical world is not an end in itself, but is relative, as means to spiritual ends towards which is the outflow of God's love. Thus the divine love cannot rest in creative activity through the successive stages of the inorganic and animal spheres till it has embodied in its works a realm of self-likeness in personal constitution and character. "Man is made in the image of God, because he is the analogue in creation of the uncreated Son whose working is in him consummated."

In the light of this analogy of human personality with the divine, the incarnational assumption of humanity, while not divested of mystery, is relieved of contradictoriness. Nothing forbids the conception that the Infinite Spirit, the Eternal Revealer, may take the limited human capacities within the movement of the Infinite Divine, so as to blend the two natures into a single personality. God could not communicate to the human nature self-existence; for that would obliterate the very distinction between Himself and created being; but He, conceivably, can communicate all communicable attributes to the Divine Human Person within the measure in which humanity has been capacitated to receive, which shall fill them with the Divine. We are without warrant, then, should we undertake to say that the Logos could not personally identify Himself with and reveal Himself through humanity. The eternal Son of God could unite Himself with the humanity of created sons of God formed after the divine likeness. Very significant is it, too, that we must add that, along with the fact of man's "religious nature" with its deep sense of need of divine fellowship, and, perhaps, growing out of this, different ethnic natural religions have developed belief in some manifestation of God in human form. Incarnation has not been contradictory to, or even wholly alien from, human thought. The logic of the mighty need has been the logic for the conclusion involved in the conception. Incarnations appear in the Buddhas of Buddhism and the Vishnus of Brahminism; but paganism's false concepts of both Deity and man made possible only gross and distorted ideas of the divine reality.

(c) The third presupposition *is the fact of sin*. The incarnation was not for creational work, but redemptory, providential, soteriological. Though part of the eternal purpose, it was eternally in foreview of the lapse of man out of the status and competence which creation had given him. It was to recover to the life and destiny for which God had formed and capacitated him.

The question arises, could not the needed recovery have been accomplished except through this divine incarnation? To this we answer: First, that no man can know the possibilities of God so as to be able to say that it was absolutely impossible. But, secondly, no one can show that it could have been accomplished in any other way than through the incarnate Son. Reasoning from the actual fact, we are entitled to conclude, with Augustine and general Christian thought since his day, not only that it was an eminently fitting way, but also that it was really necessary. God does nothing in vain. And we are warranted in adding that, as nothing else than the manifestation of God's love in such an approach and appeal to the human soul as was presented therein, and in all that it involved, can be conceived of as victoriously inspiring faith and restoring real communion between God and man, we are justified in the conclusion that just this was the first great condition of human salvation. The denial of the true Deity of Christ, reducing Him to a mere man or some semi-deified creature, leaves the rupture made by sin unabridged.

But a further question has been raised and claims notice: Whether sin was its sole ground, or whether it does not rest on a deeper and non-contingent basis, and would have taken place if sin had never entered the world? Speculative theology has here and there been setting forth the conception that the incarnation rests not alone in a redemptive need and work, but belongs to God's creative work and its necessities as required for the perfecting of human nature, irrespective of the fall. The first appearance of this is found in the scholastic age, in Rupert, Abbot of Deutz, a theologian of mystic temper. He was followed in its maintenance by Alexander Hales, Duns Scotus, Raymond Lullus, John Wessel, and others, and earnestly confuted by Thomas Aquinas and Bonaventura. At the Reformation Osiander adopted it. No advocacy of it is found during the period of Protestant dogmatic theology until its modern revival by Lieber, Martensen, and Dorner, in Germany and Denmark, and by some "progressive" theologians in England and our own country. The aim of the theory is to offer what its supporters think better ground for speaking of Christianity as the "absolute religion," by lifting it above the contingent basis of dependence on man's lapse into sin through abuse of his freedom. And while its advocates formulate it in different types of view, these have converged in conceiving of the incarnation as an immanent necessity of the love of God, or as involved in the best possible creation—as determined by the necessities, not of redemptive need, but creative love. Its fundamental and supreme end is the *perfecting* of man, while subordinately and incidentally it answers the need that has contingently occurred through sin. But neither the Scriptures nor reason authenticate this view, as a few points suffice to show.

To begin: the asserted *necessity* of the incarnation for "perfecting humanity," apart from man's fall into sin, is a pure assumption. The intimation that God's "creative" action was incompetent to perfect His creative work according to His "purpose," has no warrant in Scripture or reason. The anthropology of both the Old and New Testaments negatives the idea. It represents man as actually made "in the image and likeness of God," declared "very good "(not "*a torso*," simply pointing to the future, "merely destined" to ethical goodness, as Dr. Dorner puts it), called a "son of God" (Luke 3:38), placed, in fact, in living fellowship with God. He was endowed by creative love and power for all that he was to become and enjoy. When the regenerative and restorative work of redemption is defined by St. Paul, it is in being "*renewed* unto knowledge—after the image of Him who created him, in righteousness and true holiness "(Col. 3:9–10; Eph. 4:24). Christ Himself puts it as "being born again"

(John 3:5). The only perfecting function asserted for the God-man is with respect not to unfallen, but fallen men, and for these marked as a *restoration* into the "image and likeness "with which human nature was originally endowed. The Headship of the "second Adam" exhibits a necessity for a *redeemed* humanity, not for the natural as something which God's creative power failed adequately to endow or put in right and necessary relation to Himself.

Perhaps the evolutionary hypothesis of the genetic origin of man and the unity of creation may seem to some to give a scientific place and justification to the asserted necessity of this completing step. Dr. Dorner's suggestion concerning the original man, that the creative work made him "innocent" but "*not yet pneumatic,*" might appear thus to obtain real force. It might be imagined that the genetic origin from physical and animal existence failed to endow with a true πνεῦμα or pneumatic principle, and that nothing short of a personal incarnation in humanity could confer it. It is said: "More stress is laid in recent theology upon the cosmical relations of the incarnation. The old truth of the natural headship of Christ receives new significance in view of modern theories of the origin and unity of creation. If theistic evolution be assumed, the Christ is not dethroned, but exalted as the goal of the whole ascent of life, the end and completion of all conceivable development, the perfect Man, beyond which there can be none higher, the Head of all, in whom Humanity is raised to the throne of Divinity, the second Man, who is the Lord from heaven." But the intimation in this representation is gratuitous, that the necessity of the incarnation was primarily to help out the failure of the eternal Son, by whom "all things were made" (John 1:1–3), by *creative* power to endow man with spiritual or pneumatic principle. It not only reflects on God's creative work as inadequate, but is compelled to abandon the very principle of evolution to which it appeals. For that principle, even theistically viewed, is that the creative and perfecting processes are purely *naturalistic, i.e.,* found simply in the forces and interactions of nature under law. From monera to fish, from fish to reptile, from reptile to mammal, from brute to man, with whom Christianity has come to deal, the process is naturalistic only. When Professor John Fiske, as its prophet for the "destiny of man," interprets theistic evolution, he finds, as we have seen, the reality of what theologians term "original sin," in the incomplete evolution, as "the brute inheritance which every man carries with him"; and he sees redemption and regeneration in such further transformation that "nothing of the

Christian Theology

brute can be detected in him; the ape and the tiger become extinct." The process of natural evolution is thus the true progress toward salvation—'the creation and perfecting of man being the goal toward which nature's work has been all the time tending.' In locating the primary direct function of the supreme *miracle* of the incarnation in the necessity of completing the creation of man, this new theology, we repeat, contradicts the evolutionist principle itself, that the formative and perfective cosmic powers belong to nature by original divine constitution and reach their goal by simply *natural process*. Whatever may have been the *mode* of God's creation of humanity, there is no warrant for assuming that it was left without its right endowment for its high position and blessed life. And still further, it must be noted that should human nature *per se* be thought necessarily to require incarnation for right endowment, must we not, on parallel logic, hold that the perfecting of the nature of angels demands it in their nature also? But an apostle declares: "He took not on Him the nature of angels."

But further, the Scriptures positively give another and different reason for the incarnation. They make sin its distinct presupposition. The given relation is: "incarnation in order to redemption." Everywhere from the *proto-evangelium* in the forfeited Eden to the song "unto Him that loved us and washed us in His blood" in the new heavens of the restored state, the explanation of the glorious phenomenon presented in the person of Christ as "God manifest in the flesh," is declared to be the world's need of a Savior. Take the classic text in which Jesus Himself expressed the whole Gospel of the divine love: "God so loved the world that He gave His only begotten Son, that whosoever believeth on Him should *not perish*, but have eternal life" (John 3:16). The object in view was that men might not "perish" in want of that regeneration just spoken of to Nicodemus. Jesus makes the affirmation still more explicit when He says: "The Son of man has come to seek and to save that which was lost" (Luke 19:10). Again, He is come "to give His life a ransom for many" (Matt. 20:28). He pictured His own mission and the reason for it in the parable of the lost sheep—the fact of its being lost forming the definite and alone ground of His leaving the ninety and nine and going after the wandering one. Christ's own distinct answer, thus given, why the Word was made flesh and dwelt among men, thenceforward clearly formed the regulative conception on the subject in the minds of the apostles, and it is the monotone of of their statements throughout the Epistles. "For what the law could not do," writes St. Paul, "in that it was weak through the flesh, God, sending His own Son in the likeness of sinful flesh, and for sin, condemned sin in the flesh," etc. (Rom. 8:3). "But when the fullness of the time was come, God sent forth His Son, made of a woman, made under the law, to redeem them that were under the law, that we might receive the adoption of sons" (Gal. 4:4–5). "Since then the children are sharers in flesh and blood, He also Himself in like manner partook of the same, that through death He might bring to nought him that had the power of death, that is the devil; and might deliver all them who through fear of death were all their lifetime subject to bondage. For verily not of angels doth He take hold, but He taketh hold of the seed of Abraham. Wherefore it behooved Him in all things to be made like unto His brethren, that He might be a merciful and faithful High Priest in things pertaining to God, to make propitiation for the sins of the people" (Heb. 2:14–18). Could it be more definitely and explicitly stated than it is here, that the revelation of the Son in human nature had its great end in His *priestly* action, to *make propitiation for sin?* "Faithful is the saying," further explains St. Paul, "and worthy of all acceptation, that Christ Jesus came into the world to save sinners" (1 Tim. 1:15). "To this end," declares St. John, "was the Son of God manifested, that He might destroy the works of the devil" (1 John 3:8). "Herein is love, not that we loved God, but that He loved us and sent His Son to be the propitiation for the sins of the world." "And we have beheld and bear witness that the Father hath sent the Son to be the Savior of the world" (1 John 4:10–14). Many other passages might be quoted. Indeed, the web and woof of the Gospel representation is woven to this pattern.

It is to be borne in mind that all this is but the culmination of the voices that, in the long centuries of the Old Testament preparation, had been prophesying of the needed Messiah as the Immanuel, God with us. From the first and all through, the promises marked the coming blessing as a Deliverer, a Savior, through whom the sinful and guilty might have hope. His mission was centralized in a royal priesthood, His work typified in altars and sacrifices, in atoning and reconciling blood, in self-offering, in being bruised for men's iniquities, and making intercession for the transgressors. Through great preparing dispensations, the people had been taught that the promised One, who was at once the seed of the woman, the Son of David and the Son of God, was coming that He might bruise the serpent's head, and by the one offering of Himself for sin forever

Christian Theology

perfect them that believe; so that when John the Baptist discovered in Jesus the long-looked-for Messiah, he but expressed the ages of divine shaping thought in announcing Him and His mission in the characterizing terms: "Behold the Lamb of God which taketh away the sin of the world" (John 1:29). Thus we have the spirit of prophecy in the Old Testament, the words of Christ Himself in the New, continuously and constantly, instead of seeing and announcing a reason for the God-man back of sin and redemptive need, connecting the divine coming with the "eternal purpose" to provide salvation for fallen man.

It is but fair to note that several Scriptures have been offered in behalf of the new view. They are: Eph. 1:9–12, 22, "Having made known unto us the mystery of His will, according to His good pleasure which He purposed in Him unto a dispensation of the fullness of the times, to sum up all things in Christ, the things in the heavens and the things upon earth; in Him, I say, in whom also we were made a heritage, having been fore-ordained according to the purpose of Him who worketh all things after the counsel of His will; to the end that we should be unto the praise of His glory, we who had before hoped in Christ ... And He put all things in subjection under His feet, and gave Him to be Head over all things to the Church, which is His body, the fullness of Him that filleth all in all"; and Col. 1:15–17, "Who is the image of the invisible God, the first-born of all creation; for in Him were all things created, in the heavens and upon the earth, things visible and things invisible, whether thrones or dominions or principalities or powers, all things have been created through Him and unto Him; and He is before all things and in Him all things consist." Now it seems to us impossible to read this new ground of the incarnation out of these passages without first reading it in. There is neither distinct assertion of it, nor fair implication of it. For they simply declare relations of the Son to other orders of intelligences than man—relations of creation and government—without even a suggestion that these relations have come only by virtue of the incarnation, or that the incarnation was necessary to them. The Logos, of course, by becoming the God-man, is none the less thereby the eternal Son in whom all things consist, their natural Head by creation, under whose dominion they are forever. There is no assertion that it has been through the incarnation that the Son became or eternally is the Head of the angels, or that only thus He became revelatory of the Godhead to them or the center of their union in God. Moreover, the incarnation for *redemption* is the only consistent idea that will explicate the apostle's statement of Christ's purpose to "sum up," "gather together again" (ἀνακεφαλαιώσασθαι) all things in heaven and on earth. The ἀνα, *iterim* "again" in the compound word points back to a state in which no separation as yet existed. The disharmony came by *man's sin and fall*. The redeeming work of Christ, annulling this disharmony, re-establishes the unity of God's kingdom in earth and heaven. The gathering together is "in Christ." He is the central point of the union. But it takes place by the recovery of *man* and the necessity was *redemptive*. There is not a word in all this that legitimately implies that the harmonization of the things in heaven and earth, or the gathering of them under one blessed headship, required the incarnation apart from the lapse of humanity. To connect the necessity of a God-man with the placing of the *angels* in right harmony would not only be *per se* singularly inept as implying that *man* is the center about which the things in heaven are to be summed up, but utterly incongruous also with the non-relation of the purpose of the incarnation to the angels clearly indicated in the declaration: "Not of angels doth He take hold, but He taketh hold of the seed of Abraham." These texts, critically examined, give no different conception of the incarnation from that for redemption. The most that can be claimed for them is that, if the theory we are studying were elsewhere distinctly taught, they *could* be interpreted in accord with it. But in themselves they are utterly inadequate to establish it.

The theory, moreover, is unnecessary for the very purpose for which it has been formulated and urged—a supposed better and absolute basis of Christianity. The supposed gain is illusory. If the aim is to lift the reality of the God-man out of all relation of contingency into that of eternal certainty and sure divine purpose, this, in all essential features, clearly belongs to it without this new view. As we have seen, the prevailing understanding of the Scriptures has been that they teach that God's foreknowledge, whether based on fore-ordination or not, is absolute and eternal. It covered the fall of humanity and the need of redemption as completely as it did the purpose of creation; and this at once gives the same absolute certainty to the redemptive basis as belongs to the creational and perfective. For all theology acknowledges that creation is a free action of God—not an absolute reality like the immanent activity or *opera ad intra* of the Trinity. Absoluteness of that kind is not sought or supposed in the necessity for the

Christian Theology

incarnation. The only absoluteness is that of the free eternal purpose of love in Jesus Christ. And as the foreknowledge of God covered the future fact of sin as truly as the creation, though He stood in a different causal relation to the two, His love could act as absolutely in the purpose to redeem as in the purpose to create. Each purpose was a purpose of free love, and eternally chosen in the same absoluteness of love's foresight and free fore-determination. Redemptive Christianity is the "absolute religion."

Further, transfer of the motive of the incarnation to the creative aim would take from it the unique and incomparably inspiring significance it has as a *specific revelation of God's love to recover and save a self-ruined and undeserving race*. No merely cosmic working can disclose such a view of the reach and possibilities of the divine goodness. It has, indeed, been urged that since the incarnation is so transcendently the world's greatest exhibition of God's love, it is something that cannot reasonably be supposed to have been left contingent on human sin. But the impressive fact is rather that it is just in its relation to the necessities of the race as self-ruined and guilty in sin, that it *becomes* such an unequalled exhibition of the heart of God that we have no calculus to measure it. The sore heart of a lapsed humanity, struggling in the faith that has caught a glimpse of the vision and hope it offers, is not easily ready to surrender it. It has even an apologetic value, as having in itself the very reason why we may believe it. The soul opens in confidence toward God through the very thought of such supremely Godlike goodness. There is a correspondence between means and end. "The incarnation, apart from the *cross of redemption*, would lack precisely that revelation of God's love which is to us the most immediately impressive and soul-subduing—His yearning compassion for the unworthy." "God commendeth His love toward us in that while we were yet sinners Christ died for us" (Rom. 5:8). It is this all-surpassing vision of redemptory self-manifestation that has inspired the mind and shaped the songs of the Church, breathing out even in the rapt strains of "*O felix culpa quae talenm ac tantum meruit habere redemptorem,*" as being a vision that more than compensates for the damage done by sin, and forms the supreme environment of the moral universe. The ecstatic strain is no bewildered concession to sin, but a recognition of the superlative reach and triumph of God's love. And it is in line with the truth of the incarnation for recovery, that philosophical thought is beginning to obtain, if not a solution of the mystery of moral evil in the world, yet glimpses that offer some light for the problem.

For it is conceded that the problem is inseparably connected with God's creation of free personal beings capable of abuse of freedom in wrong-doing. Such creation, indeed, raised creature existence into attributes kindred to God's own life, with correspondent fellowship and blessedness. But, as already pointed out, with this supreme endowment, in His "image and likeness," and its correspondent exaltation of the world system above the mere aggregations of matter—"things," or forms of material or physical motion—into the sublime realm of intelligence, reason, ethical character, and the blessedness of holy communion in love, came also necessarily the possibility of the misuse of freedom in sin. The elevation of life into this realm involved the possibility of lapse into moral evil. But God, as we must conceive, could not find His true measure of satisfaction in a universe of mere mechanics and incapable things, unable to respond to creative love or share in its meanings. The only kind of creature that could satisfy a Being of absolute personal goodness would be a creature capable of the highest form of excellence, in filial relation and blessedness. "Creation, to be agreeable to Him, must be of creatures like Him; spirit as He is Spirit, intellect as He is Intelligence, love as He is Love." The material creation is only relative and subsidiary. "The only creation worthy of a personal God is a universe of persons," freely obedient to duty and love, respondent to their motives, and advancing in the high life of free goodness.

Some further things need to be distinctly perceived. (1) God's purpose in forming a creature world in the supreme grade of exaltation of life and excellence, was neither to introduce sin nor as *necessitating* it. At the fullest import, sin thereby becomes a possibility, to the *actuality* of which through creature will, God's will is an eternal moral antagonism. He neither created sin nor any necessity for it; on the contrary, He incorporated in the dowry of a moral personality kindred with His own, a law of utter condemnation of it and of absolute obligation to righteousness. (2) If the ethical world-system is, indeed, the best, and the only one worthy of God, His eternal self-consistency and goodness forbid us to think that He could then, by acts of preventive interference with freedom, have secured against the possibility of any but right moral choices. For such system of control would annihilate the very principle of free self-determining personality. The intervention would be destruction. The lofty grandeur of self-moving spiritual life in holy love would be lost in a show of will-less automata. (3) The term "permission," often used to state God's relation to the entrance of sin, needs distinct interpretation before its use can be true to the truth. It suggests a degree of "consent" that cannot possibly have been involved. "Nonprevention" would better express the reality, as accordant with the principle of responsible freedom in which He Himself had constituted human life. The moral law, with its behests and prohibitions, had been written in that life. The moral elevation had been given for blessed preservation and its fellowship of holiness. The creature's use of it for sin was a direct antagonism to God's will or eternal purpose of creative love, and God's attitude permitted the sin in no more positive sense than simple abstention from physical prevention. Sin is eternally that with respect to which God says to those made in His image of freedom: "Thou shalt not." (4) But here, from the incarnation, enters light upon the mystery of unprevented creature disobedience. While God did not, foreseeing the disobedient purpose, arrest it by annihilation of the creature freedom which His wisdom and love had created, and, going back upon His plan, drop His world-system down to the low grade of impersonal things, with no capacity of fellowship in thought, aim, or love, He *did*, just as truly as He fulfilled His purpose to create with foresight of a possible or even actual fall, also, in the same foresight, determine to establish a providential administration of redemptive grace and recovery of the fallen, through this remedial incarnation and its otherwise unreveealable love. The true theodicy of creation must include, with the foreseen possibility of sin, the predetermined incarnate manifestation of love for restoration of moral life. God thus gave the universe the supreme revelation both of His love and of His opposition to sin. He turned the creature's self-ruin and guilt into occasion for transcending creative goodness by the new glory of the compassionate and self-sacrificing goodness of redeeming love. He thus added to His creational expression against moral evil, in the ethical behests made constitutional for guidance of human freedom, the infinitely surpassing expression of antagonism to it given in the incarnational and redemptory administration for salvation from it. Though God could not fail creationally to lift the world-system up into the worthy range of ethical life, nor retract the system by annulling freedom, yet in His infinite resources of wisdom, power, and love, He could establish a providential economy of recovery through motives appealing to personal freedom itself.

Milton Valentine

The incarnation stands for this whole economy of provision and persuasion for man's return from self-wreck to the true relation and life to which his creation looked. It has its appropriate agencies, means, and spiritual influences. "Marvelous was the absolute primal creative love, which made something, nay, everything, out of nothing. But still greater is redeeming love, still greater is God as the Redeemer, inasmuch as He conquers the contradiction of Himself (Heb. 12:3), the enmity of sin, by His divine *love of His enemies, or grace.*"

This view explains and justifies the fact that the conservative evangelical theology of our day is increasingly emphasizing the incarnation. Its significance and value are more and more clearly seen. It is viewed not only as a necessary prerequisite to the teaching, ministry, and atoning sufferings of Christ, but as itself, in its place and aim, the sublimest and most assuring revelation of the holy character and love of God. In it, sin-smitten and enslaved humanity is given a vision of His goodness and beneficence, than which nothing can be conceived more impressive or appeal more mightily to the soul for abandonment of sin and new life in righteousness. It is a vision the world cannot afford to lose. Yet over against this supremely needed, significant, and inspiring truth is the fact that evangelical theology is facing an active movement appealing to science and philosophy against acceptance of it Materialistic evolutionism and idealistic monism or pantheism, also evolutionistic, have been elaborating cosmogonies that, even if claiming to be theistic, wholly exclude from the creative process for both the world and man any forces but those that operate under the form of natural causation, and leave no place for any direct divine working or supernatural manifestation in the world—God forever remaining, either apart from it, an absentee God, or pantheistically self-revealed in it, in all its naturalistic forms and individualities of being, but without any direct, miraculous self-manifestation. This teaching deletes the whole supernaturalism of Christianity, to which the incarnation pre-eminently belongs. In the law of cosmic creation and procedure God is regarded as self-barred from all direct working or transcendence of natural causation. We are told: "The modern perception of the uniformity of nature and the unbroken domain of law makes the idea of miracle inconceivable, save in the line of natural causation. We do not, and we ought not to expect God to act otherwise than in accordance with those modes of His action which we have learned to designate natural law." If natural law be

Christian Theology

understood, as rightly, the unbroken uniformity of causation established by God's creational will and work, the incarnation, the redemptive self-manifestation of God, is absolutely excluded from His administration, or is strongly discredited to faith, and we are pointed to Christ only as the divinest of men and the best religious teacher of the world. The miracle of the incarnation is eliminated from Christianity, and Christianity is reduced to a natural religion, though the highest that human thought has thus far read from God's self-disclosure in nature. No wonder that conservative theology resists these destructive urgings, based only on speculative science or pantheistic theorizings, tending to darken out of sight this vision which the incarnation gives of God's redeeming love and saving aim for humanity—the vision that, above all others, has been the inspiring power of Christianity and remains the supreme appeal to the human soul to forsake sin and turn to righteousness.

2. The Historical Preparation for the Incarnation claims some notice. As redemption realizes the divine purpose from the foundation of the world, all history preceding the incarnation was a progressive providential preparation for it, prophesying of it, and providing the fitting conditions for it. This historical movement, in accordance with the two great courses of human history, presents two lines of development.

(*a*) In the *ancient pagan* world, humanity, through its rational faculties and religious constitution, so far as the depravity of its sinful state had left the elements of its spiritual constitution still operative, was striving to realize the divine fellowship for whose right possibilities the incarnation was ordained, but without true success—only exhibiting its semi-conscious *need* of this form of God's self-manifestation. Glimmerings of the conscious need of it appear in almost every system of heathen religion, showing man's sense of broken fellowship with his Creator, and developing proof of the greatness of the evil and the inadequacy of human effort to secure and make known the remedy. Through the experiences of highest civilizations and natural culture, as well as of grossest ignorance and degradation, was given demonstration of the necessity of some divine self-revelation that should show the true way of salvation, and prove to be Love's victorious power of moral and spiritual recovery.

(*b*) Among the *Jewish people*, with its special providential dispensation and training, the preparatory unfolding was of a much more direct and positive kind. The movement looked to providing the immediate conditions for the divine advent. The incarnation was voiced, as a keynote, in the very first promise that assured of grace and redemption to fallen man: "The Seed of the woman shall bruise the serpent's head." In clearer and clearer statements the great fact took shape in Jewish history. It matters not that through want of spiritual apprehension the people failed to see the distinct and full import of the unfolding truth, and largely misconceived the real purpose of the Messianic coming as well as the true lineaments of the promised Savior. The mystery of the divine event had to await explanation and true understanding through its realization. Enough that it was foretold and marked for sure identification. The preparing Promise ran through centuries of prophecies and reminders, assuring a Divine Deliverer or Savior, with His great offices and work defined and emphasized (Gen. 12:1–3; 22:18; Deut. 18:15; Ps. 2; Isa. 11; Isa. 53; Micah 5:2; Dan. 2:44; 9:26; Mal. 3:1–4). Supporting and interpreting the Promise itself there was an established order of national worship in a system of typical sacrifices and institutions pointing to His redeeming mission, and surely identifying His personality.

This double preparatory movement deserves some measure of emphasis. In the pagan line, the insufficiency of naturalism, or man's native powers without direct revelation or special divine redemptory provision, was demonstrated through a length and breadth of history justly entitled to settle that question for the whole race and for all time. The issue certified human helplessness before the task. For it sufficed to test and bound the ability of the human faculties in relation to the transcendent realities and problems involved in the question of God's forgiveness of sin and recovery of free moral agents to loyalty to Himself and holiness. The solution lay in a realm beyond the reach of these finite faculties, and *ex necessitate* could be made known only by the All-knowiug God through a supernatural teaching. The culture of the human mind and its scientific findings in the physical and intellectual realms of the cosmic universe, can never of themselves reach up into the realm in which that problem lies. So the pagan trial was wide enough and long enough not only to develop for that time a prevalent sense of human need of more light by direct divine manifestation—a condition favorable to the reception of the Gospel—but also to furnish a permanent demonstration of the insufficiency of naturalism.

Christian Theology

In the movement of supernatural providence in the Old Testament history, the aim was more specific and direct, looking to and positively effecting the best attainable conditions for a recognition of the divine reality, a response of faith in the incarnate Son and the gracious redemption, and for successful planting and initial work of Christianity in the world. Though this preparation was of supernatural order, yet, as it had to be secured in harmony with human free agency, it required the use of means in the way of instruction and spiritual influence. It trained the Jewish mind into the great truth of monotheism; it clarified and exalted the divine attributes, especially those of righteousness, power, eternity, and supremacy, yet assured God's goodness, compassion, and grace; it taught and disciplined the moral and religious consciousness into increasing sense of responsibility to Jehovah's law and the guilt of disregard of its requirements; it sought through its system of sacrifices and confessions of sin to beget a true conception of God's holiness as necessarily to be kept uncompromised in remission of transgressions; and through prophecy assured of the sending of salvation, in a Messiah-Redeemer who should bear the people's iniquities and bring in a dispensation of forgiveness and holy life. This development was through the Church or community of Old Testament believers, which contained enough "prepared people" (Luke 1:17) to receive the accomplished redemption, and form the ordained agency for the evangelization of the world.

Of course the incarnation is to be viewed primarily as a fact rather than a doctrine. If it is a truth at all, it is the truth of a great historical event, the greatest of the earth's history, an event that, in the divine order, stands back of the Scriptures which record it, and of the doctrines that rise out of it. It needs to be perpetually emphasized that Christianity is not a system of thought-out truths, or a philosophy of history or of life. It is grounded primarily in a series of supernatural facts, of which this is the center or heart—the reality that integrates and inter-relates them all. The coming of the God-man, His teachings, miracles, sufferings, death, resurrection, and ascension, underlie all the doctrines that are legitimately derived from them. The power of Christianity is not in the power of abstract truth or theory, but of redeeming action, as believingly apprehended. Our first business with this truth is, therefore, to recognize it as a fact, certified in its appropriate and fitting evidence; only as thus certified and vindicated are we to seek to understand

and trace out the doctrinal realities or practical truths involved in the meaning and bearings of the stupendous event

3. THE MODE OF ITS BECOMING A FACT.—As an event, we must conceive of the mode of incarnation according to its historic records as divinely stating it. As in the supreme sense it was a supernatural movement, our imagination cannot inform us of it. From the divinely-given account of it we may mark a number of essential features or elements in the mode.

(*a*) As it was a process in which the Son of God voluntarily surrendered a state or condition that belonged to Him as divine, and took on Him human nature, He entered it through a *human birth*, becoming the "seed of a woman." In this He assumed true and full human nature, the humanity in which the race is constituted. He became "Immanuel," God-with-us (Gen. 3:15; Luke 1:30–33; Gal. 4:4; Heb. 2:14). He entered personally into the life of the race.

(*b*) The conception was without human fatherhood, the immediate power of God, the Holy Spirit, super-naturally effecting the quickening for birth (Matt. 1:20–23; Luke 1:35; Mark 1:1; John 1:14; Heb. 2:16). Though skeptical criticism has lately been seeking to discredit the genuineness and historic authority of the Scripture passages asserting this feature, known theologically as the "miraculous conception," the general and best critical judgment sustains both their genuineness and credit. Moreover, the fact itself, so far from being incredible and inviting unbelief, is so thoroughly accordant with the supernatural character of the incarnation, and, we may say, justified and even demanded by its generic principle and bearings, as to commend it strongly to acceptance. For, as simple suggestions in this line, we may recall that birth of woman is itself and alone sufficient to convey true and actual "human nature" in its integrity; that ordinary or natural generation carries the inheritance of a corrupt moral condition; that such a corrupt nature would have voided the possibility of Christ's presenting a sinless and perfect manhood, either as the divine model, or as a sinless sacrifice for redemptive atonement; that it is not difficult to conceive that God, for spiritual ends so sublime and glorious as those centered in the incarnation—the event of divine eternal counsel, about which the earth-history revolves—should work this miracle of a human birth from woman by supernatural power, but entirely in keeping with the whole transcendent movement; that, furthermore, it is *easy* to conceive that in this virgin birth—this birth entirely due to the "power of the Most High"—the miraculous power, thus efficiently present, could and did annul the transmission of the element of sin as no proper part of true human nature, and the transmission of which to the Christ would have been in conflict with the revelation of a sinless and perfect Savior, whose consciousness the sense of sin never invaded during His whole life, nor led, so far as we know, to a single prayer for forgiveness.

(c) The Son of God, "the Word," "Logos," was a Person, self-existent in the Trinity from eternity, but His human nature had no personal or individual existence prior to its creation in the incarnation. The act did not consist in uniting two personalities already existing, a divine and a human, but two *natures*—the Son of God uniting with His own Divine Nature also the fullness of the nature belonging to mankind or the seed of Abraham. The mode of the assumption acted creatively for the true reality of that nature, yet appropriated it from the midst of the race, the union realizing the theanthropic personality, the God-man.

(d) In forming the union the Divine Nature was *active*, the human *passive*. It was entirely God's work in behalf of a humanity wholly helpless. "He took on Him the seed of Abraham" (Heb. 2:14–17). "He took on Him the form of a servant" (Phil. 2:7).

(e) These things imply, further, that it gave the personality of Christ from the *divine* side. The Son had eternal personality in the Trinity, carrying it in the assumption of the incarnate state. The personality of the human nature, if realized, was not self-given, but consequential on the completion of the act or process of incarnation. The question whether, in the completed union in the divine-human person of Christ, the human nature as therein perfected attained real personality, or remained "impersonal" (*anhypostasia*, non-personal) as often represented since John of Damascus, must be left for a later page.

(f) It involved a certain reality of *self-limitation* or emptying of Himself on the part of the divine Son. This is distinctly taught us (Phil. 2:6). "Being in the form of God, ... equal with God "in the fullness of the divine attributes and activities, He, in some way, "emptied Himself" (ἑαυτὸν ἐκένωσεν) not of the divine *essence* (οὐσία) or *nature* (φύσις) with its attributes, but of that "form" of being; and, further, in this state "humbled Himself" to an order of service and "obedience unto death." He accepted mysterious limitations which involved an actual human life in human form, development, and experiences, all the privations, trials, labors, and sufferings that marked His history to death on the cross and descent into the grave. While the constitution of human nature after the "image of God" removes the incredibility of the incarnation, this self-limitation thus involved, nevertheless, covers a mystery for whose speculative or theoretical explanation theology presents us with somewhat differing views. This need not disturb us. Human inability to point out the actual mode cannot be claimed to annul the fact, inasmuch as while the fact is distinctly revealed, the manner of it, lying in a realm of transcendent divine possibilities, has not been descriptively declared to us. Unquestionably there was a divine self-limitation, as in themselves the divine and the human, the infinite and the finite, have not equal diameter or comprehension; but the mode of bringing them to coincide in their personal union in the theanthropic Christ, we may well regard as so far humanly inscrutable as to make it impossible for theology to determine definitely how it was effected. It is one of the secrets of God's love and power "past finding out" and beyond our descriptive definitions.

Christian Theology

Milton Valentine

CHAPTER II
THE DIVINE-HUMAN CONSTITUTION OF CHRIST

The fact and mode of the incarnation, as thus presented in the Scriptures, bring us right into the whole mystery of the Person of the Redeemer as constituted in that incarnation. We make a distinction between the act and the *state* of the hypostatic union. We must endeavor here to fix in our minds more clearly and fully the realities or truths that are incorporated in this mystery, and the evidences that assure these truths and justify them to our faith. The truths must be ascertained through the records and divinely-given teachings of the Christian Scriptures. We are, nevertheless, justified in approaching the great subject by recalling the advancing formulation of the doctrine by the early Church out of these Scriptures, in connection with doctrinal traditions in the earliest congregations. We will thus be prepared to understand the significance of these formulations and to appreciate the Scripture basis upon which they were rested, as well as the aberrations against which they were placed. It will open the way to understand also the discussions of the subject in the Reformation period, and especially the various divergent speculative theories that have been developed and offered these late years by prominent theological writers, aiming at thoroughly reconstructed conceptions of the divine reality. And above all, this method is fairest alike to the content of the Christian consciousness of the church from its earliest time, and to the authority of the sacred Scriptures with whose records and teachings our doctrinal formulations must accord.

The doctrine of the person of Christ has been one of the great themes of thought and discussion from the apostles' days to ours. The controversies in the early Church led progressively to the unfolding and distinct formulation, in the ecumenical creeds, of what was believed to be the teaching of the Scriptures on the subject. The occasion was not simply the Church's felt need of an intellectual understanding of the import of its own faith, as a bond of fellowship, but also the fact that here and there, among speculative leaders, dissentient explanations appeared which were felt to be untrue, even destructive, to the fundamental verities of the Gospel. From the first the Christian consciousness may properly be

Christian Theology

regarded as holding two points concerning the Son, or Logos, who became incarnate. First, His real divinity, and secondly, His personal distinction from the Father. The points involved the Trinity of the Godhead and the equality of the Father, Son, and Spirit. But they were not always consistently maintained. A tendency developed to regard the propositions of the unity of the Son with the Father and the personal distinction between them as contradictory, leading some writers to the idea of a "subordination" of the Son, and others to a denial of the personal distinction. The former appeared in the anti-trinitarianism of Paul of Samosata, who made Christ a mere man, and the latter in Sabellius, who recognized His full and essential divinity, but denied His hypostatic distinction from the Father, holding that He was but a form or mode of the self-manifestation of unitarian Deity. These and allied views were ranked as "heresies," as at variance with fundamental realities in the necessary faith of the Church. But the immediate occasion of the Church's formal setting forth its understanding of the truth, on these and associated points with regard to the person of Christ, came with the great and subversive error of Arius, a presbyter of Alexandria, in the early part of the fourth century. Contending, as he did, with popular force and persistence, from the word "begotten," that the Son cannot be conceived as eternal nor truly divine, but must be regarded as only an originated or created being—though, indeed, the first and greatest of begotten or created beings—the Church became so violently and injuriously disturbed by the controversy, as to lead to the calling of the first Ecumenical Council, at Nicæa, A. D. 325, in order to let the truth of Scripture teaching, as lodged through the Holy Spirit in Christian thought and consciousness, have expression, with whatever force or authority may belong to such expression. Against the Arian heresy, and all modifications of it, the Church there proclaimed, and has since maintained, its doctrine of ὁμοουσία, declaring Christ's consubstantial divinity, and proclaiming Him as very God of very God. Whatever subordination may seem to be involved in certain Scripture passages is to be regarded as official and not essential, as marking His redemptory work, not His divine nature. As other questions concerning the constituents of His person and their reality in the union became subjects of controversy, further Ecumenical Councils were convened, in which the Church, as a whole, through its representatives, gave expression to its understanding of the truth. Thus, beginning with the Nicene Creed, set forth by the Council of

Nicæa, in A. D. 325, as above, followed by the fuller statements of the Council of Chalcedon, A. D. 451, and those of the Council of Constantinople, A. D. 680, one point after another was settled and embodied in the Church's Creed concerning the Person of Christ. The truths thus reached, over against heretical or infidel views, are the following:

1. THE TRUE AND ABSOLUTE DIVINITY OF CHRIST. According to His eternal nature, He was the second Person of the adorable Trinity—*God*, with no lowering whatever of the idea conveyed by that untransferable name. The progressive formulation of this is marked in the ecumenical creeds.

The traditionally formed so-called *Apostles' Creed* simply implied the doctrine in its statement of faith concerning the second Person of the Trinity: "I believe in Jesus Christ, His (the Father's) only begotten Son, our Lord," with an enumeration of the chief facts in His redemptive work.

The *Nicene Creed:* "And in one Lord Jesus Christ, the Son of God, only begotten of the Father, that is, of the substance of the Father, God of God, Light of Light, very God of very God, begotten, not made, being of the same substance (ὁμοούσιον) with the Father, by whom all things were made in heaven and in earth." This was reaffirmed at the second General Council at Constantinople, A.D. 381.

The *Council of Chalcedon:* "We, then, following the holy fathers, all with one consent, teach men to confess one and the same Son, our Lord Jesus Christ, the same perfect in Godhead, and also perfect in manhood, truly God and truly man, of a rational soul and body, of the same essence with the Father according to His Godhead, and of the same essence with us according to His manhood, in all things like unto us without sin, begotten before all ages of the Father according to His Godhead, and in these latter days, for us and our salvation, born of the Virgin Mary, the mother of God according to His manhood; one and the same Christ, Son, Lord, only begotten, to be acknowledged in two natures, *inconfusedly* (ἀσυγχύτως) *without change* (ἀτρέπτως), *without division* (ἀδιαιρέτως), and *inseparably* (ἀχωρίστως); the distinction of natures being by no means taken away by the union, but rather the property of each nature being preserved, and concurring in one Person and one Subsistence, not parted or divided into two persons, but one and the same Son, and only begotten, God the Word, the Lord Jesus Christ; as the prophets from the beginning [have declared] concerning Him, and the Lord

Christian Theology

Jesus Christ Himself has taught us, and the creed of the holy fathers has handed down to us."

The Scripture warrant which justified and necessitated the Church in an early fixing, with such dogmatic positiveness and emphasis, this side of the Person of Christ has been already condensed before the reader's view in connection with the doctrine of the Trinity.

2. HIS TRUE AND FULL HUMANITY. There was little disposition to deny this. Yet it was denied, in whole or in part. The *Docetæ* (from δόκειν, to seem) of the first and second centuries, claimed that His body was a phantom, or, if real, was of celestial origin, so that He suffered in appearance only and not in fact. The Eutychians, or monophysites, asserted it to be of composite nature, resulting from a union of humanity with the divine nature, a *tertium quid*, different from our nature. Apollinarius, with his followers, made the Divine or the Logos Himself take the place of the rational soul in the God-man. St. John seems to have discerned the rise of this failure to recognize the real and true humanity of the Christ, and placed the admission of it as so fundamental that he asserts: "Every spirit that confesseth not that Jesus Christ is come in the flesh is not of God" (1 John 4:3). There was occasion, therefore, for theology to define its understanding of this truth.

The *Apostle' Creed* involved it in affirming: "He was conceived by the Holy Ghost, born of the Virgin Mary, suffered under Pontius Pilate, was crucified, dead, and buried."

The *Nicene Creed*, in asserting: "Who, for us men and for our salvation, descended from heaven and was incarnated by the Holy Ghost of the Virgin Mary, and was made man; and was crucified also for us under Pontius Pilate; He suffered and was buried."

The *Council of Chalcedon* became explicit, paralleling the completeness of His humanity with the completeness of His divinity: "Perfect in Godhead, and also perfect in manhood, truly God and truly man, of a rational soul and body, of the same essence with the Father according to His Godhead, and of the same essence with us according to His manhood, in all things like unto us, without sin, begotten before all ages of the Father according to His Godhead, and in these latter days, for us and our salvation, born of the Virgin Mary, the mother of God according to His manhood, one and the same Christ, Son, Lord, only begotten, to be acknowledged in two natures, *inconfusedly, without change, without division,* and *inseparably,* the distinction of natures being by no means taken away by the union, but rather the property of each nature being preserved, and concurring in one Person and one Subsistence, not parted or divided into two persons, but one and the same Son, and only begotten, God, the Word, the Lord Jesus Christ." We repeat this quotation in order to call attention to the completeness with which all the elements of perfect humanity are included. When later, the sixth Ecumenical Council, that of Constantinople, A.D. 680, condemned monophysitism and monotheletism, it simply maintained the faith declared at Chalcedon more than two centuries before.

The true humanity of Christ, therefore, means that the divine Son took on Him not a mere appearance of human nature, but the reality in all its essential parts, as included in a true human body and rational soul. As to His true human *body*, the truth is Scripturally reflected and evidenced in such Biblical records as speak of His conception and birth of a woman (Gen. 3:15; Matt 1:25; Luke 1:35; Gal. 4:4); His circumcision (Luke 2:21); His growth, like other children's, from childhood to manhood (Luke 2:40–52); His necessities and experiences, both physical and psychical, marking and identifying human life, as shown in hunger and thirst (Luke 4:2–4; John 19:28); weariness (John 4:6); need of sleep and rest (Matt 8:24); suffering, wounds and pain, crucifixion, death and burial (John 19:1–3, 34, 36–42; Luke 23:33, 50–56). Even "flesh and bones" are specified to identify His human personality (Luke 24:39–40). His possession of a *true rational human soul* is proved by His growth in wisdom, or true knowledge, the intellectual correspondent to His growth in physical stature (Luke 2:40–52); by the antithesis presented between "body "and "spirit" (1 Pet 3:18); by His human affections and sympathies (John 11:5, 35; Luke 19:41); by His habit of prayer (Mark 1:35; Luke 3:21; 9:18; 11:1); by limitation in knowledge (Mark 13:32); a "soul" (ψυχή) belonged to Him (John 12:27; Matt. 26:38; Mark 14:34); and also a "spirit" (πνεῦμα) (John 11:33–38; John 13:21; Mark 8:12; Luke 10:21), etc. Whether, therefore, we adopt the theory of human dichotomy or trichotomy, He possessed the human rational principle or constituent Throughout His whole recorded history, even in closest conjunction with the manifestations of His supernatural character, the elements and witnesses of His true humanity come into view. Indeed, the denial or doubt of this side of His personality has disappeared from the thought of our times, in a false tendency to emphasize it into the totality of His being. But the whole truth is that through the incarnation Jesus Christ, the perfect

Christian Theology

Son of God, became the perfect Son of man. With one consent Christendom has come to recognize in Him an actualization and presentation of perfect or ideal humanity, the full and faultless example of true manhood, elsewhere unequalled and impossible to be surpassed.

3. THE ONENESS OF CHRIST'S PERSON.—This point settled itself according to the definitions of the two constituent natures, and the historic portraiture of His individual personality. The two complete natures, the truly divine of the Logos, and the truly human by birth from Mary, form, not two persons, a divine and human conjoined, but one Person. The unity was not by a "*fusion*" or conversion of the two natures into a resultant that is neither identically divine nor human but a *third* something (*tertium quid*), in which the integrity and purity of both are merged and are lost. Nor was it a union that was incomplete, a close association merely—the natures conjoined but not made a personal unit. The Chalcedon and Constantinopolitan determinations provide against both these conceptions. The union was not a simple conjunction, but one that effected a true hypostatic unity. Nor did this unity take place by any impairment or alteration of either nature. The Chalcedon Confession multiplies words to make these two points precise and emphatic: "without change," "without confusion," leaving "no separation," and becoming "inseparable "—guarding against the error of Nestorius on the one hand and of Eutyches on the other. The Council of Constantinople, 680, reaffirmed these explanations by condemning both monophysitism and monotheletism. The incarnation thus made no changes, brought no impairment or confusion in the essential properties of the two natures, but gave as the resultant *one* Person, who is neither simply a divine Person, nor simply a human person, but a theanthropic, Divine-human Person. As a Person, Christ was and is the God-man, with a divine-human consciousness, the divine and the human concurring or acting in unison. The Church thus guarded the oneness of His Person against the Nestorians, who denied a true and real union, and against the Eutycheans, who destroyed the natures in the union.

The oneness or unity of *consciousness* must be specifically noted. It means that Christ had not two personal consciousnesses, as consciousness of two persons conjoined, but *one personal consciousness*, continuous from pre-existent state, and covering the realities of both the divine and human natures. He knew Himself as a Person, *one* Person, not two, and knew Himself as both human and divine in essence or nature. His personal consciousness included the realities of His experience from both sides of His constitution. "This personal consciousness as much distinguishes the condition of the two natures as unites them in love" The proofs of this oneness are found in the clear and necessary implications of the Scriptures. For example, Christ always used the singular personal pronoun as covering the action of the two natures in His selfhood: "Before Abraham was, *I am*" (John 8:58); "Glorify Thou *Me* with Thine own self, with the glory which I had with Thee before the world was" (John 17:5); "*I* and My Father are One" (John 10:30), etc. Everywhere the duality of natures in Him becomes apparent; everywhere also the oneness of His personality. Moreover, the records never even suggest the idea that in Him the divine and the human had relations to each other as persons, as of converse with each other, as in the case of the persons of the Trinity (Gen. 1:26; 3:22). The designation "hypostatic union" is framed from the *resultant* of the incarnation, that the two natures are united in one ὑπόστασις, one Person.

This personality, as already stated, was formed from the divine side of the union—by the Logos. The eternal Word, Son of God, assumed, not a human person already actually existent, but human *nature*, whose elements were non-existent until creatively originated in the act of incarnation itself; therefore constituting the theanthropic personality in the very act of taking on Himself all the parts of our complete nature, the faculty of will included. The constitutive act for Christ's Person was the assumption of the human nature—the nature of the Son being eternally personal and His human nature being created *potentially* personal in the process of its origination. The Son of God, eternally personal, thus creatively assumed into union with His own divine nature, the entirety of *human nature*, so becoming a theanthropic Person, a divine-human Person. Dr. Liddon justly says: "The perfect Manhood of Christ, not His body merely, but His soul, and therefore His human will, is part of the One Christ. Unless in His condescending love, our eternal Lord had thus taken upon Him our fallen nature in its integrity, that is to say, a human soul as well as a human body, a human will as an integral element of the human soul, mankind would not have been really represented on the cross or before the throne." Sartorius explains: "The Divine nature, then, in this union, is the taking, the personifying; the human, the taken, the nature into which the self-consciousness of the Divine Son thought and fashioned itself, so that His *ego* is the central point of both the Divine nature, which was

Christian Theology

proper to Him, and of the human nature which He took unto Him, the latter being indeed not personal of itself, but being so in and with the Divine nature. Thus is He conscious of the divine and human nature, and of their different properties in individual personal unity, and for this very reason Christ, the God-man, and as such the one and only Mediator between God and man."

The doctrine of the impersonality of the *humanity* of Christ thus set forth in the early Church with the purpose of guarding against the idea that His Person was formed by a union of two persons, instead of its being by the Divine Son's assumption of generic human nature creatively produced in the act of assumption, was, in the progress of current tendencies, afterward so extended, under influence of John of Damascus, as to be held applicable to the *permanent* condition of His human nature. The tendency to lay the chief stress on His Divinity led to a compromise of the importance of His humanity, and, as more easily conceivable, to the notion that it never became personal. Hence the theory of the permanent impersonality (*anhypostasia*) of His human nature. But the modern inclination to emphasize His true and full humanity has largely broken with this conception of its impersonality in the accomplished and abiding union. Dr. Dorner tells us: "The doctrine frequently advocated in the older divinity, though expressed in no church symbol, of the non-personality of the human nature of Christ, has been pretty generally given up." Its abandonment seems to be required both by the records of the Scriptures and the logical necessities of His mediatorial relation. We may look at it thus: It is conceded that the Person of Christ was a personal unit, one Person. The Logos, the Divine Nature was personal *before* the union and *in* it, being causative and active in the creative assumption of the human nature—the human, therefore, not being personal before its assumption. But the act of incarnation, assuming the nature in all its parts, in their wholeness and integrity, necessarily aggregated all the elements of genuine, full personality in that human nature. Now, if Christ is One Person, a single personality, and the two natures are both in that One Person, He must be personal on both sides; else He is not *One* Divine-human Person. His personality would be *only* Divine, if the human nature were not an element of it. How could He then *represent and act for us as "persons,"* the only character in which we have any interest in the redemptive work?

Several truths are properly recalled here. The first is that the profound *mystery*, acknowledgedly in the incarnation and Person of

Milton Valentine

Christ, belongs not to the elements or facts which the Christian faith holds as necessarily embodied in it, but to the impenetrable transcendency of these facts to exact and final definition and explanation in our measures and terms of thought. The incompetency of speculative thought to picture the *how* of the reality should suggest modesty in our dogmatic settings of the truth, without affecting the very truth itself of the facts and our faith in them. The framing of the Creed statements was not in speculative aim, to explicate the *method* of the incarnation, but to assert its full reality. It is an apt remark of Canon Gore that "there is no more signal evidence of a divine providence watching over the fortunes of the Church, than the Church's persistent loyalty, *in its authoritative decisions*, to the true humanity of Christ, in spite of strong individual prepossessions." The decisions of the ancient Councils must be viewed in this light, not as an analytic removal of the mystery of Christ's Person, but as assertions of the fact in its integrity, in order to save the essentials in the truth of the incarnation for the faith of the Church against various speculative theories which sought to reduce or eliminate the mystery. The mysterious is, and must forever be, an object of faith. Because of human finiteness and limitations of knowledge, the realities of the universe, within us and about us, clasping us closely as the air and reaching us from far-away worlds, compel us to believe and trust far beyond our ability to penetrate the ultimate constitution, essence, and reasons of the system of nature and life which holds us every hour. We must, in part, "walk by faith." Faith is not made absurd by mystery, but required and justified. The grand ethical need of redemption warrants this faith. To eliminate all mystery would reduce from reality, whether in the realm of the natural or supernatural. In either realm faith is precluded, not by the mysterious or transcendent, but only by absolute self-contradiction.

And some faint illustrations have been well employed to suggest the conceivability of the incarnation and its resultant in Christ's person, or at least to open a line of approach toward the mystery. (*a*) Man's own constitution is a mental nature and a physical nature united in one personality, the one personal consciousness, the individual ego, embracing the experiences from both sides. (*b*) We see in the single soul of St. Paul two principles of volition, one animated by remaining carnality and the other by reason quickened by grace—a spiritual dualism which he describes as if in a conjunction of two wills (Rom. 7:14–15). Though not an exact analogy, this is suggestive. (c) How humanity may be assumed without being destroyed or the personalizing Divinity made human, is suggested by Martensen's statement: "He did not possess His Deity outside of His humanity, but His true humanity was grounded in His true divinity "[*i. e.*, made in the "image of God," and, therefore, receptive of the divine presence and thought]. "It is the idea of human nature not to be independent, but to be an organ, a temple, for the divine nature. To the extent to which human nature is filled by the divine, to that extent does it attain its true idea; and we may say with perfect truth of every human individual, that he is a true man only in proportion as a divine word becomes incarnate in him. The capacity of an individual to realize and manifest true humanity must, therefore, be measured by his capacity for receiving the divine, by his capacity for becoming an organ of God. And that individual alone will be the perfect revelation of humanity, or the Adam, who is able to embrace in himself the entire fullness of Deity.... Not that the human nature of Christ had the capability of rising by its own power to this union with the divine. The divine nature must be conceived as taking the initiative in the union; and the entire conception of Christ first acquires steadiness and fixity, when we recognize with the Scriptures that it is God Himself, the eternal Logos, who has here made Himself man."

A second truth belonging here is the *sinlessness and impeccability* of the theanthropic Person. The Scriptures declare Him to have been without sin, connecting absence of human depravity with His miraculous birth, and asserting His actual life to have been without fault (Luke 1:35; John 10:36; 8:46; 2 Cor. 5:21; Heb. 4:15; 1 John 3:5). The records of His life never suggest natural depravity in His sentiments or tendencies, or the idea of Theodore of Mopsuestia that He took on Him our humanity with its sinful affections in order to overcome them and thus elevate it into victory over them. The simple narrative of His conduct, in deeds and words, revealing His inmost self and outward bearing, forms a portraiture of purity, righteousness, holiness, and love which has justly impressed the conscience of the Christian mind as that of a sinless man. Though He everywhere showed the most sensitive appreciation of moral distinctions, He nowhere confessed sin or any fault He never prayed for forgive-ness, though He taught others so to pray. He was not only without sin, but He *could* not sin. As to Christ, it is not enough to say, "*Posse non peccare*" and "*non peccasse,*" but we must add, "*Non posse peccare;*" because, exempt from original sin, His human nature was holy, and the union of the divine with the human lifted Him above the possibility of sin. To some minds the last feature presents an apparent difficulty, as seemingly incongruous with the admitted fact that He suffered "temptation," trial, testing (Matt 4:1-2; Mark 1:12; Luke 4:1-13; Heb. 4:15). But closely viewed, there is no inconsistency involved. Between being tempted and sinning, *per se*, there is a distinct and radical difference. To be tempted is no sin. Sin begins only in yielding to the temptation. He was tempted "without sin." When the tempter came to Him, there was no depravity in Him ready to respond. So that with respect to His humanity He was "able not to sin." But we must, nevertheless, remember that that same humanity opened Him to temptation. The parallel of His position with that of the first Adam is illuminating. Adam's sinless humanity opened him to the possibility of being tempted, and sin came only in yielding. Apply the realities in his case to the experience of Christ in that occurrence which is pre-eminently recorded as His temptation, the trial in the wilderness. There may be unsolved elements of mystery as to the divine purpose in including those strange trials in Jesus' life, though it seems at least partially disclosed as designed to present to the confidence of faith a merciful and sympathetic Savior and Helper who knows what temptation and trial are, and who brings the power of victory over them. But, clearly, through the distress of "hunger," which is no sin, but a divinely-given feature of unfallen humanity, there was brought into Christ's experience the temptation of the natural impulse toward relief. But to secure it by the method proposed—the use of His miracle-powers for personal and private end, to escape the sufferings incident to His assumed condition of manhood, and thus break the principle of *example* that belonged to His redemptive and saving mission on earth—would have violated the divine law of His earthly life. So the temptation and tempter were rebuked away. The temptation failed to bring forth sin. We may say, indeed, that this victory over the trial was possible on the simple basis of His untainted human nature, as Adam *might* have preserved his integrity in virtue of the pure freedom given him. But we are entitled and obliged to say more. He was not only able, viewing His personality on its human side, to triumph, and thus reverse Adam's failure, but, viewing it on its Divine side, in which the theanthropic person arose and which is forever the central and ruling fact of His being, Christ *could* not have sinned and fallen. He was as truly God as He was man. God cannot sin. The Divine safeguarded the human nature and made Him absolutely impeccable. So we need to think of Him.

4. There is a further problem in the unity of the Person of Christ—*the relation of the attributes of the two natures to this One Person.* It is the question of the *communication of attributes* (*communicatio-idiomatum*). The relations sought are conceived as arising out of the communion of the natures in the personal union. All orthodox Christendom has been wont to accept part of the teaching here involved. But Lutheran dogmatics in the sixteenth and seventeenth centuries developed some special features, one of which at least has not been accepted by general theology. Three kinds of communication have been defined.

(*a*) The first kind is that termed *idiomatic* (*genus idiomaticum*), whereby the attributes of both natures are communicated and belong to the One Person. All the essential divine attributes and all the essential human attributes belong to Christ. His person is Divine-human, the God-man. This has been the common doctrine of the Church, in accordance with the statement of the Creed of Chalcedon: "The diversity of the two natures not being at all destroyed by their union in the Person, but the peculiar properties (ἰδιῶται) of each being preserved and concurring in One Person." This kind of communication seems involved in the very necessities of the personal union. Not to attribute both classes of attributes to Christ would destroy His individual personality, leaving the two natures, as two persons, only standing in juxtaposition, as in the error of Nestorius and his followers. And it is sustained by the Scriptures. In these, sometimes the human properties give designation to the Person; sometimes the Divine. For example, in Rom. 9:5, we have the human designation, with divine predicate: "As concerning the flesh, Christ came, who is God over all." Similarly in John 6:62: "Ye shall see the Son of man ascend up where He was before." In Rom. 8:32, the divine gives the designation with human predicate: "He that spared not *His own* Son, but delivered Him up for us all." So also in 1 Cor. 2:8: "For had they known it, they would not have crucified the Lord of glory"; and in 1 Cor. 15:47: "The second man is the Lord from heaven." Sometimes the whole Person is made the subject of divine predicates, as John 8:58: "Before Abraham was I am"; and sometimes of human predicates: "I thirst." Sometimes the whole Person is made the subject of predicates from both natures, as brought into single view, as in John 1:1–14; Rom. 1:3–4.

Milton Valentine

(*b*) The second kind of communication is what is termed the *genus apotelesmaticum* (κοινοποιητίκον), whereby the redemptory functions or actions which belong to the whole Person are predicable, not of one nature alone, but of both natures, or of each with communication of the other. This, too, is in harmony with the Creed of Chalcedon, which says: "Each nature does or performs whatever belongs to it with communication of the other, and is the common doctrine of the Church." The Form of Concord puts it: "As to the execution of the office of Christ, the Person does not act or work in, with, through, or according to only one nature, but in, with, according to, and through both natures." It means that Christ executed His office in the unity of His Person; so that, for instance, when He suffered He suffered both as man and as God, in the oneness of His theanthropic Person. For the Person suffering was the God-man, and in the unity of consciousness the whole Person suffered (1 Pet. 3:18; 1 John 1:7; Acts 20:28).

This second aspect of communication really only explicates, in analytic way, what is already included in the first kind. "The whole work of Christ is to be attributed to His Person and not to the one or other nature exclusively. The Person is the acting subject; the nature, the organ or medium. It is the Divine-human Person that wrought miracles by virtue of His divine nature, that suffered through the sensorium of His human nature. The superhuman effect and infinite merit of the Redeemer's work must be ascribed to His Person because of His divinity, while it is His humanity alone that made Him capable of and liable to temptation, suffering and death, and renders Him an example for our imitation."

(*c*) The third kind is called the *genus majestaticum* or *auchematicum* (from αὔχημα, glory), in which the attributes of the Divine nature are said to be communicated to the human nature. In this, which is peculiar to Lutheran dogmaticians, is developed a view which goes beyond the Ecumenical Creeds and was not accepted by other divisions of the Church. A prompting occasion for its development was the support it seemed to give to Luther's affirmation of the omnipresence of Christ's body, and thus to the doctrine of its real presence in the Lord's Supper. It is stated by different writers in somewhat different terms—some representing it in extremer and others in more moderate form. To rightly estimate it, it must be looked at under these differing representations.

First, in the extremer statements; that of Hollaz is a fair example: "The Son of God truly and really *communicates the idiomata of His divine nature to the assumed human nature.*" Prof. Heinrich Schmid explains: "The impartation of the divine attributes to the human nature occurs at the very moment in which the Logos unites itself with the human nature." This communication of attributes is asserted as only from the divine side to the human, and is constantly accompanied by denial of a so-called *genus kenoticum,* or communication of properties of the human nature to the Divine, in accordance with the maxim that while the finite is capable of the Infinite, the Infinite cannot be increased or diminished. "For there cannot be an emptying or lessening of the divine nature," says Quenstedt.

Secondly, in a more cautious and moderate form; by the Form of Concord: "The human nature in Christ, inasmuch as it has been personally united with the divine nature in Christ, has received, over and above its natural, essential, permanent properties, also *special, high, great, supernatural, inscrutable, ineffable, heavenly prerogatives and excellences in majesty, glory, power, and might* above everything that can be named, not only in this world, but also in that which is to come." By Gerhard: "That which is communicated, the holy matter of communication, is divine *majesty, glory,* and *power,* and on this account *gifts, truly infinite and divine.*" "*Gifts* truly infinite and immeasurable have been imparted to Christ the man through the personal union, and His exaltation to the right hand of the Father." By Quenstedt: "We do not say that there is any transfusion of divine properties into the human nature of Christ (whereby the reproach of Eutychianism is repelled) or that there is any change of the human nature into the divine, or that there is any equalization or abolition of natures, but that there is a personal communication." The Scriptures cited for this communication are mainly Matt. 11:27; 28:18; John 3:13; 3:34; 5:27; 6:51, 54; Rom. 9:5; Phil. 2:10; Eph. 1:20.

This third kind was not distinctly formulated by either Luther or Melanchthon, though its substance was maintained by Luther. The Augsburg Confession, the Apology, the Smalcald Articles, are silent on the subject. Only by the Form of Concord (1580) was a measure of confessional position given to it, in the modified type. The dogmaticians formulated and pressed it with special view to the stronger foundation which it was thought to give to the Lutheran doctrine of the Eucharist, through its involved omnipresence of the body of Christ.

Milton Valentine

As to this *genus majestaticum*, as stated in the extremer form, as a communication of the attributes of the Divine nature to the human nature, it is to be remarked:—

(1) The Scripture passages quoted for it scarcely reach the grade of proof. They clearly prove the first and second kinds, viz.: that the attributes of both the Divine and human natures truly belong to the *One Person*, the God-man; and that in the redemptory work this One Person acts through each of the two natures, or through one with communication of the other. But they fail to assert the point of a real communication of the properties of the one nature to the other "nature" as such.

(2) The assertion of a communication of the attributes of one nature to the other *nature* comes dangerously near the Eutychian error which in the union confused and destroyed both natures. It is impossible to conceive how the divine properties could be given to the human nature, as real attributes, without making it something else or other than human nature. For the reality of anything, the substance or the "essential" of it, is determined and marked by the sum of its attributes; and when the sum of its attributes is changed, the substance or nature of it is changed. Human nature is not full human nature, the truly self-identical nature of mankind, if any of its attributes are wanting; for instance, "rational soul" or "will." It is more than human nature if any are added. It is the essence of human nature to be finite; to add to it omnipresence is, to the necessities of scientific thought, to constitute it *per se* infinitely beyond the self-identity of human nature. It becomes deification of human nature.

(3) The Form of Concord, despite its eucharistic prepossessions, sees the trouble and utters repeated warnings against this danger of Eutychianism, confounding the two natures or obliterating the true human nature. For example: "*The two natures of Christ are so united that they are not mingled one with another or changed one into the other, and each retains its natural, essential property, so that the properties of one nature never become the properties of the other nature.*" "Therefore in Christ there is and remains only *one* divine omnipotence, power, majesty, glory, which is *peculiar alone to the divine* nature; but it *shines, manifests,* and exercises *itself fully yet voluntarily, in, with, and through* the assumed exalted human nature." The very terms thus used concede that the attributes of the divine nature are truly and *really* attributes "peculiar alone to the divine nature," and only "manifest" themselves "in," "with," and "through" the human nature. They have not become real attributes

"of" the human *nature*, in any other sense than that the Divine nature uses and exalts the human in the *functions* of the theanthropic Person and office. This, indeed, avoids Eutychianism; but at the same time asserts nothing to justify the use of the extreme forms of statement here under criticism.

(4) Proof that the Form of Concord never meant any such doctrine as the extreme terms express, is seen in the fact that the "Catalogue of Testimonies" (prepared by Andrea and Chemnitz) explains what was sought to be affirmed, and declares: "The essential attributes of the one nature, which are truly and rightly ascribed to the whole Person, *never become the attributes of the other nature.*"

(5) The most discriminating Lutheran dogmaticians explain it so as to disclaim the idea of a real impartation of the attributes of one nature to the other nature. They make it a communication and communion of "gifts," a sharing in "prerogatives," "excellences," "powers," "glory," etc., a participation in the exaltation and activities of the God-man, *e. g.*, Gerhard and Quenstedt, as already quoted.

If we remember this fact, that no transfusion of divine properties into the human nature of Christ is meant, but only a participation by the human in the *action* of the divine through the unity of the theanthropic Person, the difficulty of this species of communication disappears. There is a clear difference between a communication or communion in the *activities, exercises, glories,* and *prerogatives* of the divine idiomata, in and through the One Personality, and the supposed impartation of the attributes themselves to the human nature as such. Interpreted in this, its true light or sense, it is really only a necessary explication and issue of the functional action taught in the second kind of communication, arising from the real personal union, or true oneness of the God-man—this Person acting with no reduction from His true humanity, but with the fullness of His essential Godhead, a union in which the humanity is made to share in His personal activities and powers, and is thereby exalted and glorified. This is substantially the putting of the doctrine by Sartorius: "But God in Christ not only made the poor properties of human nature His own, and endured them in His state of humiliation, but also lets that human nature share the abundant glory of His divine properties. Though itself only a creature, it was, nevertheless, after the work of reconciling even the most extreme contrasts had been performed in humiliation, raised, in consequence of its abiding personal union with the Godhead of the Son, above all creatures in heaven and on earth, to a participation of divine majesty and honor (Phil. 2:8-11).... It is not with His exclusively and directly divine presence, which, because it is this, is neither mediatorial nor reconciliatory, but with His divine and human personal nearness, that the Mediator and Reconciler is, according to His own good pleasure, with us always, even to the end of the world, so that He is not withdrawn from us by the ascension, but on the contrary, is efficaciously near (Matt. 28:20).

Looked at in this light, this kind of communication surely belongs to a full Christological view. The theanthropic Person cannot be divided, and in the unity and wholeness of Christ's Person since His exaltation, *He* is almighty, omnipresent, omniscient, and infinite in all divine perfections. This gives all that is necessary to a correct view of the Lutheran doctrine of the Supper.

At a later date, but connected with this controversy concerning the *communicatio idiomatum*, another difference was developed. Both parties agreed to the first kind (*genus*), that by the incarnation the attributes of both the Divine and human natures were united in the Person of Christ. *He* was at once true God and true man—divine-human by the full possession of the divine and human properties. But the Scripture representations of the growth and development of Jesus called for possible explanation. How, with absolute possession of the attributes of Godhead, "God manifest in the flesh," can the phenomena of normal infancy and advance to manhood both physically and mentally be made conceivable or intelligible to faith? The problem opened in two solutions: one, through a distinction made between "possession," "use" or "exercise" of the divine properties and powers, found the possibility and fact of such human growth and progress in the theory of an early *non-use* of these attributes and powers. Though fully possessed, they were not fully exercised. So the Giesen school of theologians held. The other party, the Tuebingen school advocated the doctrine of a hidden, secret use of all the divine attributes. They were fully possessed and fully exercised. According to this, Christ, even according to His human nature in virtue of its union with the divine, was actually, though invisibly omniscient, omnipotent, omnipresent, during the whole state of humiliation from infancy to the grave; actively, with the Father, participant in rulership of the world, in all divine powers, through all His progress from the manger to His ascension and session at the right hand of God. The difference between the two theories is the difference between a temporary renunciation of the

Christian Theology

use of His divine attributes, except as they were called for by the redemptory functions themselves, and an invisible concealed exercise of them all, in an unseen side of His divine-human life. The manifest fact that this kryptic view, when analyzed to its ultimate reality, is found to involve essentially a Nestorian denial of the real union of the two natures into a single personality, and also a living of two separate lives in different spheres at the same time, with docetic human aspect, leaves the *first* view—that of non-use of His divine powers in the state of humiliation—far preferable for interpretation of the genuine reality of that state as exhibited in the records of His life and death, and in the apostolic assurances of some divine *self-emptying* of what belonged to His "form of God" (Phil. 2:6–8; John 1:1, 2, 14; Heb. 2:9, 18). For the New Testament portraiture of His life exhibits the possibilities of His supernatural action or use of His divine powers, as being at His own option, in the service of His holy freedom, reason, and will. He held its employment as subservient to His divine mission, and at His choice. This accords with His true divinity, for it belongs to our highest conception of God to think of Him as the infinite, absolute Personal Being, and as using all His attributes and powers, with sovereignty of freedom, for the service of His own holy reason, love, and will. He is not Fate. His attributes are all centered in His intelligent, rational, personal selfhood, in which He determines His holy purposes after the counsel of His own will. He is not an automaton, acting *ex necessitate* and eternally exhibiting all the divine possibilities in every conceivable direction. He owns Himself for infinite potentialities of goodness and power. We dare not think of Him as always doing all He can do, as creating all the worlds or creatures He can, or as evermore exhausting the potencies of His attributes. His self-possession means self-control and self-direction for the aims of His free love and choice. Not all the divine thought passes into effect. It is part of His immutable, eternal nature to act in freedom—to hold the exercise of His divine attributes in an order of reserve, according to His purposes and plans. And so nature exhibits Him as making history by progressive working out of His free counsels of love. In short, it is normal to our conception of God to think of Him as exercising His eternal powers under a principle of self-reservation, using them or not using them in self-determining freedom, for the realization of the aims of His wisdom and choice—or as abstaining from action that would be apart from or in conflict with His purposes. And this principle seems to be eminently applicable for the explanation of this phenomenon of the humiliation of Christ. In the solution of the problem of the growth and progressive development of the Person who was the incarnate Son of God, a divine-human Person, true God-man from infancy to His full Godmanhood, we are justly and fully entitled to think of the eternal Son in becoming the Redeemer and accomplishing the earthly stage of the work, as renouncing, in measure, the *exercise*, the *use*, of the divine prerogatives and powers in His possession. For this self-reserve, this *non-use* of the divine attributes and powers belonging to Him, is seen to be but a reflection and illustration of a divine possibility and reality of freedom that belongs forever to the very conception of God. It presents a section of the divine method which is normal to our idea of God's eternal employment of His free powers.

The modern "kenoticism," originated by Thomasius, and adopted with modifying changes by various theologians, replaces this doctrine of the "non-use" of the divine prerogatives and powers possessed by Christ, with the theory that the incarnation involved a renunciation by the Son of the "*possession*" of the Divine attributes. It was a "self-emptying" of the attributes themselves. The "depotentiation" was not merely of the "exercise" of powers, but actual dispossession of them. Whatever claims may be made for this theory in any of the forms in which it has found following, or has been made plausible by acute tracing of the consciousness of Christ in the New Testament records of His thought and conduct, it lacks assuring Scripture testimony, and breaks too strongly across the law or necessities of human thought in its fundamental conceptions of the Divine nature and attributes. The eternal *freedom* of God in the "use," both positive and negative, of His attributes and powers, is normal to our necessary conception of Him as the absolute, immutable, eternal, free Personality, the purposive Creator and Ruler of the universe; but we cannot conceive of His laying aside the *very attributes* by virtue or possession of which He *is* God. His free "exercise" or direction of these attributes or prerogatives in the service of His holy will or plans, or even His "non-use" of them in relations in which their exercise would not coincide with His purpose, is one thing—a thing easily and consistently conceivable. But to lay aside their *possession* is quite another thing—is, in so far, to annul the *reality* of the Deity, to extinguish the *existence* of the Godhead. God is not capable of increase or diminution of the essential Being that He absolutely and eternally is. This new or

Christian Theology

modern *kenoticism* postulates conceptions at variance with Christian Theism, and involves inconsistent and contradictory thinking. It thus shows itself incompetent as a guide to Christological truth. Compared with the old and widely prevalent dogmatic teaching of a temporary *abstinence from use* (*abstinentia ab usu*) of the divine attributes and powers by the incarnate Logos or Son, in His humiliation, this new theory has no merit that should entitle it to supersede the old. In all the advantages of both Scripture implication and rational consistency and coherence, the old must be held as the far better interpretation. Dr. Dorner's theory of a gradual incarnation, in avoiding the difficulties of this offered kenotic theory, also fails to deserve the place of the older view.

It is proper to summarize here the relations of this constitution of the Person of Christ to the work of redemption to which it looked. We have already noted that the incarnation had its reason in the woeful fact of human *sin*, and that so far as the Scriptures have given distinct affirmation, it was conditioned on the need of recovery and salvation, and is not to be looked upon as primarily, and apart from that need, involved in creational or metaphysical necessities. To this great end of redemption, therefore, we will find the divine-human constitution of His person to be in vital and assuring adaptations. We need simply define the points here, as they will be developed and illustrated in tracing the work of Christ.

1. The incarnation places him in true adaptation to the office of *mediation*. This term expresses His aggregate office, His generic position. In all that He did, He acted as Mediator: "There is one Mediator between God and man, the man Christ Jesus, who gave Himself a ransom for all" (1 Tim. 2:5). His divine-human Person put Him into actual union with both parties—able both to act for God in providing and revealing mercy, and to make His work stand for man by doing His vicarious service as Man (Heb. 2:14–18).

2. Specifically, it adapted Him to the great work of *atonement* or "*propitiation*," in that He could both obey and suffer in the nature that had sinned, and by His divinity give value to this obedience and suffering as a testimony against sin and vindication of the claims of righteousness. Rom. 5:19, "By the obedience of One many were made righteous." Rom. 8:3, "God sending His own Son in the likeness of sinful flesh, and for sin, condemned sin in the flesh." Also Rom. 5:8–10; Heb. 2:16–17; 9:15.

3. It gave a *Teacher* who could speak the things of God authoritatively, knowing both the mind of God and what is in man.

4. It opens the way to, and furnishes, a close and living *fellowship* with God. In the theanthropic Person, the divine and human natures have come together, and God and man can evermore meet in living communion. A point of union is created in Christ, and in our union with Christ through faith, we are united again with God in most vital way—as members with the Head, as branches with the vine.

5. In relation to the race, Christ thus becomes a *second Adam*, as the Head of a redeemed humanity (Rom. 5:12–21; 1 Cor. 15:45–47). This Headship of Christ stands over against the headship of Adam in nature—Christ's headship giving spiritual life where Adam's gave sin and death. In a second Adam, a true man, the seed of the woman is bruising the serpent's head, destroying the work of the destroyer, recovering humanity, and becoming its true type of relation and destiny.

6. It furnishes the true *Model* for human imitation and ethical conformity. He is the Perfect Man, with all human virtues, not in abstract standard, but in real personal life. This is, indeed, a most impressive form of teaching, and Christ's pattern has had wonderful uplifting and transforming power. In Him the ideal perfection has been made the actual human character—the perfection of humanity historically realized by and through the fullness of the divine life. It has won the admiration of the world.

7. It adapts Him for the divine *Judgeship* belonging to the moral government (Matt. 25:31–46). "The Father judgeth no man, but hath committed all judgment unto the Son" (John 5:22; Acts 17:31). The judgment that shall be the award to all men will be at once that of the eternal God of love and holiness and that of the moral nature or reason of perfect Man. There is a supreme adaptation of His Person to this office. "Christ's perfect love for justice, which sacrifices itself in order to glorify the divine justice, and which He attested by suffering and death, was His consecration to the office of theanthropic Judge of the world."

The simple enumeration of these leading adaptations in the divine-human Person of Christ not only shows with what impressive directness they look to His redemptive work, but suggests how the very mystery of the incarnation, in itself so perplexing to thought, nevertheless becomes, in its great meaning and fitness, a grand evidence of the divine truth of Christianity.

Christian Theology

Milton Valentine

DIVISION III
THE STATES OF CHRIST

As preparing the way for us to understand His total redemptive work it is needful to fix in mind the states of Christ as embraced in that work. These are usually spoken of as two, but it seems better to mark them as three. Considered simply with reference to His divine-human Person, two states may comprise all; but viewed in relation to the scope of His work, three ranges of movement are covered, viz.: The State of Pre-existence, the State of Humiliation, and the State of Exaltation or Glorification.

1. THE STATE OF PRE-EXISTENCE was that of "the Word" (ὁ Λόγος) (John 1:1–3), as the second Person of the Triune God, before the incarnation. This has been sufficiently set forth in the doctrine of the Trinity. To this state belong all the work, or divine self-revelations, that appear in the Old Testament economy, preparing the way for the actual coming in the flesh. We properly include this as embraced in a state of Christ, because it covers *mediational* function and action in the pre-advent government or administration of the world. The movement of redemptive, saving grace began at once on the fall of man into sin and guilt, according to purpose before the foundation of the world. The movements of the Old Testament dispensation of grace, its instructions, theophanies, training, and salvation, were in and through Him. No man had seen God, the Father, at any time; the only begotten Son had revealed Him. He dates Himself as "before Abraham." It was He whose "glory" Isaiah saw in vision (John 12:41). In plan, purpose, and power, He was already the "Lamb slain." His work was already active and efficient as "the Christ," the "Anointed," in the redemptive economy (1 Pet. 1:10–11).

2. THE STATE OF HUMILIATION (*Status Humiliation is*, or *Exinanitionis*). This has already been explained, to some degree, in the incarnation and constitution of the Person of Christ. It is to be held as including the entire condescension of the Word's becoming flesh, *i. e.*, the descent from the "form of God" (μορφὴ Θεοῦ) into the "form of a servant," and "being made in the likeness of men," as well as all the subsequent self-privation when, "being found in fashion as a man He humbled Himself" in conditions of poverty, weakness,

Christian Theology

sufferings, to "the death of the cross" (Phil. 2:5–9), and descent into the grave. Lutheran dogmaticians, generally, have been peculiar in restricting the "state of humiliation" to Christ's *human nature*, as a temporary renunciation of the use or exercise of the Divine attributes and powers with which that nature was at once, in the incarnation, actually invested, according to their theory of the *communicatio idiomatum*. They have made it appertain only to the assumed nature, while affirming that according to the *divine* nature Christ was from infancy to His death fully participant in all divine powers and activities. And they excluded the assumption of humanity as such from constituting a part of the humiliation of the Son—alleging that as the union of the two natures is *permanent*, continuing in His exaltation, the incarnation itself must not be counted constitutive of this state. We cannot, however, so understand the Scriptures, nor concede the logic which was thought to require such a view. "Numerous more recent Lutherans abandon it" It can be made plausible only from strained and extreme notions of the *communication of attributes*. The preexistent Son, Logos, Word, was the *subject* of the humiliation or self-emptying. Sartorius distinctly and justly includes the incarnation as itself forming the fundamental reality in the state of humiliation, involving as it did the whole actual human life of the Son of God as incarnate on earth.

From the point of view thus gained of it, we may specify the following features, sketched in Phil. 2:6–8. (*a*) It was *voluntary*—a thing of self-sacrificing love, to meet the needs of a fallen race (Phil. 2:5–8; 2 Cor. 8:9; John 10:11–18). (*b*) It included a real birth, a gradual growth and advance to manhood, the acceptance by Him of all the real and innocent experiences of human nature, as hunger, thirst, weariness, human sympathies, pains, etc. It seems to have been necessary, or at least fitting, that He should live and act in a real human life, and thus present Himself a merciful, sympathetic, and faithful High Priest, actually touched with a feeling of man's infirmities (Heb. 2:16–18; 4:15). (*c*) It included a divine self-limitation, or "emptying" on the part of the eternal Word, a surrender, in some way, of the plenary exercise of divine powers or attributes—*not* of their *possession*—in order that He might be truly and really man and have a true human experience. Thus He could "increase in wisdom and stature" (Luke 2:52); thus He could say: "Of that day and that hour knoweth no man, no, not the angels which are in heaven, neither the Son, but the Father" (Mark 13:32). "He was made a little lower than the angels, for the suffering of death, ... that

He by the grace of God should taste death for every man" (Heb. 2:9). (*d*) It allowed such manifestations of His Godhead as were needful to show and prove Him to be the Son of God, and were necessary to accomplish His divine teaching and redemptory work. He declined to use His supernatural powers for private ends or out of relation to the purpose of His incarnate mission. (*e*) It included a real *death*. "He became obedient unto death." As we shall see, this was necessary to the great peculiar redemptory function to which the incarnation looked: "Except a corn of wheat fall into the ground and die, it abideth alone, but if it die it bringeth forth much fruit" (John 12:24). That *He laid down His life of Himself* is not inconsistent with this reality, but rather deepens the depth to which His voluntary love condescended. (*f*) As to its time-extension, it began with the incarnation and continued all through His earthly life and ministry to the moment of His revivification in the tomb.

3. THE STATE OF EXALTATION. This expresses the full resumption of the "form of God," in the infinite divine glory which He had with the Father before the world was. In its time-relation we may properly conceive of it as beginning with the moment of His reanimation in the grave, and as consummated, through transformation and the ascension, in His "session at the right hand of God" (Acts 5:31; Phil. 2:9–11; Eph. 1:20–22; Matt. 28:18–20). It is to be borne in mind that this state of exaltation, like the others, is marked by its representing a special relation and activity in the accomplishment and consummation of the redemptive economy. In specific statement, it means: (*a*) The glorification of the whole *Person of Christ* as the *God-man*. *He*, the Theanthropic Christ, was exalted. It is of *Him*, in His whole personality, that the predicates of the state of exaltation are affirmed. "If any man sin we have an advocate with the Father, Jesus Christ" (1 John 2:1); "That at the name of Jesus every knee should bow," etc. (Phil. 2:10; John 5:27–29; Matt 24:30; 25:31; 26:64; Mark 13:26). When the end of this dispensation comes, it is "the Son of man" that shall come in the clouds and sit on the throne, (*b*) The exaltation is *official*, as well as personal. Christ is Mediator, exalted into relations of official power and activity, above time and space, above all things that He may *fill* all things. These are the essence of what is meant by "the right hand of God" (Rom. 8:34). "The right hand of God is not any definite place, but the omnipotent power of God." It expresses redemptive dominion, in full, divine, efficacious power. In this relation, He (1) sends the Holy Spirit (John 16:7; Acts 2:33); (2) endows men and calls them into the work of the

church and service of His kingdom (Eph. 4:11); "He gave some apostles," etc.; (3) is Head over all things to the church, providential Ruler (Eph. 1:22; 1 Peter 3:22); (4) He is Judge, as already mentioned. As these brief statements of the states of Christ make evident, they all have their designations and reality in connection with the redemptive necessity and moral needs of man.

In this State of Exaltation, and at the beginning of it, Lutheran dogmaticians usually put what the Apostles' Creed terms the "*descent into Hades*" (*descensus ad inferos*). The doctrine of a descent by Christ was developed in the early Church. It appears in Clement of Alexandria, and in Origen. It is found in the Formula of the Fourth Synod of Sirmium (359) and in the Creed of Aquileia in the fourth century. It appears in some subsequent baptismal formulas, and was inserted in the Apostles' Creed some time after the fifth century. It was incorporated in the third article of the Augsburg Confession. The Form of Concord amplified the statement.

The conception of it is considerably varied in theology. In the Greek Church it is represented as "a voluntary passage of Christ's human soul, in union with His divinity, when separated from the body, into Hades (*ad inferos*) in order to offer, through the preaching of the Gospel, redemption to such as were held there under uncleansed sin, and to transfer believers to Paradise, especially the saints of the Old Testament". In the Roman Catholic Church it is held that the whole divine-human Personality of Christ descended into the *Limbus patrum*, or the place where the saints of Israel were detained, in order to deliver them into the full enjoyment of blessedness. The Reformed Churches of Protestantism have generally given it a metaphorical interpretation, as a figurative expression of Christ's extreme humiliation and sufferings in connection with His death, the depth of woe He reached in dying for sin and sinners. Some have made it a mere synonym for "dead" and "buried," by addition of a phrase indicating a separation of the soul from the body. This conception of the Reformed theology means, as it explains, that they place the *descensus* as a part of the State of Humiliation.

The prevailing Lutheran view, as stated in the Form of Concord and general dogmatics, is distinctive in Protestantism, in respect both to its position in the states of Christ and its generic conception. This connects it with His State of Exaltation, placing it, as His first act in this state, between His reanimation, or resumption of life in the grave and His resurrection from it. He is viewed as, in His whole person, descending into Hades, the realm of death, and exhibiting Himself as Conqueror. It thus belongs, not to the passion, but to the glorious victory and triumph of Christ. And it is an act, whatever obscurity and mystery may enshroud it, accomplished in His entire divine-human Person as having overcome death. It is enough to know that He has thus descended and taken the keys of death and Hades for those that come to God through Him. And it is fitting when the Form of Concord advises against curious speculation or dogmatism about points left unrevealed and beyond determination. The Scripture passages for it are too incidental and their interpretation too uncertain to justify anything more than a very general statement. The literature of its past discussion is immense, but the conclusions established by it are exceedingly small. We may well accept the general statement of the Apostles' Creed in the Greek form, for thus far the Scriptures plainly warrant; but many of the special theoretic amplifications of the divinely stated fact are too unwarranted to be counted as theology. Especially must it be regarded as utterly without right and profane to build up upon the "*descensus*" a scheme of purgatorial grace, through penal sufferings and priestly absolutions, in derogation of the all-sufficient propitiation and righteousness of Christ.

Of another thing in this connection we may hold ourselves as fully certain—that the English word "hell" should not be used as a translation of hades in this clause. As the equivalent of the Hebrew *sheol*, hades stands in the Creed in the generic sense for the "spirit-world," the place of departed spirits irrespective of condition. It is not a simple equivalent *gehenna;* propriety and accuracy forbid its use as such. It is true that the *old-English* word "hell," from the Saxon "*helan*" (concealed, invisible) meant the same as hades or sheol; but it has lost that meaning in present English and popular understanding, and its use now constitutes a distinct mistranslation. Accordingly the revisers, giving us the revised version of the Bible, have refused the world "hell" where the Greek has hades, or the Hebrew sheol.

Christian Theology

Milton Valentine

DIVISION IV
THE WORK OF CHRIST

The constitution of the Person of Christ, being a divine adaptation to a work of love, at once emphasizes that work as an end of transcendent importance. The mystery of incarnate Deity bespeaks an aim worthy of itself, and to which it presents itself as a justifiable means. The grandeur of importance and value of the work of Christ is thus thrown before our view in measureless impressiveness. It should be traced out, therefore, and accepted in the features of spiritual reality, in which He Himself and those whom He taught, whether directly or by His Spirit, have presented it.

Approached in this conception, His work may properly be divided into two parts—one which He accomplished in his states of pre-existence and humiliation, the other which He fulfills in His state of exaltation. The first has been finished, a work done once for all; the second continues through the whole of the mediatorial sovereignty, until the office of saving and judging is all accomplished, and the mediatorial kingdom is surrendered (1 Cor. 15:24–28). The second is based upon the first, using the divine verities and powers it provided, and carrying them to the consummation of the divine purpose.

It is to be noted, in preliminary way, that His entire work is *mediatorial*. This stands as its general designation. The whole work comes under it. Christ is Mediator, and this expresses His generic office. "There is one Mediator between God and men, the man Christ Jesus." (1 Tim. 2:5). All parts come into unity in this all-inclusive office, for which He was prepared by His threanthropic Person. Quenstedt's statement is good: "The mediatorial office is the function belonging to the whole Person of the God-man, originating from theanthropic actions, by which Christ, in, with, and through both natures perfectly executed, and is even now accomplishing, by way of acquisition and application, all things that are necessary for our salvation."

But the work of this all-inclusive position and office necessarily divides itself according to the specific requirements involved in providing, applying, and completing the salvation which He came to bestow. As an activity of love it is determined by various teleological needs. There is no sufficient reason to displace the threefold division, termed the *Munus Triplex*, almost universally followed by theology, viewing Him as Prophet, Priest, and King. It is simple and

Christian Theology

all-embracing. It covers all parts of both His earthly and heavenly mediatorship. It is very ancient. The Jewish rabbis ascribed to the expected Messiah the threefold dignity: "The crown of the Law, the crown of the Priesthood, and the crown of the Kingdom." Eusebius, in the fourth century, gives it as a summary view of Christ's redeeming work: "Christ, the divine, heavenly Word, the only High Priest of all men, the only King of all creation, and the Father's supreme Prophet of all prophets." It is recognized substantially by Chrysostom and Theodoret appears among the scholastics, and has been followed generally by theologians of the Protestant Church, both Lutheran and Reformed. Indeed, it so reproduces and unites the Scripture affirmations and portraiture of both the Old and New Testaments, as to stand as a simple rehearsal and explanation of the revealed teaching. The guiding lights for the threefold division in the Old Testament are: Deut. 18:15–18; Ps. 110:4; Zech. 6:13. In the New, the commonest representations portray His work so as to throw it into this order. And it is impressively confirmatory of its correctness that these three functions form a complete adaptation to the fundamental constitution and condition of fallen man, and are essential in the process of redemption and salvation. They provide and employ the very things absolutely necessary to the great end. They conform to the great, all-inclusive functions of the human mind, the intellect, the sensibilities, and the will. As salvation is an ethical and spiritual change, God can accomplish it, not by abrogation or disregard of the essential faculties given man, but by entering into his soul with moral truth and motives. So the saving work requires the information and instruction of the prophetic or teaching office, the atoning reconciliation of the priestly service, and the subjection of will to the rule and authority of the kingdom of God. These three things are the requisites to the supply of man's need—giving him a knowledge of God's will, providing forgiveness, and working deliverance from sin under divine government and care. As a Prophet Christ reveals, as a Priest He atones and reconciles, as a King He subdues to Himself and confers the blessedness of His kingdom of love.

It is worthy of note, in confirmation of the value of this threefold division, that most of the defective or misleading theologies arise from not holding to each part in reality or in due proportion. Some, as in Pelagianism and Unitarianism, exalt the teaching function so as to exclude the priestly or atoning office. Some practically depend only on the priestly work of atonement, and care not to be taught and guided in duty by Christ. Still others practically refuse Christ's kingly function and think of being saved, though they make it apparent every day that they are not ruled by Him. If men are to be saved, it must be through the joint action of *all* these functions. This adds force to the importance of maintaining this classification. For it gives full and balanced view of His whole work, in form at once adapted to popular impression and production of the well-rounded Christian life. We must trace these functions.

CHAPTER I
THE WORK OF CHRIST AS PROPHET

By this, as already apparent, is meant all that He needed to do, has done, and will do, in the way of giving men true and saving knowledge—the knowledge of God, of His will, holiness, and love, of human obligations, of the way of salvation from sin, and of the duties and blessings to which we are called—all, in short, that is necessary to be known and believed in order to be saved and attain our right character and destiny. *Predictive* prophecy is but an element in this great teaching function, in which He is "the Light of the world," in ethical, spiritual, saving truth. Its domain is not physical science or the arts of secular life. He was designated to it in the Old Testament Messianic descriptions and promises: Deut. 18:15–18; Isa. 60:1–3; 61:1–2; compared with John 8:12; Acts 3:22; 7:37; Heb. 1:2: Luke 4:18–19. The reality of this work is reflected in the way in which He accomplishes it In the Jewish economy, in which He was mediatorial Revealer, Logos, or Word, before the incarnation, He effected it through Theophanies (Christophanies) and through the Holy Spirit in the prophets, through the teaching power of the divine Law, through the ceremonial ordinances as types and shadows of the saving plan, and by means of all the providential discipline through which He took His people. In His incarnate state, during His humiliation, the work of teaching was that with which He began His ministry and which occupied Him all through it. At its close He said: "I have given them thy word." In His state of exaltation He effects it through His teaching as recorded in the Scriptures, through the office of the ministry proclaiming the Gospel, the Holy Spirit using this to show the things of Christ, and make the truth effectual for the enlightenment and faith of men.

Christian Theology

Since His ascension the instruction in truth is not direct, but mediate.

The greatness of this prophetic work of Christ becomes evident in the fact that it has to maintain and give victory to the truth in perpetual conflict with sin, error, and darkness of the world, a conflict with enemies and false teachers within the Church as well as without it, and a triumph that shall make the progress of the Church an ever better realization of the power and fullness of the Gospel. The preservation of the truth and its progressive illumination of the earth and uplift in knowledge which Christendom is displaying, are testimony to the real and mighty teaching power which the exalted Christ is actually exercising.

CHAPTER II
THE WORK OF CHRIST AS PRIEST

This, manifestly, in the light of the Scriptures, is the central and chief part of His work, that for which His teaching prepared and which it uses, and the meaning of which His kingly function brings to realization. We must arrange our consideration of it under the distinct topics: The reality of His Priesthood; the nature of it; its several parts; and the results or effects of it.

1. *The reality of His Priesthood.* His office is called sacerdotal or priestly, because He truly accomplished the priestly functions implied in the instituted sacerdotal services in the Old Testament order—services which *prefigured* His work. He turned their types into reality. Of this fact, and the consequent fact that Christ's office is really priestly, we have abundant Scripture proof. Prophecy pointed to Him: "The Lord hath sworn and will not repent, Thou art a priest forever after the order of Melchizedek "(Ps. 110:4). This connection of Christ's priesthood with that of Melchizedek is not a denial that He fulfilled the import of the sacrificial activity of the Aaronic priesthood, but means simply that He was in the office, not as one among many, but in a peculiar way, without predecessor, without successor, the alone offerer of the effectual Sacrifice, to which the Hebrew sacrifices pointed, and from which they have

their real value. See Heb. 1:3; 2:17; 3:1: 4:14–16; 5:5–10; 6:20: and chs. 7 to 10.

He was a Priest because, as we shall see, the sacerdotal function was a *real necessity* for human salvation. The necessity rests back on the fallen and guilty condition of man. The Old Testament priest's function arose out of this fact, and rested on a felt and clearly recognized sense of need which developed priestly action even in all the natural religions of the world. One of the largest and most self-revealing facts in universal humanity is the sense of sin, with felt need of reconciliation with offended Deity, requiring sacrifices of expiation and propitiation, and giving rise to the priestly idea and function. However crude the conception or ill-adjusted or even shocking the rites, the practices of pagan peoples have ever testified to the necessity to be met. The universal reality of sin and guilt is the explanation of the existence of priesthood everywhere. As a Priest Christ became the "desire of all nations"—desired in the sense of being a felt necessity of the race. And since the incarnation itself was in order to redemption through sacrificial self-offering, as the propitiation for sin, the reason of the *central* character of priestly functions already asserted becomes clear. It is not simply an equal function with the prophetic and kingly, but the *heart* of the redemptory service, to whose aim and consummation the other two are needfully conjoined. It is conceivable that the Son of God could have accomplished the teaching and kingly functions without incarnation, but not the priestly. The priestly office thus ranks with the all-surpassing importance of the incarnation itself, and subordinates as collateral or tributary all His other activities in the work of human salvation. It marks the central and determining function of the Savior of mankind. It is instructive to observe how the apostles put their emphasis on this and hold it before the reader's mind.

2. The *general nature* of the priestly work appears in noting a few features of it. (*a*) Its generic function is that of *reconciliation;* "God was in Christ reconciling the world unto Himself, not imputing their trespasses unto them" (2 Cor. 5:19); "When we were enemies we were reconciled to God by the death of His Son" (Rom. 5:10); "For it pleased the Father that in Him should all fullness dwell, and having made peace through the blood of His cross," etc. (Col. 1:19–22; Heb. 2:17). (*b*) The formal mode of its accomplishment is reflected from the ritual types of the Old Testament which, as ceremonial action, pointed to this divine work of reconciliation. The

priestly office, as mediatorial, presented the sacrifice of propitiation in atonement for the guilt of the offender, opening the way to assurance of forgiveness and restored relation of peace with God. In themselves these Levitical sacrifices could not expiate sin or compensate for its wrong, but were accepted as instrumental reality envirtued from the "Lamb of God," already, in plan and efficacy, "slain from the foundation of the world" (Rev. 13:8; 5:9–10; John 1:29–36). The full presentation of this belongs to the doctrine of the atonement. (*c*) A distinct feature in the form of Christ's priestly work is that He *sacrificed Himself,* uniting in His own Person the offering and the Offerer. He came in the flesh to be the antitype of both the priest and the sacrifice of old. The world could bring no adequate sacrifice—could furnish no competent priest. Only He could act in priestly mediatorship, to open the way for human return to reconciliation with God, in His propitiation "taking away the sin of the world." But He actualized, completed, and absolved the whole priestly function, in the sense that no official priest is now needed or has any place. By the "one offering He hath perfected forever them that are sanctified "and there is "no more sacrifice for sin" (Heb. 10:14, 26; 1 Pet. 3:18; 2 Cor. 5:21; Heb. 1:3; 7:23–27; 9:24–26). (*d*) The priestly work being so distinctly an intervening for conditions of forgiveness and peace, it is in this pre-eminently that Christ's work becomes mediatorial. Mediatorial relation holds, indeed, in His prophetic and kingly functions, but most clearly and thoroughly in His self-offering for the sin of the world.

THE PARTS OF HIS PRIESTLY WORK
I. THE ATONEMENT
The opposition in our day to the use of the word 'atonement' in this connection is not justified either by the Scriptures or the logic of reason. It comes sometimes as a natural consequence of Socinian denial of the true divinity of Christ; sometimes from superficial interpretation of the Biblical truth of sin and the relation of God's holiness to the conditions of forgiveness of it. We are pointed to the fact that the word is found but once in our common English New Testament (Rom. 5:11), and that in the revised version even this disappears, as it should, in the word "reconciliation." But the reality which theology employs it to express remains, organized into its continuous representation of Christ's work. And over against the absence of the word in the New Testament, we count its employment in the Old sixty-three times for direct designation of

the priestly function opening the way to God's forgiveness of sin and grace to sinners. And what is more, the entire New Testament doctrine of forgiveness of sin is directly and fundamentally drawn by apostolic pens from the procedure of "atonement" divinely incorporated in those Old Testament typical rites. The apostle's declaration (Rom. 5:11), "We joy in God through our Lord Jesus Christ by whom we have now *received the reconciliation*," expresses joy in the *result* of Christ's work, and, as he makes emphatically clear elsewhere, as in Rom. 3:25–26, rather implies than denies His mediatorial and priestly function by which the conditions for reconciliation were opened and the blessing made possible. The resultant reconciliation, and the work opening the way to it, are different things, which the apostle does not confound. The truth to be inquired into here is not the blessing made possible, but what lay back of it and was needed to provide the necessary conditions for it, viz.: the nature or elements of Christ's high-priestly work as its procuring antecedent. For designation of this work theology has fittingly employed the term atonement (derivatively, at-one-ment), under which to bring into view the teaching of the Scriptures.

It is to be noted here, also, that theology must rightly recognize the distinction between the essential reality or truth of atonement as presented by the Scriptures for the faith of men, and the speculative *theories* which have been, or may be, elaborated to explicate the philosophy by which it has validity and operative power. The "theory" is a theologic formulation or systemization of some, more or fewer, of the features of revealed truth discerned in the Person of Christ—His relations to God and to man, His love and holiness, His mediatorship, obedience, sufferings, death, and resurrection, framed together according to some human conception of adaptation which is made to stand ideally for the atoning efficiency. But the constructed theories vary and stand apart, some finding the explaining principle in one feature, others in another. The process of speculative construction is usually a narrowing movement, and exhibits truth only in parts or fragments. The atonement, as to its divine philosophy or grounds of validity as it lies in God's thought, is apostolically recognized as part of the "mystery of godliness, without controversy great" (1 Tim. 3:16). The fact of His provision of an effective atonement has been abundantly assured; but He has not lifted it out of all mystery by adding an explanation of its philosophic ground or how it is that it actually provides a basis for God "to be just and the justifier of him which believeth in Jesus"

Christian Theology

(Rom. 3:26). Its essential reality, in a historical manifestation of the eternal Son of God in human nature, condemning human sin and providing in His own perfect obedience and innocent suffering even unto death an adequate moral satisfaction for man's failure and guilt, opening the way to forgiveness and peace with God—this is the practical gospel message offering a provided salvation. Men are not saved by accepting a formal philosophy of the atonement, but through faith in the revealed fact and the divine promise. The fact and promise, in their revealed and historic form, are comprehensible by all men and suffice for faith; the partial, narrowed, fragmentary theories of its *rationale* are not the essential thing for saving efficacy. To the masses of men they are unknown, and scarcely interpretable. However valuable any one of them may be in theologically elucidating some aspect of truth in the atonement, or all of them may be in conducting systematic thinking to a comprehensive view of the philosophy of redemption, no one of them is to be allowed as itself the full and absolute Gospel. The atonement as God's provision, of adequate force and breadth, is one thing; a theory of it is another thing, and may be partial, one-sided, or even obscuring.

We must primarily, therefore, read the reality of the atonement in the form presented to our faith in the Scriptures. But it will be helpful to preface this with definitions of some of the chief terms employed in connection with the subject, whether fixed distinctly by the Scriptures or by the usage of theological discussion. (*a*) *Sacrifice.* When used in relation to forgiveness of sin, this specifically carries the conception of a substitutionary endurance, by innocence, of the ill-desert or consequences of guilty wrong-doing, and so opening the way to remission for the offender. In both typical symbolism and in effective redemption, the term sacrifice denotes an offering that provides conditions for pardon. Lev. 4:15-21; 5:14-18; Deut. 21:1-9; Heb. 9:11-28. (*b*) *Satisfaction* is a theological term, used to express the precise thing accomplished for us through Christ's obedience and suffering unto death. He satisfied the claims of divine and necessary righteousness with respect to sinners, so that they may be consistently released from the sufferings due their guilt. (*c*) *Expiation* is an equivalent to satisfaction, designating the cancelling of guilt, or so satisfying for it as to take away the necessity of its deserved punishment. It effects an opening to forgiveness. It has no reference to the *defilement* of sin—only to its liability to punishment. (*d*) *Propitiation* relates to God as ethical Ruler or Father, and refers to the fact that the expiatory sacrifice or offering, while satisfying for the guilt of sin, opens God's way to an actual acceptance of the repentant sinner. "The offense is expiated; God is propitiated," *i. e.*, the reparation made by the vicarious endurance of the consequences due to the sin and sinners by the Son in human flesh, makes it possible for God consistently to show grace and love to the guilty or ill-deserving. It is not necessary, however, or even allowable to include the idea that in the "propitiation" any change is wrought in God's essential mercifulness or desire to graciously forgive and save. Such an idea is to be rejected as utterly false and misleading. As a designation, propitiation throws into specific view, not at all that God does not love His creature or desire to save sinners, but that in the atoning work of Christ the ethical and governmental hindrances are taken out of the way of His pardoning and saving love. It was His love, or graciousness, that opened the way: "God so loved the world that He gave His only begotten Son" (John 3:16). (*e*) *Vicarious* expresses the idea and reality of substitution, *i. e.*, that in His high-priestly work Christ put His divine-human obedience and suffering in place and instead of what was due from sinful man, to be the ground upon which sin has been made pardonable and men are saved. It does not, therefore, simply mean, as Socinians explain, "on our behalf," or "for our benefit." (*f*) *Justice* or *righteousness* is employed in two different relations. One is to express an ethical attribute of God. He is righteous in His nature or being. The other is with respect to His government or objective moral administration. This is *administrative* justice. It is, further, discriminated as of two kinds: *first*, distributive or particular justice; *secondly*, public or general justice. The first refers to the special punishment which each wrong-doer owes for his sins; the second to such penalty or punishment as shall vindicate the supremacy of the law, so as to maintain the authority of government, making manifest the ill-desert of transgression. Penalty is not, in and for its own sake, a good, but is a means of enforcing righteousness and repressing the wrongs of sin. The chief good of the moral universe is in character; and punitive action falls into the relation of means to an end. Love, as well as justice, requires this. (*g*) *Redemption*. In the Scriptures this word seems sometimes to have about the same meaning as atonement, as in Gal. 3:13; 4:5; 1 Peter 1:18; Eph. 1:7; Col. 1:14. But it has wider meaning and application, covering the result as well as the process, *i. e.*, the entire *deliverance* gained, not only from the *penalty*, but also from the *power* of sin (Tit. 2:14, Heb. 9:12). We are

Christian Theology

redeemed through both atonement and regeneration. In tracing out the reality of the atonement in the form in which the Scriptures present it to our faith we will have the proper tests of the correctness of these definitions, as well as a view of the doctrine itself.

Necessity of the Atonement
As already evident, the revelation that proclaims an atonement rests the necessity of it back upon the terrible fact of sin. Everywhere, from the beginning to the close of the volume which has accredited itself to Christendom as a record of God's supernatural self-manifestation for the spiritual life of man, the need of redemptory action is connected with humanity's lapse into the guilt and corruption of transgression. Record of the fact of this guilt and corruption is placed in its opening pages, and then on to its end is made to underlie and determine the necessary provision for recovery through divine forgiveness and renewal. Whatever may be the reality of the atonement, as marked in the Scriptures, it has its necessity in the sin and guilt of man.

The *necessity* is here specifically asserted over against the representations of some who deny it, and teach that God can forgive sin simply in His own sovereign will or good pleasure, in absolute right to do as He pleases. This teaching comes from various sources and is grounded on various bases. Sometimes it is based on the conception that the moral law is a product of the mere volition of God, and that it is in His power to enforce or annul it, as taught by Duns Scotus; sometimes on the idea that simple mercy on God's part and repentance on man's suffice to meet all the exigencies in the case; sometimes on the representation that forgiveness is purely an act of God in His character and relation of *Father*, without any connection with legalistic or governmental ideas or realities, as by Ritschlianism; and largely upon the denial or minimizing of the Biblical doctrine of sin, as is found in much of current naturalistic ethicalism or evolutionism. The open departure of these teachings from fundamental Christian theism and the Biblical view of sin and the necessary antagonism of God's very nature to it, allies them rather with rejection of Christianity than with the question of the correct interpretation of the atonement. They shift away from basal views so widely as to propose another Gospel. The "ground of right," or immutable morality, in the *eternal nature* of God, is swept away by the first. All the rest de-ethicalize both God's nature and administration, by in some form implying that there is nothing in that nature or its action requiring account to be taken of moral necessities. They assume that God can pass over sin and guilt, and through forgiveness take the guilty to the bosom of His love, without regard to anything He owes to Himself and His government with respect to that holiness which, along with love, is the grandeur and glory of His being. Surely these offered conceptions are not even an echo of the doctrine of the long list of teachers, including Christ Himself, whose words or writings Providence has preserved as the record of the divine redemptive work. If we accept this record we must respect its teaching as to this necessity of atonement in order to forgiveness.

First, the Old Testament sacrifices *assumed* and *implied* it. It was made organic in the instituted order of worship. Atonement through sacrifices was the normal precondition of sin's remission and the grace of reconciliation. Readers of the Old Testament discover what a large fact this is.

Secondly, the necessity is distinctly *asserted* in a way that makes the principle hold for both the Old and New Testaments: "Without shedding of blood," *i. e.*, sacrifices of atonement, "there is no remission" (Heb. 9:22). "For every high priest is ordained to offer gifts and sacrifices; wherefore it is of necessity that this Man have somewhat also to offer" (Heb. 8:3). "Christ, through the eternal Spirit, offered Himself without spot" (Heb. 9:14).

Thirdly, this redemptive atonement was treated by Christ as a necessity for the very end of His coming. He distinctly connected that coming with His sufferings and death. He spoke of these as giving His life a "ransom," as His "body given" and "blood shed for the remission of sin." It is instructive to trace the increasing explicitness with which, in His later ministry, in order to correct the error of His disciples as to an earthly Messiahship, He felt it needful to make clear His true Messianic destination. "From that time forth Jesus began to show unto His disciples how that He must go unto Jerusalem and suffer many things of the elders and chief priests and scribes, and be killed and be raised again the third day" (Matt. 16:21). Here we manifestly have Christ's culminating idea of His earthly function. When Peter protests against such ending of His work, He treats him as another tempter dissuading Him from His great mission: "Get thee behind me, Satan, for thou savorest not the things that be of God" (Matt. 16:23). The transfiguration is made an occasion of reference to this function, in the high scene in which

Christian Theology

Moses and Elias were in conversation with Him concerning "the decease which He should accomplish at Jerusalem" (Luke 9:31). "As they came down from the mountain, He charged them that they should tell no man what things they had seen, *till the Son of man were risen* from the dead" (Mark 9:9). After this, again to correct false hopes and carnal rivalries for the highest places in a temporal kingdom, He repeated the assurance of His approaching death, and added an explanation of the meaning and need of it: "The Son of man came not to be ministered unto, but to minister, and to give His life a ransom for many" (Mark 10:45). We are not here seeking the elemental realities in the atonement, but the Savior's view of its necessity; and in this relation the bearing of this incident is explicit. For His assertion is that the voluntary act in which He gives His life a ransom is made the very end of His becoming incarnate in the world, the Son of man. Onward from that time, and after finally going up to Jerusalem with His Messianic thought clear on sufferings, there to end His life, His converse and parables hold the view of His disciples steadily to this purpose of His existence, centered in His death. The infliction of that death is credited to the sin and wickedness of men. But He pictured His own *presence* and *submission* of Himself to the deathworking power as opening His chosen way to human salvation and the kingdom of God. The parable of the wicked husbandmen portrays them as casting out and killing the owner's son, but only to the exclusion of themselves from the vineyard, and its passing over to a people that would render the divine fruitage. The breaking of the alabaster box is made to signify an anointing for His approaching burial, not as the point of failure of the divine purpose of His life, but of a success that would carry His name "throughout the whole world where the Gospel shall be preached." But passing by other instances, the most significant of all is His institution of the Holy Supper, through which He places the emphasis of His work in the world upon the sacrificial *giving of His body and the shedding of His blood for the remission of sins*, and establishes a perpetual memorial of this to centralize the thought and faith of men in looking to Him as the Savior. This act was an emphatic testimony to the necessity of the provision to be made.

Fourthly, in the apostolic teaching this atonement is represented as the actual and alone ground of remission of sin and reconciliation. St. Paul declares of Him: "Who was delivered for our offenses and was raised again for our justification;" "Being now justified by His blood we shall be saved from wrath through Him" (Rom. 4:25; 5:1-9; 3:24-25; John 3:14-15).

Fifthly, the possibility of divine acceptance on the ground of man's own innocence or goodness is positively denied (Rom. 3:20-23; Gal. 2:16; 3:10-11).

It is of absolutely corroborative force that this necessity of the atonement is identical with the necessity of the incarnation. We have found that the theory which asserts the incarnation as absolute in God's plan for humanity, apart from the contingency of sin, rests on no Scripture authority, but is counter to its distinct and positive affirmations, and breaks down when tested on rational grounds. There was in the lapse of humanity into sin and guilt a necessity to be divinely met, if man was to be saved. And the point of the necessity was not in those functions met by Christ in His prophetic or kingly offices. It is conceivable, as we have said, that God could have opened adequate channels of instruction of men in respect to His own will, human duty, and destiny. It is conceivable, also, that the kingly office in the "kingdom of heaven," might be exercised apart from the Word's becoming flesh. But the priestly function of making in Himself a sacrifice for the sin of the world, a propitiation through vicarious suffering and death—even though the conception of the atonement should be reduced to that of the moral influence theory—is *not* conceivable apart from the incarnation. The necessity of the atonement, therefore, becomes identical with the very essence of the necessity for the incarnation. Thus it becomes one with that moral need to meet which God sent His Son into the world, and is the explaining reason for the existence of Christianity.

This evidence of the necessity goes far toward suggesting the *grounds* of it. These open to view and are best marked as *proximate* and *ultimate*. They differ as between what is immediate in the relation of God to the world, and what is back of that relation and as absolute as God Himself. Thus, the "proximate," presenting itself in twofold relation, appears, *first*, as *moral, i. e.*, that the moral requirement of holiness and equity need in some way to be satisfied before the sinner can be acquitted and held as in acceptable relation; and, *secondly, governmental*, that the necessary authority and sanctity of the divine administration be properly vindicated against moral evil and its destructive work. The divine government, it would seem, could not consistently remit sin except through some sacrificial tribute to the moral law that recognizes sin's demerit and is attended with a power that reforms the sinner. But the "ultimate"

Christian Theology

ground of the necessity must be in God Himself—that there is that in the perfections of His own nature which requires the atonement in order to make it possible or consistent to proclaim the gospel of forgiveness. The question of these grounds will necessarily come again into view in further tracing the nature of the atonement.

It is proper to note here that the Biblical teaching of this necessity is not without support in clear principles of human life and reason. The necessity being a moral one, it finds echo in the intellectual and moral nature of the race. The groping movement of pagan religions into the use of sacrifices reflects this fact. And there is a rational response to the representations of revelation. The moral judgment of mankind affirms sin or wrongdoing to be ill-deserving. Experience discloses it to be destructive of virtuous character, ideal excellence, and both personal and social welfare, and as working untold injury and suffering, even unto death. Scientific thought observes in the working of sin the movement of a natural law of "cause and effect," of action and its reaction or injurious consequences, akin to the regularity of the law of cause and effect in physical nature, only that in moral causation free-will changes, modifies, and obscures the direct line of sequences. The penal sufferings fall not only on the guilty, but often, through the solidarity of human life, on the innocent, and spread in far-reaching lines. The moral reason consents that to let sin go unpunished or unrebuked by penal suffering, or to make the guilty happy in their sins, is a failure in justice and a contradiction of both holiness and goodness. The maintenance of righteousness alone can satisfy the decisions of our moral nature, which asserts the rightful supremacy of holiness. Hence our moral reason comes into accord with the Scripture teaching of the necessity of the atonement.

The Nature of the Atonement

This will appear by tracing successively the ends to be secured by it, the way in which it is declared to have been accomplished, and the different theories which have sought to explicate the *rationale* of its effectiveness.

i. THE ENDS TO BE SECURED. These were necessarily twofold, because there were two sides in the relation made abnormal by human sin. This sin broke at once the true and necessary relation of man to God, and, by law of inevitable ethical consequence, made God's relation to him one of just condemnation or reprobation. Man was out of right relation to God because he had changed, and God, out of approving and complacent relation, because He could not change. God's relation cannot be the same to the evil and the good. His love cannot governmentally treat righteousness and sin alike. Sin is at once alienation from God, and an ill-deserving unrighteousness that cannot justly be passed over in simple compassion for the sinner. And so the New Testament teaching is that the atonement needed was such a work by Christ as should, on the one hand, reconcile divine forgiveness of sin with the unlowered supremacy of holiness and righteousness; and, on the other, reconcile estranged man to God. Thus its primary and fundamental purpose was in its *Godward* bearing—to remove out of the way all ethical and governmental obstacles to a gracious forgiveness and acceptance of sinners. It was, in its transcendent realities and bearings, to make such satisfaction to God's holiness and righteousness as to render if possible for God consistently to act in pardoning love to penitent guilt. "Whom [Christ Jesus] God hath set forth to be a propitiation through faith in His blood, to declare His righteousness for the remission of sins that are past; to declare, I say, at this time His righteousness, that He might be just and the justifier [accounter just] of him which believeth in Jesus" (Rom. 3:25–26). "For Christ also hath once suffered for sins, that He might bring us to God" (1 Peter 3:18). "Christ was once offered to bear the sins of many" (Heb. 9:28). "But this Man, after He had offered one sacrifice for sins forever, sat down on the right hand of God "(Heb. 10:12). "There remaineth no more sacrifice for sins" (Heb. 10:26). In its *humanward bearing*, the end sought through the atonement, as distinctly indicated by the supreme manifestation and appeal of redeeming love, is to overthrow man's alienation and inspire trust, love, and, obedience. "God was in Christ reconciling the world unto Himself, not imputing their trespasses unto them" (2 Cor. 5:19).

These two ends are inseparable in a full Scriptural view of the atonement. They have often been torn apart, one or the other denied, or they have failed to be held in adjusted relation to each other. Theology sometimes, especially in its older Latin and earlier Protestant forms, brought scarcely anything but the first into view. The love of God was hidden behind strong delineations of His anger and wrath, and the impression frequently left that God's disposition or nature had to be changed toward mankind by the sufferings of. Christ The idea that "*God so loved* the world" as to give His Son to the work, that "*God was in Christ* reconciling the world to Himself," had small place in this connection. On the other hand, Socinian and rationalistic theologies have shown a tendency to deny or underrate the bearing of the atonement on the Godward side, and resolve it all into a manifestation of the divine love to win the human heart and inspire faith and obedience. This has run into a claim that the "Moral Influence Theory" presents the entire reality of the atonement, and a denial of any bearing of it on the possibility or fact of forgiveness. But the decisive point which divides all false or partial theories from the true and full conception is right here—in this denial or omission of the Godward side. Whatever may be the philosophy of the atonement, any account which makes such denial thereby takes its position outside of the requirements of Scripture orthodoxy. Whatever way it was accomplished or whatever elemental realities were necessary and included in the process of provision, this double aim must be recognized and held in view for correct and full explication of the doctrine.

II. How the Atonement was Accomplished. The *mode* reveals to us the very core of the *nature* of this work. And this must be explained and seen in respect to both the ends to be secured. Though both are accomplished by one and the same atoning work, this becoming efficacious on the Godward and manward sides, we will have a clearer view by considering them separately.

As to the Godward Bearing. In this we find a double work accomplished:

1. Christ came in our room and stead "under the law," the law of human duty, and through His entire life fulfilled it all for us, thus by vicarious action providing for us a perfect righteousness, imputable to all who receive Him as their Savior. The righteousness due from man, but which he, as sinful, could not attain, was provided by Christ. Jesus' perfect holiness was not maintained simply that He might be ready to present Himself as an unblemished sacrifice at last, but as actually working out and exhibiting an unbroken or sinless obedience that should at once honor the law and be an element in the vicarious satisfaction opening the way to forgiveness and acceptance of the unrighteous. This is part of the atonement properly called Christ's "active obedience" (*obedientia* or *satisfactio activa*), and necessarily included in the ground of *justification.* Hollaz defines: "By His active obedience Christ most exactly fulfilled the divine law in our stead, in order that penitent sinners, applying to themselves by true faith this vicarious fulfillment of the law, might be accounted righteous before God." This is the usual representation of our Lutheran dogmaticians. The Scripture warrant for it is clear and abundant. St Paul's view includes it: "That I may

win Christ, and be found in Him, not having mine own righteousness, which is of the law, but that which is through the faith of Christ, the righteousness which is of God by faith" (Phil. 3:8–9); "But of Him are ye in Christ Jesus who, of God, is made unto us wisdom and righteousness" (1 Cor. 1:30); "As by one man's disobedience many were made sinners, so by the obedience of One shall many be made righteous" (Rom. 5:19). This may include "obedience unto death" (Phil. 2:8), but as St. Paul uses it as an all-comprehensive term, parallel with Adam's transgression, which was active, it must necessarily include the obedience of His life. Christ Himself says: "Think not that I am come to destroy the law or the prophets; I am not come to destroy, but to fulfill" (Matt 5:17).

But as many theologians exclude Christ's active obedience as a distinct part of the ground of justification, the truth needs fuller statement. *First*, it must be remembered that the entire truth of the atonement rests upon the Person of Christ as the God-man. As the divine Son He was God and represents God's love in making an atonement for sin. As true Man, the universal humanity of the race having been assumed, He also *represented* mankind, and lived and offered His whole life, not for Himself, but for the gracious work He came to effect. This representative position was no ideal fiction, but sublime reality. Hence His whole earthly work must be regarded as actually and thoroughly mediatorial. The incarnation put Him in vicarious position, with all His official activity. He was "made of a woman, made under the law, to redeem them that were under the law, that we might receive the adoption of sons" (Gal. 4:4–5). He was "under the law," not for His own sake, but for man's sake, for the total vicarious redemption or propitiation. In it by His perfect obedience He confessed the authority of the law upon man, honored it, and condemned sin in the flesh—acting "for us" in it all. *Secondly*, simply the vicarious suffering of the Divine Redeemer, expiating the guilt of sin, satisfying justice against it, and thus providing forgiveness of it, would not of itself be the provision of a perfect righteousness for the forgiven. It could not provide all that they need. They need more than to be brought into the *negative* condition of release, by mere cancellation, from the guilt and penalties of sin. This would not in itself constitute them righteous. Yet for "justification" they need at once a *positive status* of acceptance. Even perpetual forgiveness alone would not make them either holy in themselves, or cause them to be *looked upon and held by God as righteous*. Yet they need both these things. Beyond the negative state

Christian Theology

of exemption from sin's penal consequences, they need endowment, by impartation, of a positive righteousness, whose perfection accords with the divine requirements. To say nothing, at this point, respecting the relation of the atonement to the restoration of believers to a *new life*, progressively advancing but never perfected on earth, it is proper to observe that that new *life*, in its faulty attainments and yet clinging sins, is not and cannot be the ground of their justification (Rom. 7:18; Phil. 3:13–14). Their justification, evangelically a "counting righteous," is based in the provision of Christ's atoning work. Moreover, righteousness has, *per se*, a positive and eternal significance and worth, which He could as little drop out of the satisfying provision as He could drop out of it the necessary expiation for the forgiveness of sin. Thus the provision of a vicarious righteousness, through Christ's divine-human, official, active obedience to the law of holiness, in inseparable jointure with His passive obedience in the suffering of death, is properly regarded as included in the atonement.

We find this inclusion from the early periods of Christianity. Thus Irenæus seems to have put it in the foreground as carrying deep significance, in the well-known passage in which he represents Christ as advancing through infancy, youth, and manhood, saving all ages by living and acting through them. Gregory, of Nyssa, mentions it as an element of redemption that Christ maintained a pure disposition in all the moments of His life.[2] The early and long-persistent theory of the payment of a ransom to Satan greatly hindered just conceptions of the atonement down to the scholastic era. In the Reformation theology the distinction of active and passive satisfaction was not sharply and strongly drawn until necessitated by the erroneous teaching of Osiander. The emphasis then laid upon the recovered evangelical truth of justification by faith threw into clear view the guiding principle for correct interpretation of the nature of the atonement. In Lutheran theology this principle put the distinction in clear and permanent ascendency, though dissent appeared and has continued in measure among the Reformed branches of Protestantism. The prolonged discussion has made it evident that the objections urged against this side of the atoning satisfaction have been due to the double fact that its advocates have often given it crude or unspiritual form, and its opponents have misinterpreted its significance. The right way of combining and applying the two sides has often been misconceived, giving rise to attacks or criticisms. Thus, for instance, the notion which interprets Christ's vicarious righteousness as meaning that personal righteousness is no longer due from *believers*, is by no means involved in the doctrine or legitimate as an inference from it. So, too, the objection to it which alleges that if the law has been satisfied by Christ's active obedience—this being a perfect righteousness, offsetting and answering for all our unrighteousness—there is no need for His vicarious *expiation of its guilt* by His death, has its plausibility only by reason of an exaggerated notion of the separate force of the *obedientia activa*. On the other hand, when criticism asserts that since the *penal sufferings* of Christ have fully atoned for all guilt, even the guilt of omitted good, there is no necessity of an imputed righteousness—sin's unrighteousness needing now only the provided forgiveness—the suggestion has its seeming weight because of failure to reach a true view of the bearing of the satisfaction on the two sides of its relation—to God's justice and man's need. It is fundamental, as theological thought is increasingly recognizing, that the *unity* and *self-consistency* of the atonement be preserved by a true and non-contradictory adjustment of its significance to both of these relations. The relation between the *obedientia activa* and *passiva* cannot be such as to allow the supposition that either of the two *without the other* effected a special part of the expiation or covered a special defect without respect to the other. Christ could not have expiated the guilt of sin apart from His own sinless obedience for man's sake, nor have provided a vicarious imputable righteousness by merely enduring the penal consequences of sin. Christ's personal and mediatorial righteousness was contributory to His expiatory function, and the expiatory function was at the same time contributory to working out a vicarious obedience that, according to St. Paul, is connected with the very end of the total atonement: "Who was delivered for our offenses and was raised again for our justification" (Rom. 4:25). These two designations of action express, not an absolute, but only relative difference. The whole Christ in the unity of His divine-human Person acted in that *unity;* and it was "action" as truly when by choice He accepted suffering and death for sin as when He maintained an unblemished holiness and obedience in His life; and the two sides of His work which we name by the two terms were indissolubly one, in interblending and contributory adaptation to the total need in both aspects, spanning, for true reconciliation, the entire chasm which sin had made between God and man.

Christian Theology

But some of these statements anticipate the second element in the Godward bearing. In our room and stead *Christ also suffered and died for our sins, expiating them by satisfying the divine holiness and justice against them, so as to make forgiveness possible and consistent.* This is His passive obedience (*obedientia passiva*). It is the sacrificial element of the atonement, the Just suffering for the unjust and vicariously satisfying for them. Having kept the law, under which He came for the whole vicarious redemptive service, He submitted to *its penalty*—not for Himself, for He had no sin of His own, but for us, thus paying the debt, *i. e.*, what was due to the demerit and evil of sin, for all who make Him and His work their own by faith. "By His death He hath satisfied for our sins."

This, as redemptive provision, holds logical precedence with respect to the vicarious righteousness. For it looks to securing the human state of forgiveness, to which the vicarious righteousness is imputable and imputed. Righteousness is not imputed to such as remain unforgiven. To the forgiven, and to them only, the imputation of Christ's substitutionary obedience becomes real and actual, and thus supplies the completing reality in justification, carrying this beyond a merely negative state of release from the penalty of sin into positive endowment of righteousness. So we may properly regard the *primary* import of the atonement as consisting in this passive obedience, furnishing that which is first and basal in justification.

Of the *fact* that Christ's passive obedience, His willing acceptance and endurance of suffering and death, is constitutive of the atonement in chief measure, the teaching of the Scriptures is explicit. The most casual reading of the Bible is sufficient to impress every unprejudiced mind with the vital and paramount relation of this to the salvation of men. Text follows text and declaration is added to declaration, to keep Christ before men's view as the Lamb of God that taketh away the sin of the world. The Old Testament points to this part of His work in type and shadow, bleeding victims and smoking altars, temple order, and prophetic announcements. Isaiah directs to a suffering Savior, stricken, smitten, making His soul an offering for sin, and justifying many by bearing their iniquities. Daniel beholds Him as "Messiah, the Son of man, cut off, but not for Himself." In the New Testament we hear Christ Himself declare, as He approaches the dreadful suffering: "For this purpose I came to this hour," and see Him appoint a memorial of His self-sacrifice, as for "remission of sin." And although His disciples at first could not understand it, yet, after the outpouring of the Holy Spirit, leading them into the truth, they were ready to exclaim: "God forbid that I should glory save in the cross of Christ"

The sufferings of Christ were not a mere incident in His mission—an incident to a simple mission of teaching and example. They were a "cup," the drinking of which stood in some necessary relation to provision for man's salvation. As He fulfilled the requirements of the law in our stead, by His sufferings and death He satisfied the claims of justice against our transgressions. It is sometimes alleged that we owe this teaching to Paul, as a development of doctrine beyond the teaching of Jesus. But we have already given sufficient evidence that it was not to Paul, or any of the apostles, that, primarily, we owe this conception, but to Christ Himself, who put this clear stamp upon the meaning of His sufferings and death. The apostles merely emphasized that upon which Jesus had already placed culminating stress. As proof that we owe this doctrine to Christ's own teaching, the following Scriptures fully suffice: Mark 9:9; 10:33–45; Matt. 16:21–23; 20:18–19, 21–23, 28; Luke 9:30–44; 12:50; 18:31–33; John 18:11; Matt. 24:26–29; Mark 14:22–25; Luke 22:19–20; Matt. 26:30–46. Apostolic affirmation of it: Acts 20:28, "The church of God which He hath purchased with His own blood"; Rom. 3:25–26, "Whom God hath set forth to be a propitiation through faith in His blood, to declare His righteousness for the remission of sins that are past, through the forbearance of God; to declare His righteousness, that He might be just and the justifier of him which believeth in Jesus"; Rom. 5:6, "For when we were yet without strength, in due time Christ died for the ungodly"; 1 Cor. 15:3, "Christ died for our sins according to the Scriptures"; 1 Cor. 5:7, "Christ our Passover is sacrificed for us." See also Rom. 5:8–9; 2 Cor. 5:21; 1 Pet 1:18–19; Heb. 9:12–14, 26–28.

These passages, and scores of others all through the New Testament, set forth unequivocally that Christ made His own sufferings a real sacrifice for the sins of the world—that, acting in vicarious capacity, He bore the sins of men, expiated their guilt, honored and satisfied the law and divine holiness, and opened the way to pardon. If the Scriptures do not teach this, then the whole science of exegesis must be false and misleading. For this is, in fact, what the Scriptures say. Dr. South was right when he wrote: "And this I am sure is spoken so plain and loud by the universal voice of the whole Book of God, that the Scripture must be crucified as well as Christ to give any tolerable sense to it."

Christian Theology

The Manward Bearing of the Atonement. This is simply the truth which the Moral Theory, dropping the Godward necessity and provision, mistakes for the whole atonement. It expresses its relation to reconciling *men to God.* It looks at it only in its adaptation as a divine appeal to the human conscience and heart, Love's means of overcoming human alienation and inspiring the faith that will return love for love. It is in this, through the Holy Spirit's regenerating power, that pardon of sins is guarded from becoming an injury to man's ethical nature.

III. EXPLANATORY STATEMENTS TO REMOVE MISCONCEPTIONS
1. The Scripture teaching requires, as the very core of the atonement, the reality of a vicarious *satisfaction of the divine justice and holiness against the guilt of sin.* God could not compromise His righteousness by simply passing over its unspeakable ill-desert. Tendencies to obscure and exclude the elements of sin's guilt and juridical satisfaction for it, and confine the scope of the atonement to a simple display of God's paternal love for trust and obedience, have appeared in various forms. But the very discussions which have revealed these tendencies have made increasingly certain the inadequacy of the views they offer. The reconciliation of forgiving grace with the divine righteousness remains a necessary and cardinal element in the atoning provision, if we are to retain the truth of God's absolute holiness, justice, and moral government. The divine love that redeems cannot be conceived as setting aside the holy claims of the divine righteousness in so doing. The divine attributes of love and righteousness are essentially not inconsistent, but in harmony with each other. There is a distinction between them, but no conflict. They agree and combine in the unity of God's perfection. They coincide and blend in the divine purposes. Love cannot desire what would overthrow righteousness. For, righteousness, which is synonymous with the honor of God, is of greater value than the whole world, and requisite to the order and welfare of mankind. Love is equally God's glory and the fountain of all creature good. They agree in working for the same ends. Love seeks man's redemption for the sake of human character and happiness. Holiness seeks it for the sake of the same. God's compassionate love cannot disregard or set aside the law of righteousness, on which all ethical welfare and blessedness depend. Only by maintaining and honoring it can that love hold the creature view to the very kind of life to which the redemptive work seeks to

restore. The justice of God must not only be preserved, but emphasized in the divine work of salvation. An adequate satisfaction must be recognized as rendered to that "justice" as revealing "the righteousness of God for the remission of sins." His very nature, as well as the untarnished sanctity of his government required it.

2. The entire work of atonement is *a work of love*. Though the divine holiness and justice appear and are vindicated in the movement, it was self-sacrificing goodness that initiated and accomplished that movement. Its direct aim was a gracious recovery of guilty and unworthy man to blessedness through forgiveness and restoration to true life. That it might reach this without surrender of righteousness was indeed essential in the atoning work; but the motive or "eternal purpose" was one of pure, and we must say, self-sacrificing love. And the truth that this very end of the redemptory kindness, the salvation of the lost, includes *recovery to holiness*, adds its testimony to the supremacy of the action of love in the movement effecting the reconciliation. The love is Holy Love, flowing in ethical channels for holy blessedness. Holiness is kept unimpaired, while Love, which is at one with it, acts in self-sacrifice in order to the sinner's restoration to holy blessedness. There is no conflict in God's nature when His goodness desires for lost sinners a gracious return to righteousness, and self-consistently opens a way. And there is no need for the suggestion that, in the vicarious movement in which the incarnate Son suffered as penal satisfaction for human sin, God was *directly punishing* Him in wrath. That suffering belonged, indeed, to the divine "counsel and foreknowledge." But it was inflicted by the hate and "wicked hands" of men. Peter, under the inspiration of the Spirit given to show the things of Christ, declares: "Him whom *ye* have taken and with wicked hands have crucified, *God* hath raised up" (Acts 2:23). We know of no Scripture whose legitimate interpretation teaches that God immediately inflicted suffering on the innocent Redeemer. What He endured was the wrong and violence of ungodly men and came as the onworking of wickedness. "The contradiction of sinners" through which He had reached this stage of His saving work, at last brought Him to the cross and to death. It was sinful man that caused it all. The love of both the Father and the Son foresaw all the strife which sin would wage against even Holy Love, and that the Savior's way and work would be through such an experience. Christ foreknew that He had only to place Himself in the path of the sinful perversity of men, and He would be on the

Christian Theology

way to die for humanity. The culminating wickedness of the world, thus foreseen, was voluntarily met and endured by redeeming Love. The Father was showing no displeasure with the Son in those awful sufferings—rather, if conceivable, *more love*, as this redemptive work was the common counsel of the divine goodness.

And here must be recalled the transcendent and transforming truth that the death of Christ was not that of a mere martyr. It was chosen and purposive. It was spontaneous and with design. The martyr's death turns on the will of others. This turned on Jesus' own; and this fact changed His death from a martyrdom to a *sacrifice*. "Sacrifice is possible only when there is perfect freedom—where a man surrenders what he has both the right and the power to withhold." Jesus distinctly declared His course and the issue of it to be free: "Therefore doth My Father love Me, because I lay down My life, that I might take it again. No man taketh it from Me, but I lay it down of Myself. I have power to lay it down, and I have power to take it again. This commandment have I received of My Father" (John 10:17, 18). He had only to fulfill His chosen mission of teaching the truth and reproving sin, to insure the certainty of suffering and death. He was voluntarily and expiatorily receiving the curse of human guilt into His own bosom. And it is to be observed that Christ affirmed this spontaneity of love, in enduring all this, to be identical with the very purpose of His incarnate mission: "The Son of man *came* not to be ministered unto, but to minister, and to give His life a ransom for many" (Mark 10:45). It was the supreme wisdom of love, in the drama of redemption-history, to transmute the appearance of martyrdom into the reality of an expiatory sacrifice for the sins of the world. It reveals Love's conquering wisdom and power.

3. The *representative position* of Christ needs to be emphasized and conceived in truer and more vital connection with His vicarious function. It is often represented in a too abstract and formal way, leaving it without the force of a substantial and effective reality. Inadequate thought makes it little more than a fiction, or lowers it to a mere official appointment. The simply *legal* or *appointive* idea, guiding many minds, fails to suggest the essential and vital reality in which Christ's representative character consists. It is, indeed, official, but in an office not merely by *legal* or *appointive* powers, but *grounded in the very constitution and nature of His Divine-human Person*. The conditions for effective atonement were provided in the God-man, who not only represented, but really *was* both God and

man, divine and human. The representative relation was based in the actuality of the being of the Savior. Since Christ was "God manifest in the flesh," His work and sufferings in accomplishing the atonement were fully and perfectly divine, God Himself making the provision, at once meeting the requirements of His own attributes and the needs of man. The sacrificial sufferings and death were not merely human, but divine also; since Christ necessarily *suffered in the unity of His personal divine-human consciousness.* Only a *divine* self-sacrifice of suffering, an offering of infinite ethical value, to counterpoise the ill-desert of human sin, could be a complete atonement and answer to the demands of righteousness against it. And that divine satisfaction, vicariously real, becomes imputable, because wrought *in* and *for* the humanity which the divine Love laid hold of with the atoning aim. For that humanity, preserved sinless in Jesus, having no sins of its own to expiate, became sharer in the divine sufferings through which Christ expiated as well as condemned sin in the flesh.

4. This point connects itself closely with another—that the atoning value of the sufferings of Christ is to be seen and estimated not simply or chiefly on their physical side, but mainly in their *spiritual elements* and significance. The aim looked to physical redemption only secondarily and consequentially. It sought spiritual or ethical relations and life. It meant spiritual recovery from sin and sinfulness; a moral redemption from the evils and woes in which man's true life is wrecked. The woe of all the woes of humanity—the grief, so to speak, of God with respect to man made in His image and for His fellowship—was the spiritual ruin of disobedience, whose evils could be arrested only through a pardon which should open the gate of return. And the atoning sufferings are not be conceived or measured in the terms of *physical* pain, of either scourging or cross. Terrible as this was, Christ could and did accept it and uncomplainingly endure it. But long before this He had, in the spirit of love, "emptied Himself of the form of God," and humbled Himself to trials of compassionate service, had taken into His "soul" (Isa. 53:10) the burden, grief, and misery of sin's "contradiction" against God and against His own loving endeavor to lead men into true spiritual life. Without entering into sin, He had entered into sympathy with the wretchedness of man's alienated, unspiritual state and hardness of heart (Mark 3:5; 16:14), which met and distressed Him at every turn, until He bore an inconceivable weight of sympathetic sorrow, troubling Him and bruising His soul, forcing

Christian Theology

tears of grief over the sacred city and bloody sweat in Gethsemane. For years already He was carrying His atoning passion before He came to the scourging, the thorny crown, the torturing cross. And even when these physical sufferings smote Him, it was the spiritual aim that He had His eye upon, and the spiritual side and quality of His sufferings that constituted the essence and measure of their atoning worth and effect Not physical suffering in itself, but the spiritual worth and merit of Love's endurance of it lifts it all into atoning value. It is this spiritual quality that made *all* His divine-human sufferings the true "sacrifice," the adequate "propitiation" for the sins of the world, so that now God can be just and yet the justifier of the ungodly.

In these sufferings in which Christ vicariously became bearer of the curse of sin, we seem fully entitled, if not necessitated, to include the anguish of forsakenness on the cross: "My God, My God, why hast Thou forsaken Me" The mystery of this experience must be interpreted in the actual relations in which He was suffering. He had reached the culminating hour of sin-bearing—was within its darkest shadows. Through His sympathy He had entered into the world's misery and ill-desert, assuming it all for substitutionary expiation. That sympathy was moved, above all, in view of the guilt and deserved punishment of humanity—and that in far stronger sense than men themselves feel. And it is truly part of the reality of man's fallen and guilty state, to be without a sense of the divine approval and fellowship, without consciousness of God's loving presence and help. In making His own what belongs to our sinful state, and thus drawing on Himself the penalty due us, Christ is here revealed as having entered into this human reality of being without the light of the Father's face. Not that the Father positively or directly withdrew His love in fact, but that under this darkest cloud of suffering the wages of sin and tasting death, His vision of it was obscured and momentarily lost. Thus He bore the very worst of sin's curse. The order of "substitution" became complete, Christ covering man's sinful condition to the uttermost with His vicarious work and suffering.

5. This *spiritual quality* of Christ's sufferings reaches beyond the question of their expiatory value, and helps us to a proper revision of the *quantitative representations* of the atonement. These arose from not making clear distinction, in the doctrine of sin, between *generic* and *personal* sin, or between the universal and common guilt of mankind and the personal sins of the members of the race, as

creating the need of this redemptive provision. Many writers have estimated the necessary satisfaction through consideration of the countless multitude of sinners, and the innumerable kinds and grades of sin whose guilt is to be expiated. The tendency was to assume that the satisfaction of divine justice consisted in the same amount of suffering befalling Christ as would have to be endured by those to be saved, or to whom the way of salvation was to be opened. It involved the view that the amount would be greater or less, according to the number and guilt of the persons atoned for. Both the guilt of sinners and the sufferings of Christ were estimated quantitatively. Christ was conceived as having assumed each individual's sins and borne the full penalty for each and all. Thus each person's debt was fully satisfied and paid. In order to make atonement at all, an impression obtained that Christ must have endured the pains of hell—this being due from divine justice to sin *per se*—; and, further, that for each sinner there must have been measured to Him the full numerical amount of suffering due. This externalizing of the idea of punishment, making it quantitative, leads to an undue stress on Christ's physical sufferings, and proportionately to an under-valuation of the spiritual and ethical elements and the *infinite value* of these in the sphere of righteousness. The problem belongs to the realm of moral worth. The worth turns on the *perfect disposition* in which man's Divine substitute maintained, for God, the inviolability of the law of holiness in suffering the utmost injustice of human wickedness. We are not compelled to conceive the sum of His sufferings equal, in amount, to that due to all separate sins, wrongs, and crimes of all men of all ages, poured upon Him in the last few hours of His tasting death for all. If such full quantitative payment of the debt of sin was made, the logic of it would be the conclusion that, as the debt of sin has been fully paid, there is no room for pardon, and that salvation and eternal life are now due to men as their right. Much rather than this, do the teachings of Christ and His apostles go to establish the doctrine that the atonement consists in such a spiritual satisfaction and propitiation for the generic sin of human disobedience and guilt as make it consistently possible for God, in His holiness and justice, to *forgive* sin to those who accept Christ as their Savior, Righteousness, and Life.

6. The recognition of this *spiritual quality* of Christ's redeeming satisfaction undermines the basis of the current Ritschlianism, which sets aside the whole idea of a vicarious atonement by Christ,

and makes forgiveness independent of such provision, and purely an unmediated action of God's *Fatherhood*. Its contention insists on remodeling the traditional church doctrine of Christ's priesthood and sacrifice. It repudiates the legal relations and forensic character of justification, and asserts this to be, not an act of God as Lawgiver or moral Ruler, but only as a gracious Father, in simply paternal pardon. It denies that this fatherly Love needs to pay tribute to holiness or justice in connection with remission, and teaches that "the righteousness of God," to be maintained and exhibited in connection with it, is simply "His self-consistent and undeviating action on behalf of the members of His community" and is "in its essence identical with His grace." Christ's "priesthood" is reduced to maintaining 'such a character and fellowship of piety with God as to have free and acceptable approach to Him in worship, prayer, and intercession'—which priestly function was accomplished through His example of sincere and trusting faith in the Father's ever-forgiving love. All this modification of the Church's theology has been prompted by supposed difficulties in its doctrine of vicarious atonement. But it presents more serious difficulties than those sought to be removed. The first difficulty is in its palpable contradiction of the distinct soteriological statements of the Scripture. But, further, the rational demands of Christian theism forbid the negation of all the divine moral attributes but love, or the resolution of all into love. Holiness and righteousness are fundamental, and mean moral or spiritual law. The proposed exclusion of moral "law" from relation to the paternal love in forgiveness is self-contradictory to the whole Biblical conception of God. Most true, indeed, is it, that forgiveness rests in His Fatherhood and becomes its most glorious manifestation. By His creatorship men were constituted creature-sons of God. It was of Fatherhood that His love desired redemption for His fallen and sinful children. In love He gave His own Son, and seeks to recover. But while acting in Fatherhood, God is also in His eternal essence or nature Law, ethical Righteousness, and moral Lawgiver and Ruler, and can no more cease to be righteous or just than cease the reality of loving Fatherhood to beings made to bear His image. To exclude all but His Fatherhood in this work of Holy Love is not only superficial thought, but distinctly false to the whole revelation He has given of Himself. In His love He may, and does, yearn over His children, but He cannot just say to their sinning, "I forgive," and treat them as if they had never done wrong at all. He cannot, *for their sakes*, do so.

Milton Valentine

He cannot, for *His own sake*. He owes something to His own holiness. His nature can open His fatherly heart only as, at the same time, He preserves, for His own sake and His creatures' sake, His holy and righteous nature and dominion. And it is in the proper estimate or emphasis of the *ethical and spiritual* value of the holy self-devotion and sufferings of the Redeemer in maintaining and exhibiting the inviolability of righteousness even unto death, that we find the explanation of their moral worth against the worth of exacted penalties on sin.

7. The atonement is properly viewed as vitally, if not formally, including the *incarnation* of the divine Son as well as His resurrection from the dead. It has been well said that "Christ's whole work as Redeemer was of a piece." The movement was an organic unity from its beginning to its close. And it is usually conceded that the beginning of "sacrifice" by the redeeming Son is found in His self-emptying and humiliation in taking the "form of a servant"—for our sakes 'becoming poor.' He Himself declares that He "came" for this purpose, *i. e.*, to give His life a 'ransom.' From first to last His work had an objective meaning for pardon and renewal. It was by His whole humiliation, in whatever suffering it involved to its end, as inherent in His unique vocation, that He redeemed us. And just as vitally connected with the satisfying atonement is His *resurrection*. This is, indeed, not part of His sufferings. Yet St. Paul, though he makes a distinction, connects them in inseparable unity for forgiveness of sin: "Who was delivered for our offenses and was raised again for our justification" Rom. 4:25). He seems to link them in a coalescent unity, in which the second is more than a simple *witness* to the atoning reality of the first; it is also a veritable and necessary *completing* element, in such sense that without the resurrection there would *be* no adequate atonement available for mankind. "If Christ be not raised, your faith is vain; ye are yet in your sins" (1 Cor. 15:17). The completeness of the atoning virtue of His death stands in the truth: 'I have power to lay down My life, and I have power to take it again' (John 10:18). Apart from that it would be nothing. He opened the way to justification, not simply by a single phase of His work, but also through the total movement of His self-sacrifice, humiliation, and obedience, from His incarnation in humanity to His resurrection and ascension, carrying back a holy humanity into the heavens. These truths help to open to clearer view the unspeakable largeness and spiritual reality of the atoning

Christian Theology

provision and its ethical value as ground of forgiveness to returning sinners.

It seems to be needful, for correct understanding of this expiation of sin, to bear in mind also that its supreme end is, not merely forgiveness, but recovery of sinners from sin into the life of holiness. The atonement, according to the Scripture teaching, does not, in and of itself, place all men or any man in actual state of forgiveness. The realization of this state is suspended on human acceptance or the assent of faith (John 3:15–19, 36; Mark 16:15–16; Rom. 10:3; Gal. 2:16; Heb. 2:3; 6:4–6; Matt. 25:31–46). For the sin of definite rejection of Christ there is no provision. That the atonement, in its manward bearing, becomes a divine power of awakening a sense of sin, inspiring confidence and love, and, through faith, working in regenerative powers—thus redeeming from sin itself and restoring to holiness and eternal life—shows that its ultimate aim reaches far beyond the stage of simple forgiveness, and turns the atonement into a means of the overthrow of evil and a victory for righteousness as well as one of love. God's *holiness* makes love's atoning aim its own; for through the atonement it reaches its own triumph.

8. It is well to bring under the light of the foregoing truths the *special difficulty* sometimes thought to be in the doctrine. The difficulty is connected with the substitutionary position of Christ, but appears in view of two facts. *First*, that God did not *directly inflict* on Him, as representing mankind in sin, any punishment or displeasure. Jesus' consciousness, as revealed in the records, shows no signs of His being a sin-bearer, except in the sense that in a uniquely sympathetic heart He carried always a burden of sorrow on account of human sin, blindness of heart, sickness, suffering, and death. *Secondly*, that His crucifixion, as historically presented, was the work of "wicked hands," and therefore not a divine or righteous act. It was a deed of enormous wickedness. The crucifixion of the Son of God and Perfect Man, the Lord of glory, in return for His holy teaching and unselfish goodness, was the supreme sin and unrighteousness of mankind. The problem is: How are we to see and understand the sufferings of Christ, thus inflicted by "*wicked hands*" *in a most unrighteous crucifixion, as a propitiation*, satisfying God's righteousness so as to open the possibility of forgiving sin? The precise point of the difficulty is in evolving out of the crowning sin of the crucifixion the effective manifestation of "the righteousness of God" (Rom. 3:25). The solution is reached by giving just force and

right connection to the leading truths already brought to view, especially these: (*a*) The purpose of redemption by God, as Father and Son, was *one*, an organic movement, through a divine work of indivisible love and righteousness, or holy love, to redeem man through forgiveness and recovery to holiness. The Father freely sent; the Son freely came. (*b*) The gracious plan and work moved *wholly from the divine side*, and *continued wholly and purely a divine work*, save that in the incarnation the Son assumed human nature, without sin, into personal union with Himself for vicarious and representative action. Except as God saved believers, through gracious divine administration based in the Son's being, in plan and purpose, "slain from the foundation of the world" (Gen. 3:15; John 1:29; Rev. 13:8), the human race moved on in its wickedness. It was not by any purposive co-operation on the human side that salvation was to come. (*c*) The terrible unrighteousness which crucified Christ was *not inspired* by God, but, like all sin, a pure abomination in His sight, the culminating injustice and wrong in that total of human sinning which could not be forgiven without satisfaction to justice and holiness. This was a deed of human *free-will*, plotted and carried into execution with the purpose of ending Jesus' pure teaching and holy service. It was not *man's* part in the crucifixion that expressed or "manifested the righteousness of God." (*d*) Sin brings suffering and death under the natural operation of the law of cause and effect. It needs no divine intervention. The moral law against sin has been made self-executing. In itself it works penal suffering. This is part of the righteous constitution of the world—witnessing against sin and vindicating righteousness. It manifests God's holiness and justice. But suffering could thus reach Christ without any infliction of it by God. (*e*) In the *solidarity* of the race, which is such that no individual can isolate himself, can either 'live or die to himself alone,' both right-doing and wrongdoing touch in suffering or relief on others, and full room for *vicarious* action is ever open. Here Christ entered with His loving work of atonement. His voluntary incarnation for this very purpose prepared Him for it, as the One sinless member of the sin-smitten race. With clear consciousness of His priestly mission and in view of the evil purpose of His enemies, He not only accepted martyrdom for righteousness' sake, but to complete the redemptory aim, He freely bore, vicariously, the sufferings falling on Him from the working of human sin and guilt, offering Himself as a holy expiating sacrifice, maintaining the justness and honor of God's law against evil, and revealing anew holy condemnation of sin. The

Christian Theology

suffering had to fall *somewhere*. Righteousness *must* be maintained—for the sake of all human welfare and blessedness; holiness requires it; love requires it. To remove the necessity of its falling on men, the self-sacrificing love of the Redeemer opened His bosom to its bitterness, tasting death itself for universal humanity, in which and for which He was acting. The "righteousness declared" through "the propitiation" was neither wrought nor prevented by men's part in the crucifixion. It was entirely "of God." It dwelt in the Son, as revealed in all His earthly life and redeeming work for men. He embodied it all, and "set it forth for the remission of sins," becoming "our righteousness" (Jer. 23:6; 33:16), "made unto us righteousness" (1 Cor. 1:30), "the righteousness of God by faith of Jesus Christ" (Rom. 3:22). The atoning virtue came wholly from the divine side—from the infinite dignity of Christ's Person, the spiritual quality of His work, and the ethical ends, all worthy of God. Without sins of His own for which to suffer, in the substitutionary reality of love He gave His spotless innocence to the suffering due to sin, as at once the divine witness to the claims of righteousness and the satisfaction of them. This is manifestly the explanation given by St. Paul, in forms of representation drawn from Jewish types: "Him who knew no sin, He made to be sin on our behalf, that we might become the righteousness of God in Him" (2 Cor. 5:21); "Christ redeemed us from the curse of the law, having become a curse for us" (Gal. 3:13).

9. It is proper to note the *chief objections*, urged by Socinians and others for rejection of the doctrine of the atonement as understood by the Church. These have appeared mostly in connection with a denial of the Trinity of the Godhead and the Divinity of Christ. When Jesus is held to be a mere man, or even when regarded as some higher yet creature being, sent by God, there is an absence of the elemental realities for the atonement, precluding a rational conception of it. Even among believers in the Savior as the incarnate Son of God, there have been criticisms that have amounted to surrender of the Scripture teaching. But we confine our notice here to a few forms of objection meant to express repudiation of it.

(1) It has been objected that the doctrine of an atoning satisfaction is contradicted by the fact of God's *forgiveness* of sin. Satisfaction and pardon are declared to be subversive of each other. If the debt is paid it is not forgiven. If the retributive penalty is exhausted the sinner needs no pardon. If God's justice is satisfied by infliction of judicial suffering there is no room for the exercise of mercy. But the sufficient answer is: (*a*) That the objection would be

of force only if the guilty had made the satisfaction in literal and full equivalent, but not at all if the atonement be, as it really is, "a vicarious" divine provision *for* forgiveness. (*b*) The atonement is not itself pardon, but a provision preconditional for it, a *vicarious* action making forgiveness consistent with God's righteousness and His irrepealable law against sin. The actual forgiveness is suspended on human acceptance of Christ in faith. The Scriptures, as well as the Church doctrine, are clear on this (Heb. 2:3; Mark 16:16; John 5:24–40; 15:22). Were the atonement itself pardon of the sins of the race, God would be estopped from any penal administration against them in the world. (*c*) The making of the "propiation "for forgiveness was itself a work of mercy, with which remission of sins is not in contradiction, but the on-moving of the same divine grace. The atonement and forgiveness do not exclude, but imply, each other.

(2) Objection is made to the *vicarious* feature—that *substitution of penalty is impossible*. Sin and its guilt, virtue and its merit, are declared to be so thoroughly identified with personality as to allow of no transfer of merits or demerits from one person to another. Character is personal, and justice permits no vicariousness or substitution. This strikes at one of the basal points in the propitiation. It appears in two forms. *First*, assuming that the Church doctrine involves a reciprocal transference of character between Christ and men, it denies the possibility of such interchange, viz.: that Christ should suffer as a sinner or that His holiness can become ours. Dr. Martineau rejects the possibility of the "conveyance of an alien holiness by imputation." This objection misses the real doctrine of the atonement and fights a caricature. For, (*a*) the very first element in the atonement is that Christ is absolutely innocent and holy, and only thus can act meritoriously for the guilty. As innocent He obeyed and suffered *instead* of the guilty, the 'Just suffering for the unjust.' (*b*) The doctrine does not teach that God transferred Christ's personal holiness to us. We may allow that as an attribute of His character, that remained His and not ours—not transferable. Could it have been immediately transferred, His obedience and suffering might not have been necessary. But the doctrine makes, not Christ's intrinsic holiness, but His work done in man's stead and behalf, the essence of the atonement. "The righteousness," says the Form of Concord, "which out of pure grace is imputed before God to faith of believers, is the obedience, the suffering, the resurrection of Christ, by which, for our sakes, He has

Christian Theology

made satisfaction to the law and expiated our sins." The objection misses the doctrine and assails a phantom.

But a *second* form presses the objection further—that the *work of one cannot be counted to another.* It denies the possibility of transferring the value of vicarious *action.* It asserts such an absolute individualism in reference to both sin and penalty, virtue and blessedness, that Christ could neither suffer for our sins, nor we reap the benefit of such sufferings. To this form of objection we reply: (*a*) That it stands in direct contradiction to the clear teaching of God's word. We may justly hold that God knows best what may be possible and acceptable in moral order and holy government. (*b*) The objection goes in the face, not only of the religious experience of the Christian world, but the religious convictions of the race. The attack is not on church orthodoxy alone, but on the whole sacrificial idea of pagan as well as Jewish and Christian humanity. (*c*) The *natural constitution* of the world is replete with vicarious work and suffering, the saving of men or procurement of blessings by the substituted service or passion of others. This constitution is largely mediatorial, especially where evils are to be lifted off or men are to be elevated. Many of the best things men know are won for them by the self-sacrifice, even to death, of their fellows. Physicians and nurses throw themselves before the diseases which men's violation of laws of health bring on, and stay the destruction by self-sacrifice. Patriot soldiers give their lives on fields of battle and purchase blessings for other generations. The actual movement of life shows the fallacy of the objection.

(3) Objection is made, that to substitute the suffering of the innocent for the guilty *is essentially unjust.* The answer to this is: (*a*) That it is refuted by lying as much against the natural constitution of things as against the atonement. The innocent are often found suffering for the sake of the guilty and instead of them. Though, in our Christian faith, we believe these sufferers will be compensated, yet this is an actual part of the system of things in the world in moral relations, through which relief and help may come. (*b*) Christ's sufferings were wholly *voluntary.* He came as the God-man for this very purpose, in an aim of love and grace. The Father did not compel it, nor inflict punishment. Viewed in reference to the whole Godhead, we may say that God Himself undertook to make the needed satisfaction. Those who make this objection admit that self-sacrifice for the good of others is not only allowable, but is the highest and noblest thing of which we can conceive. They praise as

grandest the men who voluntarily put themselves under death-service to rescue and save others.

(4) It has been objected, further, that what Christ has done and suffered, or could have done, would not be an equivalent satisfaction for the sin of the world. Even on the vicarious principle, it was inadequate. It would not, and did not, equate with the debt of sin. The curse of the law being "eternal death," Christ could not satisfy it by anything short of that death. It is claimed that, as He did not surrender Himself to it He did not bear and exhaust the curse of sin. And it is added that, as He suffered only as man, had He accepted that death, He could not have done so for more than one person. To this objection we answer: (*a*) The terms "curse of the law," "wages of sin," and others of like import, in connection with eternal death, are of too spiritual a signification to allow any *quantitative* measurement. (*b*) Even if taken quantitatively, in the sense of "eternal" punishment, thus expressing a penalty *infinite in duration*, there is no reason why we may not believe it may be atoned for by the *infinite* value of the sufferings of the *infinite, divine* Savior. The infinite in Being may be in moral value commensurate with the infinite in time. (*c*) Satisfaction, or the liquidation of a moral obligation, does not necessarily consist in perfect identity of requital for the primary obligation, but in the *worth* of the compensation or offering—the worth of it for the ends involved. An atonement, for the end of recovering, through *forgiveness*, to new and eternal life, through a risen and triumphant Redeemer, may be of infinitely greater moment than a precisely *quid pro quo* exaction of sin's debt. And the "ransom" through which God opens to Himself a way of consistent proclamation of amnesty and forgiveness to penitent sinners, is a full showing of the love, wisdom, and righteousness of God.

Theories of the Atonement
Beyond a general statement of the essential features of the atonement, as presented in the Scripture for the acceptance of faith, theology has been disposed to develop special theories to exhibit the *philosophy* of it. They seek to give its *rationale*—a rational exposition of the principle in which its effectiveness is solved. These properly date from the work "Cur Deus Homo," by Anselm, Archbishop of Canterbury, in the close of the eleventh century. Not that no theoretical expressions are found earlier, but that that dates the

beginning of elaborate speculative effort on this subject. We sketch the chief theories:

I. THE ANSELMIC THEORY. This presents the atonement as a *vicarious satisfaction*. Its points are outlined as follows:

1. Sin is a debt, a withholding of something due to God. Man owes absolute obedience, of all his powers, all the time. Not given, it is guilt and debt.

2. This debt cannot be extinguished by simply beginning anew, in repentance and reformation, to subject our wills to God. Satisfaction is needed for the previous guilt.

3. Man cannot render such satisfaction, because it would require the double work of both fulfilling the law for the present and making up for the past. He has no surplusage of powers to diminish the debt. It stands as penalty due. The impossibility of rendering the satisfaction does not release from the obligation to it.

4. The compassion and love of God cannot come in at this point and simply remit the guilt without satisfaction. This would be irregular and unjust, giving more liberty to sin than to righteousness itself. As there is nothing greater or better than God Himself, and holiness or justice is essential to His being, God's righteousness must be satisfied before the sin can be forgiven. In satisfying righteousness God satisfies Himself.

5. There are only two ways of such satisfaction: one, the infliction of the punishment on the sinner—but this precludes salvation; the other, that justice must be satisfied by substituted or vicarious obedience and sufferings. But *who* can give such satisfaction or pay man's debt? Justice cannot be satisfied by substituting a less for a more valuable satisfaction. Something greater than all that is finite or created must be offered—greater than all that is not God. An infinite value must pertain to the satisfaction. These requisites are found in the God-man. Only Deity can satisfy the claims of Deity. Only in man or humanity can the satisfaction stand for man's sin. As God, Christ could give more than the whole finite creation could render. In the way of suffering, justice had no claims on the humanity of Christ; in the way of obedience, only a man's obedience, not the obedience of the God-man was due. Hence His divine-human obedience and suffering were a surplusage, overflowing to man's advantage, for whom they were voluntarily rendered.

6. Love acted in making this atonement, and Love acts in saving through it.

This theory, with slight variations in subordinate points, became the Reformation doctrine, incorporated in many creeds, and holding large sway in orthodox theology.

II. THE ACCEPTILATION THEORY. This came from Duns Scotus (died 1308), as a modification of the Anselmic formulation, according to his idea that the moral distinctions of right and wrong are products of the mere *will* of God and subject to its sovereignty. The following points suffice to state it:

1. It denies the infinite demerit of sin, and consequently also the infinite value of Christ's sufferings and work.

2. It assumes that God in His sovereignty could accept whatever satisfaction He might fix as proper—not that the satisfaction must be infinite or have an equally intrinsic value.

3. Therefore, the principle of sufficiency in the atonement was asserted to be: "*Tantum valet omne creatum oblatum, pro quanto acceptat Deus illud, et non plus*" (every creature oblation avails for as much as God may accept it for, and no more). This, therefore, denied real or essential fitness and adaptation between Christ's atonement and man's sin, and made its efficacy depend only upon the arbitrary consent to accept it. The theory, therefore, secures an acceptable atonement only in a surrender of the truth of God's essential, eternal, and immutable righteousness.

III. THE GOVERNMENTAL THEORY. This, since the days of Hugo Grotius (died 1645), who first elaborated it, has been stated with frequent variations. As framed by its author, it was, like the Acceptilation Theory, constructed to the idea that the moral distinctions are not internal in the divine nature, but only effects of His will; but it need not be placed in that alliance. It stands as a governmental expedient, apart from necessities of the divine holiness. Its philosophy is in these points:

1. The divine government, being necessarily by moral law, with adequate penalties for sin, needs to be sustained for the order and happiness of the creation.

2. A gracious remission of sins cannot occur without weakening the motives restraining from disobedience and wrong, and so overthrowing the necessary supremacy of the authority of the divine government, unless such an exhibition of the demerit of sin be given, as in the sufferings of Christ for it, that shall show that it cannot escape with impunity.

3. The atonement is in no sense an arrangement to satisfy distributive justice, but relates solely to *public* justice or

righteousness, for the maintenance, by requisite means, of God's authority as Ruler for the highest happiness of His kingdom. Its aim is not so much penal for the past as preventive for the future. It means so much vindication of the law of penalty, in Christ's sufferings, as shall satisfy the needs of moral government, and yet allow the remission of sins.

The chief defects of this theory are: *First*, it overlooks the truth that public justice cannot be met without, in some fair measure, at least, maintaining distributive justice. The maintaining of public justice is, in fact, only through distributive justice. *Secondly*, the atonement, under this view, has respect only to men, and not at all to God Himself. It rests the necessity of it in something *wholly* outside of God—as though *He* could consent to take no account of sin, were it not that mankind would be less happy. It drops out of view what He owes to His own holiness and righteousness.

IV. THE MORAL INFLUENCE THEORY. Abelard (died 1142) constructed this in antagonism to that of Anselm. It drops the entire idea of satisfaction with respect to God's holiness or law. The Deity can pardon on repentance alone. It has been modified in various forms, and appears in the theology of many who are dominated by rationalistic temper. It includes three points:

1. That there is no necessity on the Godward side for any satisfaction, either as respects God's holiness, justice, or government.

2. That the atonement consists essentially in God's gaining moral power or influence over the minds and hearts and wills of men by and through the voluntary self-sacrifice and sufferings of Christ on their behalf.

3. The moral power works in the double way of overcoming the alienation and rebellion of men, and of inspiring faith and love, and so leading back to obedience.

The inadequacy of the theory is that it sets aside all Godward bearing of the atonement, either as satisfaction to the divine holiness and righteousness or the necessities of moral government.

V. THE MYSTICAL THEORY. The essence of this, in its various forms, is in locating the atonement, not so much in Christ's sufferings and death, as in the *incarnation*, in which mysterious union the reconciliation between God and alienated humanity was accomplished. Christ is Himself the atonement in His very Person. His death on the cross was the completing epoch of the spotless offering of Himself for the redemption of our race which He made by coming through conception and birth into this world. The movement of "reconciliation" is laid especially in the divine assumption of humanity into fellowship with Deity in the Person of Christ, and becomes effective through faith in which Christ is formed within men as the power of an endless life. The reconciling principle is not the single fact that Christ died, but a vital, mystical union with Him.

This view was held by Osiander, the Schwenkfeldians, Schleiermacher and his followers.

In estimating the value of these theories, it is to be observed:

1. The Satisfaction Theory, the Governmental Theory, and the Theory of Moral Influence, each expresses and emphasizes a real part of the whole truth or reality of the atonement, viz.: (*a*) The Satisfaction Theory justly puts into the front the relation of the atonement to the very *nature* of God as immutably holy and righteous in Himself and as moral Ruler. (*b*) The Governmental Theory presents a true and important feature in asserting the necessity of justice or righteousness for the benevolent ends of the divine administration. (*c*) The Moral Influence Theory fastens its view on the great truth in the atonement that there has been provided a truly winning and faith-begetting power for recovery of men.

These elements in its reality are not inconsistent, but involve each other, and are severally provided for in the unity of the atoning work. And we may say:

2. That the Satisfaction Theory, in its substance and with modifying definitions, because of its emphasis upon God's unchangeable holiness and righteousness, presents the essential truth, at once uniting most harmoniously the various statements of the Scriptures and the demands of reason. This substance is, (*a*) That what is due to man's sin and guilt is a debt owed to God's essential righteousness, or rather to Himself as holy and just. (*b*) That Christ in His Divine-human Person, by His gracious and perfect obedience in man's stead and by a true vicarious suffering and death for our sins, has made real satisfaction to the divine holiness and the honor of God's law. (*c*) That this perfect obedience in our stead—this voluntary substituted sacrificial suffering of innocence for guilt, confessing and setting forth the righteousness of the law—by its infinite merit from the infinite Person, the Son of God, forms a ground on which God can forgive sin to such as accept Christ as

Christian Theology

their righteousness and take right relations to God through His grace.

But the qualifying, and to some degree *modifying*, definitions are important.

(1) That the "satisfaction" is not a commercial one, as *quid pro quo* payment. The use of the term "debt" suggests misleading analogies—quantitative and numerical conceptions, instead of moral and spiritual values or sufficing equivalents. The atoning sufficiency need not, as we have seen, mean the exact suffering in kind and measure which each and every sinner would have had to suffer. The sufferings of the Son of God, in His self-emptying incarnation, in bearing the trials and griefs of the contradiction of sinners all His life, to the giving of His blood on the cross, were *for* man's sake, not as an identical, but as an ethical equivalent in the realm of moral relations and values.

(2) That this equivalence was an equivalence *for the end in view*, i. e., to satisfy the essential holiness and justice of God against sin and to vindicate the righteous authority of His law.

(3) That Christ's obedience and suffering directly and fully satisfied public justice or the necessities of governmental administration.

(4) That they indirectly and virtually satisfied distributive justice. The giving of pardon, indeed, modifies the action of distributive justice; yet because the infinite merit of the obedience and expiation by the Son of God is graciously imputed or counted to each believer, the satisfaction becomes equivalent to the distributive penalties remitted.

(5) That the satisfaction is not simply the action through which holiness and justice have been maintained, but especially the work of Love, looking to the welfare and happiness of man and asserting the principle of self-denying goodness against the selfishness of sin. Love was moving forward in it all for the redemption of the race. While, therefore, a maintenance of holiness, it is supremely a revelation of love. So it fulfills also all that the Moral Influence Theory emphasizes.

Extent of the Atonement
The question here raised is whether, as a provision for pardon and salvation, it has been made for *all* men or for only a part of mankind. Strict *Calvinism*, with its postulate of absolute predestination, says: *"For the elect only."* But it says so with a

difference. Some represent it as *sufficient* only for as many as are actually saved through it, a provision *made* only for the elect, Christ having suffered only what they deserved, atoning for them alone. Others, that it is *intrinsically sufficient* for all, but made and *designed* only for the elect. The sufficiency for the rest is only incidental, on the principle that the adequacy for some is intrinsically sufficient for others. Both these views limit the availability of the atonement. *Lutheran*, and all non-Calvinistic theology says: "*For all men.*" And this in the sense, (*a*) *Negatively*, that there is no limitation either of its *sufficiency* or *efficiency* by any predestinating election of some to life and passing others by, as is involved in the conception of absolute decrees irrespective of foreknowledge and conditioning it. (*b*) *Positively*, that the atonement expresses God's eternal purpose, which He purposed in Christ Jesus, to provide forgiveness, eternal salvation, and all the means thereto, for real acceptance and use of all men—a provision in which, in both its nature and design, all men might be saved on condition of the assent of faith. The design of the atonement was to remove the moral and legal obstacles to the salvation of *all* men, so that it is applicable to one as well as another on terms that are open and impartial to all. This is a general or universal atonement.

This scope of comprehension must be viewed as *retrospective* as well as prospective. Christ died for those who lived and died before His incarnate work. The Scripture proof of this is clear. (*a*) From the universality affirmed of the atonement, as co-extensive with the fruits of Adam's sin (Rom. 5:18). (*b*) From passages distinctly referring to its retroactive bearing: "Whom God hath set forth to be a propitiation through faith in His blood, to declare His righteousness *for the remission of sins that are past, through the forbearance of God*" (Rom. 3:25; Heb. 9:15, 25, 26; 1 Peter 3:18–20; Rev. 13:8). This retroactive bearing of Christ's atonement is fundamentally *normal*—the law of atoning action under the typical order of the Old Testament sacrifices being that the sin-offering was made for sins already committed. The primary conception and application referred to the past, whether the sin-offering was for an individual or the people in general. It would appear to be only a secondary principle of application, when it comes to be provided in advance of the transgression for universal amnesty.

PROOF OF A GENERAL ATONEMENT. 1. Direct affirmation of provision for all in Christ John 1:29; 3:16; 6:51; 14:27; Rom. 5:18–21; 2 Cor. 5:14–15; Rom. 5:9; Heb. 2:9; 1 Tim. 2:6; 4:10; 1 John 2:2.

Christian Theology

2. Salvation is offered to all; therefore, the atonement is provided and meant for all. Isa. 45:22; 55:1-3; Matt 11:28-30; Rev. 3:20; 22:17; 1 Tim. 2:4.

3. Involved in the special guilt affirmed as due to the refusal or neglect of the gospel call. If there were no real privilege neglected, responsibility for it would be inconceivable and unjust. Matt. 23:37. There are two things in this lament over Jerusalem: an affirmation that its people might have been saved, and that their rejection of Christ formed the acme of their offense. Luke 14:17-24, the parable of the Great Supper; John 3:19, "This is the condemnation, that Light is come," etc.; Acts 7:51, "Ye stiffnecked and uncircumcised," etc.; Heb. 2:3, "How shall we escape?" etc.; Acts 13:46; Heb. 10:28-29, "He that despised Moses' law," etc.

4. From the fact that Christ is declared to have died for some that may not be saved, or are not actually saved. Rom. 14:15, "Destroy not him with thy meat for whom Christ died"; 1 Cor. 8:11, "And through thy knowledge shall the weak brother perish for whom Christ died"; Heb. 10:29, "Of how much sorer punishment," etc.; 2 Peter 2:1, "Damnable heresies, even denying the Lord that bought them."

5. From various necessary implications of gospel truth. (*a*) *God is no respecter of persons* (Acts 10:34; Rom. 2:11; 2 Chron. 19:7). (*b*) He solemnly declares He has no pleasure in the death of any (Ezek. 18:23-32; 2 Peter 3:9). (*c*) The gospel message throws the responsibility of life or death on men themselves, and puts the very point of the responsibility and issue of it on their acceptance of Christ. Unbelief in Christ as their own personal Savior is the one great condemning sin (Heb. 3:7-19). If He were not a really provided Savior for them, how could this sin be committed against Him? how could salvation be pivoted on an *impossible* acceptance, *i. e.*, acceptance of an atonement and Savior never provided or meant for us?

6. A limited atonement, a provision made or designed only for a few on the basis of an absolute election, without respect to anything foreseen in them, passing by and excluding the rest, would belittle the gospel and the grace of God. The general atonement shows its rich greatness and glory—the divine largeness and inspiring grandeur of grace. It throws a higher glory over the goodness of the Divine government.

OBJECTIONS URGED. The difficulties alleged as to the doctrine of general atonement require some notice. Whatever force these may seem to have, they are as nothing compared with those into which the theory of a limited atonement throws its adherents. The force of this fact has been, of recent years, revealing itself in revisional movements in Calvinistic churches.

1. Objection is made against general atonement, that if we hold the *design* as opening provision beyond the number actually saved, we involve the absurdity that God can be, and is, defeated in His purpose. Dr. A. A. Hodge puts it: "The design of Christ in dying was to effect what He actually does effect in the result." The sufficient answer to this is, that there is no defeat of God's "design," if that design was to provide a full, free salvation, the benefits of which should be *conditioned* on human assent or acceptance of the provision. God's design included its own limitation. He does not, when He comes to save men, set aside the supreme endowment of personality in which He constituted them by creation. There is a divine reality at the basis of Christ's declaration: "I would, ... ye would not." God's redemptive "design" does not include annulment of human personality. His attitude is revealed in the words: "Behold, I stand at the door and knock: if any man hear My voice and open," etc. (Rev. 3:20).

2. The objection is raised that the distinction between the "general" will of God, and His "special" or consequent will, on which the general atonement doctrine rests, *supposes different and conflicting purposes in Him.* The answer is, by no means. One purpose is the purpose of love to open a way of salvation for all; the further purpose is to save all who are willing to accept the loving and appealing provision. Where is the conflict? Surely, within the purpose of love to save all who, as self-determining moral personal beings, may be persuaded to consent to recovery, the actual saving of them is but the consistent on-moving of the same will and plan.

3. Objection is offered that *all God's actions, in order to their absoluteness, must be wholly from Himself;* but that *this conditioning of the results of the atonement represents His will and doings as determined by something outside of Himself.* We reply, not at all, if the *whole scheme,* with all its subordinate parts, is entirely from His own self-determination and free love. It is a complete illusion to imagine His "absolute sovereignty" trenched upon when He makes the atoning provision in harmony with the need and with the realities and relations under His dominion. His sovereignty is not arbitrariness. It is perfect intelligence, reason, and wisdom, as well as power. The objection is a relic of the old scholastic

Christian Theology

theologoumenon, the asserted *"impassibility"* of God—that He cannot suffer any influence from without, cannot be moved by external realities or conditions. The doctrine of *this* kind of sovereignty would imply that the atonement itself was not at all made in view of an objective need, nor adapted to the actual condition and endowments of humanity; would annul the possibility of a divine moral administration adjusted, in historical progress, to human deserts, and would even abolish all faith in the power of prayer. The true conception of God's absolute sovereignty *includes* His ability to adjust His work of redeeming love to the given nature of man, for the purpose of spiritual recovery.

4. Objection is also offered that it represents God as *making provision for an end beyond what He knows will be effected.* The answer is on the surface: Not if the end be recognized in its fullness as twofold. Part of the end is effected in the salvation of believers; part in the perfect vindication of God's goodness with respect to those that are lost. Those who continue in sin in the light of the gospel do so in the face of God's pleading provision and call to life.

5. It is objected, that *God's justice requires the actual salvation of all for whose sins Christ has made the satisfaction.* We reply, *first,* that the objection would be of force only if the satisfaction were such a quantitative *quid pro quo* payment of sin's debt as to leave no place for forgiveness, but not if the atonement be as the Scriptures represent, a basis on which God can *pardon* and *justify. Secondly,* that justice *owes* nothing to the sinner even under an atonement except *in the way* the atoning provision offers it.

6. It is alleged that many passages of Scripture do "teach that Christ died specifically for the elect," and that this is "everywhere stated in Scripture," *e. g.,* John 10:11–15, "I am the good shepherd," etc.; Acts 20:28, "All the flock, which He hath purchased," etc.; Eph. 5:25, "Christ loved the *Church,*" etc. But as to all these passages, it is to be observed, *first,* that while they state a real truth, they make no affirmation whatever of any restriction of the atoning provision. To say that Christ died for His "Church," "flock," etc., is but begging the question as to the point at issue. That Christ is "the propitiation for our sins" is no denial of His being "the propitiation for the sins of the whole world." *Secondly,* that the affirmation of a wider comprehension is in *positive* statements. No violence is done to the specific declarations which speak of Christ's work for believers when we see the fuller Scripture statements of its scope. But great

violence is done when the strong affirmations of a general atonement are wrested from their clear meaning.

II. CHRIST'S INTERCESSION

This part of Christ's priestly work must not be isolated from His redemptive work on earth. It is a continuation of it, a moving forward of His priestly or mediatorial activity, upon the basis of the part accomplished in His earthly life. His resurrection and ascension formed the transition, integrating into unity His whole sacerdotal office. The intercessional portion appeared already in the sacrificial function on the earth. God's "suffering Servant," as in Isaiah's vision (Isa. 53.), made "intercession for the transgressors." Christ's voice, as heard through John 17., and in "Father, forgive them," on the cross, was intercession this side of "the veil." The heavenly intercession is the reality symbolized in the Old Testament by the high priest's entrance into the Holy of Holies, presenting the blood of atonement. It is the completing of the reconciliation. "By His own blood He entered in once into the Holy Place, having obtained eternal redemption.... For Christ is not entered into the holy places made with hands, ... but into heaven itself, now to appear in the presence of God for us" (Heb. 9:12–24). "Wherefore He is able to save to the uttermost them that come to God through Him, seeing He ever liveth to make intercession for them" (Heb. 7:25). "If any man sin we have an Advocate with the Father" (1 John 2:1).

The term "intercession" is an earthly word used to express a heavenly reality which transcends earthly modes. Its form or manner is hidden "within the veil." We are not concerned, indeed, with the manner—how the intercession is made—but with its *reality and spiritual import*. If we can understand its essential nature and bearings, this will give us its vital truth. Unquestionably, as imaged in the symbolism of the Holy Place, it is employed to express the truth that Christ's priestly work of reconciling has not ceased, but, transferred to its heavenly sphere, goes on *forever*, till the divine purpose and results of redemption are accomplished. It means to hold human view to the inspiring truth that the Son who, at the Father's will, became also man, and laid down His life for us, is unceasingly active in carrying into full effect the redeeming provision made on earth. It looks to the actual reconciliation of men to God through faith, regeneration, sanctification, and eternal life. He is still and forever the only Mediator and High Priest through whom we have access to God and through whom grace, new life,

Christian Theology

and salvation reach us. He made announcement of this before He accepted the cross: "It is expedient for you that I go away," putting the Father and Himself in combined co-action for the whole consummation of the spiritual redemption: "I will pray the Father and He will send the Comforter"; "I will send Him"—at once "the Spirit of God" and "the Spirit of Christ."

We need not, and should not, understand "intercession" as implying need that God be persuaded to forgiving love. His own heart was and is the Fountain of the redemptive love and purpose. And yet it is true that all sin is displeasing to Him, offensive in His sight, and nowhere more so than in those who bear His name and offend against His grace. There is need of "grace upon grace" in giving progressive and completing effect to the saving movement. It is through Christ that God mediates it all, and therefore the Son, bearing redeemed humanity, forever appears in the divine Presence on our behalf. His very presence is a perpetual asking, as well as ministering, the grace needful for the consummation of the whole saving work, through gift of the Holy Spirit, the means of grace and providential care. Humanly speaking that presence in itself is an unending plea for a realization of the aim of the cross. And with respect to man, the revelation of the reality of the intercession is the most inspiring assurance of ever-open access to God through the Divine-human Mediator, to whom belongs all power in heaven and earth, able to keep that which we commit to Him to the day of perfect redemption—a mediatorship that needs no other (Rom. 8:34).

This general view of its essence and aim prepares us to note the chief elemental truths of His intercession.

1. *Christ is fitted for the office* through His Person, as the God-man. (*a*) In His nature He is one with God, of the same holiness and love, in unity of purpose, and is also forever joined in incarnate and sympathetic union with mankind. His nature embraces the initiation of the reconciling movement and exhibits it "In all things it behooved Him to be made like unto His brethren," etc. (Heb. 2:17). (*b*) He presents in Himself the completed *atonement* and perfect merit, on the basis of which He seeks forgiveness and salvation for sinners. (*c*) Being King as well as Priest—enthroned, at the right hand of God, in providential rulership, He can make efficacious the grace and help He asks.

2. The *ground* of His priestly intercession in heaven is the *sacrifice* or *propitiation* made and the "righteousness "provided by His own High-priestly work on earth (Eph. 1:6; Heb. 4:14–16). "His

propitiatory offering is one which He continually presents to the Father."

3. *For whom He intercedes.* (*a*) For believers (John 17:8–9). In His intercessory prayer, sure index of His perpetual intercession, He says of the believing disciples around Him: "I pray for them." (*b*) *For all men*—except such as have definitively and finally rejected the provided salvation. "I pray for them also who shall believe on Me through their word "(verse 20 and Luke 23:34). Christ's *continued* activity in His exaltation works to this very aim. His intercession is, therefore, to be viewed as co-extensive with the race. Quenstedt says of it: "In general, for all those who still live in the world, and still have the gates of grace open before them."

4. *How does He intercede?* As already said, a veil intervenes between us and the manner of it. We can conceive of this properly only through the redemptive import of Christ's progress, from His priestly self-offering for sin, through resurrection and ascension into the presence of the Father. Viewing it thus, it may safely be said: (*a*) That the "intercession" consists essentially in the very *presence of the ascended Redeemer before God,* presenting Himself as the Divine-human propitiation for the sins of the world and fully opening Love's way to the forgiveness of sin and the bestowal of all necessary grace. (*b*) The suggestion of speech by the term is not to be pressed. The idea of words or language as a vehicle of intercommunication is after our human manner. The fellowship of thought between the Father, Son, and Holy Spirit may be inconceivably other than in human modes. It is enough to know that it is real. If not in articulate speech in heavenly air, it is articulate in the counsel and fellowship of God.

It is well to sum up the *effects of Christ's priestly* work as thus exhibited. Expressed in *the aggregate,* they form a full *redemptory provision* for human salvation. And the scope of the defining term "redemptory" must include, not merely the opened possibility of forgiveness, but the conditions for a progressive actualizing of personal salvation from the dominion of sin. It comprehends the following:

(1) That an atoning propitiation for sin has been actually made, so that God can be just and justify sinners.

(2) That a dispensation of pardon and grace has been established on earth.

(3) That renewing and purifying grace has been secured for men, through the presence and power of the Holy Spirit, the conditions

for whose effective mission and work depended on the work of Christ.

(4) That in all respects a kingdom of grace has been provided for and actually established on earth, in which the means and powers of redemption are in full force and operation—delivering men from the curse and corruption of sin and training them to eternal life.

This *kingdom* of redemption, under which these effects of Christ's priestly work are exhibited, brings us to the next topic of consideration—the Kingly Office of Christ.

Milton Valentine

CHAPTER III
THE WORK OF CHRIST AS KING

It will be remembered that this kingly office is joined with the prophetic and priestly in the aggregate mediatorial relation of Christ. The progress of the redemptive work was from the first meant to move on into the establishment of a divine kingdom, the mediatorial sovereignty of the enthroned Christ, exercised for the salvation of its obedient subjects and the accomplishment of God's purposes in the world. Both the prophetic and priestly offices would of necessity fail of their end, apart from this. Its grand significance is inherent in the total meaning of human salvation. For the essence of humanity's woe was, and is, that it has fallen out of obedient temper and relation to God, not simply as Father, but as moral Lawgiver and Ruler. And the teaching and atoning functions of Christ are instrumental means for recovery of mankind to loyalty of soul and life to God's necessary and loving dominion. Redemption's look and work were for the establishment of the kingdom of God on the earth, passing on into the kingdom in heaven.

This regal office of Christ, as part of the mediatorial activity given Him, is properly defined as '*the theanthropic function by which He, in His divine-human nature, exercises real providential dominion over all things in heaven and earth, as related to the necessities of consummating the work of redemption both with respect to individual salvation and the success and triumph of the Church.*' His kingdom is usually and well represented as threefold, according to the sphere of its action: the "kingdom of power," the "kingdom of grace," and the "kingdom of glory." This division will be recalled later on to explain part of the bearings of the office. We must advance step by step.

1. The *grounds of His kingly office* are two, which need to be clearly distinguished:

(*a*) It is based in the sovereignty which belongs to His essential nature as the Son of God—a sovereignty underived, absolute, unchangeable, eternal. Dominion, rulership, is His by virtue of His eternal Sonship, His place in the Godhead.

Christian Theology

(*b*) It rests also as a special sovereignty exercised by the God-man, upon the whole will and plan of God, giving Him divine rulership for the full accomplishment of His saving work. It is connected with God's exalting and honoring the Son's self-sacrificing humiliation and atoning service, magnifying the grandeur of its love before men and angels: "Wherefore God also hath highly exalted Him and given Him a name which is above every name, that at the name of Jesus every knee should bow, of things in heaven and things in earth" (Phil. 2:5–11). "All power," Christ declares, "is given unto Me in heaven and in earth" (Matt 28:18).

2. *The time of His entrance on the kingly office.* (*a*) It being a joint part of the mediatorial relation, He manifestly assumed it simultaneously with the assumption of the prophetic and priestly offices, *i. e.*, at the fall of man and the establishment of the divine administration of mercy and recovery. The early assumption, however, was not *manifested.* It was to some degree potential, but invisible and only obscurely announced. The *protoevangelium* (Gen. 3:15) was the far-reaching but faint intimation of it. A glimmer of it appears in Ps. 2:6–8; 45:7. The pre-advent stage of the Messiah's kingship cannot, of course, be regarded as the fullness of the office in all respects—any more than could be His pre-advent prophetic and priestly functions in *their* relations—because He had not yet in fact taken on Him our nature. (*b*) A further incomplete stage of His kingship was during His state of humiliation. From His coming in the flesh He was, indeed, the "anointed" King. But, according to His chosen way of humiliation, the exercise of divine prerogatives was only partial—in occasional "signs and wonders" which gave token of dominion over nature and life and death. But these prerogatives were inherent in the Person of the God-man. Luke 2:11, "For unto you is born this day in the city of David a Savior which is Christ the Lord"; Luke 19:38, "Blessed be the king that cometh in the name of the Lord," compared with Zech. 9:9; Matt. 27:11, "Art Thou the King of the Jews? And Jesus said, Thou sayest"; also John 18:37. (*c*) The full assumption of the office dates from the ascension and session at the right hand of God. In proof of this we note: (1) That all through the Gospels the strain is "the kingdom of God has come nigh unto you." (2) Only after the atoning work were the full conditions provided for the kingly subjugation of souls to the loving authority of God. (3) So Jesus is declared to be then glorified and exalted to the throne (Acts 2:33–36). (4) In this sovereignty at the right hand of

God Christ continues until the ends of His mediatorial purposes are all accomplished (Eph. 1:20–22; 1 Cor. 15:25; 1 Pet. 3:18–21).

This truth is antagonized only by premillennialism, which denies His assumption of the mediatorial kingdom before the second advent, when it teaches Christ will really take up the royal prerogative and establish, in literal sense, the throne of David and rule at Jerusalem as the capital of His kingdom. For this premillennial view we find no sufficient authority.

3. *The importance given to the mediatorial kingdom in the Scriptures.*

(*a*) The *fact* that the Scriptures emphasize it is unquestionable. It is put in unmistakable prominence and held before our view. In the long line of Old Testament types and prophecies it is given in increasing clearness and force. It is found connected with historic events. It is assured in promise and echoed in psalms. So much had Jewish thought fastened on rulership that it obscured the spiritual offices of teaching and priesthood. In the New Testament the preaching of "the kingdom of God" or "the kingdom of heaven" is a synonym for the preaching of the gospel—as if all God's love and grace, as meant and brought by Christ, were summed up in the establishment of this and the blessings given under it. As suggestive of this, we may recall how, in setting forth these blessings and the spiritual life in which they are realized, Jesus, in His parables of instruction, was wont to shape them as parables of the "kingdom of God" or "of heaven." Christ speaks to Pilate of it as "My kingdom," and the apostles or New Testament writers designate it as the "kingdom of Christ." That the term βασιλεία, in this connection, occurs in the New Testament 162 times, shows the prominence given to the mediatorial kingdom.

(*b*) The evident reason for this high valuation of it is that it expresses the consummation of the aims of the whole redemptive economy and its agencies. In this both the prophetic and priestly work come into their fruits of blessedness to man and glory to God.

4. *The scope or comprehension of Christ's kingly dominion.* A twofold division is sometimes made of it—a universal sovereignty over the world, and a particular sovereignty over the Church of which He is head. But its range is better exhibited by the old division, already named.

(*a*) His kingdom *of power*. In this He holds the whole world in providential and judicial administration (Matt 28:18; John 5:22), exercising dominion over all creatures visible and invisible, for the attainment of the objects of the dispensation of grace (Phil. 2:9–11). Under the scope of this, especially in its judicial relation, is embraced the realm of hades. Rev. 1:18, "I am He that liveth, and was dead," etc.

(*b*) His kingdom of *grace*. This is His administration in and through the Church, for the salvation of men. It is carried on through spiritual agencies, the word and sacraments, and accomplishes through the Holy Spirit the repentance, conversion, and obedience of men through faith. It defends believers and gives them supremacy over the powers of evil. This kingdom of grace presupposes that of power. Because, for these spiritual, saving results *in* the Church and for safeguarding it from its enemies and giving it its ordained triumph, the might of omnipresent omnipotence is requisite, the supreme power of the whole world— even the keys of death and of hell—must be in Christ's hands. Hence He is declared to be "Head over all things to the Church" (Eph. 1:22).

(*c*) The kingdom of *glory*. This is the realm of the Church triumphant. The saved own Him as their king forever. In His divine power He raises the believing dead (John 11:25) and introduces them into His heavenly kingdom, where angels, thrones, principalities, and powers are subject to Him (Matt. 25:34; 13:41; Luke 22:29–30). This mediatorial kingdom will continue until all the work of redemption shall be accomplished and this dispensation closed (1 Cor. 15:24–28).

5. In what sense the kingdom of Christ "*is not of this world*" (John 18:36).

(*a*) The *derivation* of His office is not in any succession or appointment of men, but divine and mediatorial.

(*b*) Its objects are *spiritual, i. e.,* the salvation of men from sin in this world and their preparation for heaven. The kingdoms of this world have primarily secular aims, moral ones, incidentally. Christ's dominion contemplates spiritual aims primarily, and effects secular ones only incidentally.

(*c*) The *form* of it is not that of an earthly monarchy—with its pomp and show. Christ is a spiritual super mundane King.

(*d*) His *agencies and instrumentalities* are spiritual—the word and the sacraments setting forth God's holiness and love, through the truths of the Gospel, made effectual by the Holy Spirit. The sword is not invoked to secure or hold its subjects. Its administration looks to the dominion of the soul, and operates from super natural sources.

Milton Valentine

6. How far *"the Church"* and *Christ's kingly sovereignty are synonymous.* This is a point of vast moment. The movement which identified "the Church" with "the kingdom of God" on earth, through a perversion and misapplication of Scripture language, and transformed the Church from the "body of believers," in fellowship of the word and sacraments, into a hierarchical organization of priests, bishops, archbishops, and pope—a self-perpetuating official organism, governing as deputy of the ascended Christ (*vicarius Christi*), of which individual believers were only subjects and not constituents, an earthly autocracy arrogating supreme spiritual and infallible dominion over the souls and bodies of men and earthly governments—this movement suggests the immense importance of the question thus raised. It brings to view the pivotal point on which the Protestant Reformation turned—whether such external organization of priestly officials has Scripture warrant for not only denying to believers the right of personal access to God through the One Mediator between men and God, but for assuming autocratic exercise on earth of the authority of the alone mediatorial King. A few facts as to the Scripture teaching will guide us into the truth.

(*a*) There is, perhaps, a discernible distinction between the designations "kingdom of God," or "of heaven" and the "kingdom of Christ." The two former seem to have been shaped by the conception of the completed *results* of Christ's saving work; the last by the conception of this work, as carried forward through the gathering and sanctification of believers in His administration of grace in this world. The kingdom of Christ is specially designative of the kingdom of God or heaven, as in-the-making, the kingly rule of grace till it passes into the heavenly world. Under this distinction, which, however, is not very explicit, the terms "kingdom of Christ" and "the Church "might, in some measure, be convertible designations. The mediatorial reign of Christ becomes the kingdom of God, or of heaven, in its progressive realization in the Church as the collective body of believers.

(*b*) The term Church (ἐκκλησία), found three times in the Gospels and eighty-eight times in the Epistles, was chosen by Christ and used by the apostles to designate the collective body of believers in organized fellowship of faith and worship. The Church, thus formed in local congregations, in spiritual fellowship with each other, is the fruit of Christ's conjoined offices of Prophet, Priest, and King. These bodies each and all form the increasing Church of Christ on earth, as the visible body (σῶμα) of which He is Head or

Ruler, and for which He is "Head over all things." This Church is not yet coterminous with the "kingdom of Christ on earth," and only partially so with that one division, the "kingdom of grace." Because "grace" in the form of mercy, long-suffering goodness, is shown from the mediatorial throne to yet unreclaimed men and to heathen peoples, the kingdom of "grace" is something far larger than the visible Church. And a further truth must be added, that even should they be conceded to be coterminous, the Church is only the *sphere* and *subject* of Christ's kingly authority and rule, and not the authority itself or the possessor of it and its blessings.

(c) The "kingdom of *glory*," since it includes angels and the heavenly hosts as ministers of service, also embraces more than the Church.

(d) Christ's kingdom of *power* is vastly larger and more comprehensive than the rulership over believers in the Church. In its proper and necessary relation this power was taken mediatorially for the sake of the Church, but it is inconceivably vaster, embracing the whole providential ordering of the world, the subordination of all its forces, authorities, and rule. Despite the contradictions of human will and wickedness, the enthroned Christ will bend the course of human history to the issues of redemption. Dr. A. Robertson, of Oxford, well says: "Our Lord nowhere simply identifies His kingdom, or the kingdom of God with the Church He came to found. As we have seen, His kingdom is visibly represented in His Church; but there are insuperable obstacles to treating the two things as convertible. Our Lord founded a society which was to be visible, like a city set on a hill, that cannot be hid, but the kingdom of God is visible only to faith."

7. *The chief modes in which Christ accomplishes His Kingly office.*

(a) Through providential oversight and direction—not only over the Church, but over the world. Matt 28:18; Luke 10:22; John 3:35; 5:22; Acts 2:34–35; 1 Cor. 15:25.

(b) Through a dispensation of the Holy Spirit, who, through the truth calls, enlightens, sanctifies, and guides His Church. John 14:16; 15:26; Luke 24:49; Acts 2:32–36.

(c) By prescribing in general features the organization of the Church, its spiritual functions, and the duties of its chief officers. Matt 18:18–20; Eph. 4:8–11; 1 Tim. 3:8.

(d) By securing through His truth and Spirit, and the organized Church, a proper call and appointment of a perpetual succession of men to preach the Gospel and ad minister its order. Acts 1:23–24; 6:5; 20:28; Heb. 13:7–17.

(e) *By His own invisible Presence* in the Church. We should offend against one of the most vital and precious truths of the Gospel were we to ignore this. The ascension of the risen Christ to the heavens, to the right hand of God, does not mean absence from the earth. It was a withdrawing of Himself from sight, a passing into the viewless, "*far above all the heavens, that He might fill all things* "(Eph. 4:10). He rose above the limitations of time and space, to exercise the attribute of omnipresence, which is His by His essential Deity. He is exercising it in His whole mediatorial position and office on behalf of His Church till He shall come again. He is so close to us that He lives in each believer and each lives in Him, and has left us the quickening assurance: "Where two or three are gathered together in My name, there am I in the midst of them" (Matt 18:20). His presence is not an idle one.

8. *Relation between the Church and civil authority.* As the Church is only a particular sphere of Christ's mediatorial kingdom, the relation between the *Church* and the *State* must not be confounded with that between Christ's *kingly dominion* and the *State*. The false identification of the Church with Christ's kingdom on earth, and the consequent usurpation of Christ's kingly supremacy by the hierarchical Church, makes clearness here of vast importance. History has developed three distinct views as to the relation between the Church and the State.

(a) That which asserts *supremacy* of the Church over the State. This is the Roman Catholic doctrine. The Church, as a formal organization in the papacy, claims both spiritual and temporal dominion and the supremacy of the spiritual over the secular. Kings must execute the orders of the pope or suffer deposition from their thrones. This system was enforced with rigor prior to the Reformation, and still continues to be the doctrine of Roman Catholicism. This views the secular administration as only a particular range of the Church's function as the kingdom of Christ on earth. It grew out of Augustine's conception of the Church as the *City of God*.

(b) That which declares the supremacy of the State over the affairs of the Church. This reverses the order of the preceding doctrine. The civil ruler becomes the Head of the Church. The Church becomes servant to the State, subject to State regulation as to creeds, organization, administration, cultus, etc. It is called a union of Church and State; but the Church is under. This has been the leading conception in almost all the countries of Europe—also in the Greek Church. It is set forth in Article XXXVII. of the Thirty-nine Articles of the Church of England: "The Queen's Majesty hath the chief power in this realm of England, and her other dominions, unto whom the chief government of all estates of this realm, whether they be ecclesiastical or civil, in all cases doth appertain.... They (the princes) should rule all estates committed to their charge by God, whether they be ecclesiastical or temporal, and restrain with the civil sword the stubborn and evil-doers." In the Greek Church a relation of subordination of Church to State grew up under the Christian emperors, who were clothed with ecclesiastical authority and power.

This view, known as Erastianism, from a prominent defender of it in Heidelberg in the sixteenth century, holds the Church only as one phase of the State. The State being a divine institution, designed to care for the wants of men, is charged with the duty of providing for their spiritual needs, and so must support the Church, appoint its teachers, regulate its worship, and superintend its administration. Rothe holds that the kingdom of God *is* a civil as well as ecclesiastical constitution.

(*c*) *The theory of reciprocal independence.* This views the Church and State as two distinct spheres of administration—*both divine institutions*—the one charged with secular order and welfare, the other with spiritual functions. "Both instituted by God and belonging to each other," says Sartorius. The State owes to its citizens protection in all their rights, including their religious as well as secular rights. But this does not authorize it to interfere with the autonomy of the Church. At the same time the Church, as an organization, has no right to assume secular or civil functions. Both Luther and Calvin taught that the Church should stand free and self-sustaining under the protection of the State.[2] But the circumstances made the attainment of such a relation impracticable. In our country this view has been the ruling one, as it is unquestionably the correct one.

9. *The relation between Christ's Kingly Sovereignty and the State or civil government.* As the scope of this Kingly Sovereignty is far wider than the Church, the question of the relation between it and the State is quite a different question from that between the *State* and the Church. There may be independence as between the Church

and State, but not of the State with respect to Chrst's kingly dominion. A few truths will make this evident.

(*a*) The State as truly as the Church is a divine institution, and its legitimate officers are "God's ministers" (Rom. 13:1–6). This is the Christian view of civil government—divine as truly as the family, a thing made necessary in the nature of man and society, a necessity framed by God into the order of life—as much so as hunger and thirst are framed into man's physical organism. Society requires order, and order rests in law. "The powers that be are ordained of God"—not any particular form of government, but government generically viewed. Anarchy is not a privilege of the race. Magistracy, civil government, and its officers are "God's ministers for good, attending continually on this very thing."

(*b*) Christ, as Mediator, is King of kings and Lord of lords, and to His authority every knee is to bow, "of things in heaven and things in earth" (Phil. 2:10; Eph. 1:21–22; 1 Cor. 15:25). Civil governments, in any and every form, are no more exempted in their special spheres from recognition of and respect for God's authority, plan, order or laws—no more entitled to a divorce from obedience—than any other activity of man. There is no secularity beneath the stars that is absolved from harmonizing its action with the sovereignty and laws of God, carried on in the mediatorial dominion of Jesus Christ.

(*c*) Every nation should explicitly and practically, in its own sphere and function, acknowledge the Christ of God as the Supreme Ruler of the earth, and His will as the supreme law to which governmental action should always be conformed. Otherwise there is the contradiction of a divine institution in revolt against God. If the civil governments of the earth, the most prominent, representative feature of human life, the very rulership of the world, peculiarly determinative of the life and character of the nation, is to be held as excused from all recognition of, or practical respect for, the divine order, how is the harmonization of all things with that order, and the bringing of the world to righteousness and peace ever to be accomplished? The blight of many nations is that the secular power is not Christianized enough to harmonize with the ideal of the kingdoms of this world as having really become "kingdoms of the Lord and His Christ."

(*d*) All civil officers should be men who recognize Christ's authority and who conform themselves to it as supreme in all the relations of human life. Otherwise they have not the basal ideas

Christian Theology

needful for application to the moral life and secular welfare. It amounts to the absurdity of acting in the position of "ministers of God," yet repudiating God's authority and the application of His laws in His own institution. The office is taken and the owner locked out. Rulers are to hold themselves in their official duties to the sovereign Rulership of Christ (1 Tim. 2:1–2).

(e) The State as one divine institution should recognize the Church as another—not in the way of assuming any of the Church's functions or attempting to control its spiritual work, but by giving it its proper free and independent action within its peculiar spiritual sphere, and by keeping its own legislative and judicial action in harmony with the right condition for the Church's prosperity. The Christian State, therefore, should harmonize all legislation with the moral principles of the Bible, all along the lines where social welfare is connected with divine laws.

This true relation of the State to the dominion of Christ has been set forth and emphasized all through the progress of revelation and history. Not only in the early theocracy, but in the Jewish government under the kings, the civil administration was held bound to respect God's will and authority, as were the Church, the priesthood, and the common people. Any attempt to divorce the powers of the State from obedience, in its given functions, was visited with divine displeasure—forming for centuries a mirror of God's mind on the subject. The amenability of the civil ruler to God's laws was unmistakable. "By Me kings rule and princes decree judgment." Moreover, in all the prophecies of the Christian day, of the new order of things under our dispensation, Christ's kingly rule over men and civil administration was put in the forefront. The kingdom was foretold as destined to break in pieces all opposing kingdoms. "All kings shall fall down before Him, all nations shall serve Him"; "Kings shall come to the brightness of Thy rising." When Christ came, and, though accepted as King by thousands on thousands of Jews in their personal capacity, was rejected by the rulers in both Jewish and Roman administration, an official illustration of the rebellious secularism in which governments say, "We will not have this man to rule over us," the warning voice which had been uttered in the ears of Israel took effect in divine judgment: "The nation that will not serve Thee shall perish." The Jewish people remain, but the nation is gone. And just as truly does the fact stand out in the providential history of the ages since that day, that the nation that in governmental action assumes independency of God's laws of order in the world under Christ—that, for instance, instead of preserving the family constitution, undertakes to enact laws of marriage and divorce which set God's laws aside, or in its own business and agencies ignores the divine Sabbath, or adopts, or even allows, in its administrational practice the invasion of Christian morality—such nation not only offends against God, but against the fundamental principles of human welfare, disharmonizes its movement with the irreversible laws of divine order, and sends disordering influences down through society that bring into action the forces of penalty and judgment.

Christian Theology

Milton Valentine

PART III
THE APPLICATION OF REDEMPTION

PASSING on from the second part of Theology, the manifestation of the Son of God for human redemption, covering the Source of Salvation, the Person of the Savior, and the States and Work of Christ as Prophet, Priest, and King—through all of which we have seen furnished a revelation of all needed truth, a full atonement for sin, a Redeemer enthroned, a dispensation of grace established over the earth, and all things ready for salvation to the uttermost of all that come to God by Him—we need to trace yet the application and consequent appropriation of the provided redemption. This third division leads us on from Christology to a further part of Soteriology or the doctrine of salvation, the grace and office of the Holy Spirit, who carries the saving provision into effect. The order of examination will be: *I. The Agent Who Applies Redemption; II. The Movement or Process of the Application; III. The Means of the Application; IV. Eschatology, or the Last Things.*

DIVISION I
THE HOLY SPIRIT AS APPLYING REDEMPTION

As Christ, through His mission and work, provided the necessary basis for divine forgiveness and recovery of sinners, so the Holy Spirit makes that provision effectual through an established method of application. This is as essential as the Father's gift of the Son, and the Son's incarnation, obedience, and propitiatory sacrifice. For such is the alienation of man and the helplessness of his broken constitution, that no one ever would or could experience the salvation without this divine agency. The Savior recognized and declared this necessity for giving effect to His own work and the purpose of salvation: "Nevertheless I tell you the truth, it is

Christian Theology

expedient for you that I go away; for if I go not away, the Comforter will not come unto you; but if I go I will send Him unto you," etc. (John 16:7–14; 1 Cor. 12:3). As we have already seen, this departure from visible presence does not mean absence from His people on earth, but an invisible mediatorial and kingly presence; but His work actualizes its aim through the promised agency of the Holy Spirit, who turns the redemptive provision into actual salvation.³

We recall that in the doctrine of the Trinity the Holy Spirit is God, of one undivided and indivisible essence with the Father and the Son, yet a distinct personal Subsistence, co-equal and co-eternal with the Father and the Son. This includes several points:

1. *The Personal Relation of the Holy Spirit to the Father and the Son.* This is twofold.

(*a*) The *ad intra relation*—as existent within the Godhead. We recall some facts already given. The word fixed in theological science to express this is "proceeding" (*processio,* ἐκπορευσις) proceeding from the Father and the Son. Like the terms "begotten," "only begotten," in the relation of the Son, this is not used to express any *time* relation or any inferiority, but to designate an eternal, necessary, and unceasing life-mode in the essence of the Godhead, whereby the Third Person or Subsistence is eternally the Spirit of the First and the Second—the same Essence or Being, without division or change, proceeding from the Father and the Son, into a personal Subsistence. After the Council of Nice, A. D. 325, in which the Deity of Christ was formulated, and which, concerning the Spirit, only said, "We believe in the Holy Ghost," the Council of Constantinople, A. D. 381, formulated the doctrine of the Spirit, "We believe in the Holy Ghost, the Lord and Giver of life, who proceedeth from the Father, and with the Father and the Son together is worshiped and glorified, who spake by the prophets." The question was afterward raised whether the Spirit does not sustain the same relation to the Son as to the Father. As a result of the discussion the western part of the Church, in the Synod of Toledo, A. D. 589, added the word *filioque* (and the Son) to the Latin version of the Creed. The Eastern or Greek Church resisted this, and to this day rejects the *filioque.*

What Scripture evidence have we to sustain the correctness of the *filioque?* (1) The Holy Spirit is called equally "the Spirit of God" and "the Spirit of Christ" (Eph. 4:30; Rom. 8:9; Gal. 4:6; 1 Pet 1:11). (2) The *essence* of the Holy Spirit is identical with that of the Son as well as with that of the Father. The *homoousian* doctrine applies to the whole Trinity. This, however, is of force only indirectly. For the point of inquiry is not concerning *essential* attributes, but personal properties or distinctions. Yet, if the Father and the Son be of the *same essence,* the *personal* distinction expressed by "proceeding from" logically suggests "and from the Son." (3) The "sending" of the Holy Spirit into the Church is ascribed alike to the Father and the Son (John 14:26; 16:7). This, too, has bearing only indirectly. The "sending" expresses an *ad extra* relation. But this *ad extra* relation, in redemptive manifestation, is justly entitled to imply a full *ad intra* basis for the external activity. As underlying the Spirit's being "sent" by both the Father and the Son for the applicatory consummation of the work of redemption on earth, a corresponding double *ad intra* relation seems normally suggested.

(*b*) The *ad extra* relation, *i. e.,* His *office and work in the economy of redemption.* As the Son is the Redeemer, so the Holy Spirit is the *Sanctifier.* It is necessary, however, to understand this designation as expressing the entire function or activity through which the provided redemption is made to issue in the forgiveness of sin and the new life of holiness.

2. *The relation of the Holy Spirit to the purpose of the Father and the work of the Son.*

(*a*) As to the first, "the eternal purpose" which was purposed in Christ, was, as we have seen, the purpose of God, *i. e.,* of the whole Godhead. In this purpose the Holy Spirit was at one with the Father and the Son in the Trinitarian unity. There is no dissonance in the Divine Will. God is One in love and aim. The purpose of the Father in sending the Son, of the Son who came, and of the Holy Spirit who was sent, is an absolute unity, as is the Trinity itself.

(*b*) As to the second, the work of the Son, this is both the basis on which and the provision through which the Spirit's agency is conducted. Without what the Son has done in His atoning work, the Holy Spirit's work could have no place, there being in such case no opened way to life and no means through which to effect it. Only on the provision made by Christ, therefore, does the work of the Spirit come in place. And then, the *realities in the atoning work,* the opened way to pardon, the truths of the gospel provision and message, become the Holy Spirit's *means* of bringing men from death to life and recovering them to the divine sonship for which they were created: "He shall glorify Me, for He shall receive of Mine and shall show it unto you" (John 16:14).

Christian Theology

It is to be borne in mind, however, that the work of the Spirit in applying redemption does not mean any cessation of activity by the Son, as has been shown in His High-priestly intercession and Kingly dominion. The omnipotent Savior, one in purpose with the Father, is working *through* the Holy Spirit. For Christ, as well as the Father, is said to send Him; and when it is accomplished it is spoken of as *God's* work (Phil. 2:13; Rom. 8:9).

Milton Valentine

DIVISION II
MOVEMENTS OR STEPS IN THE SPIRIT'S APPLICATION

We here come to the discussion of the way in which the divine supply, in the great salvation, is brought into vital relation with the human need—the steps by which, through the work of the Holy Spirit showing and applying the things of Christ, the provisions of redemption pass into effect. As the process is an ethical, spiritual one, its movement is adjusted to the free rational constitution of man.

CHAPTER I
THE CALL OR VOCATION

This is the first thing in the order of application. For uncalled, men would not avail themselves of the provided redemption. The divine provision must be set forth and invitation given with enabling grace. To this necessity Christ directly looked, not only in assuring the Spirit's coming, but in charging His disciples: "Go ye, and make disciples of all nations." The reception of this invitation constitutes men "called" (κλητοί or κεκλημένοι).

This call is rightly characterized as:

1. *Mediate.* It is through the word or message of the gospel, "the truth in Jesus," brought to the knowledge of men. The proclamation of that message is the *means* through which the call is given. It is through this *medium* that the Holy Spirit opens a knowledge of the way of salvation and presents its invitation—which is also *His* "call"—to men. "He shall take of Mine, and shall show it to you" (John 16:13). This is the appointed way, and we have no reason to include any other as having place in the divine order for us and the world. However God may, for special reason, have called directly by supernatural manifestation, as in the case of Saul, that is not the method of the gospel. St. Paul is explicit in directing us as to the

divine way: "Faith cometh by hearing, and hearing by the word of God." "How shall they believe on Him of whom they have not heard? and how shall they hear without a preacher?" (Rom. 10:14–17). An appointed ministry of preaching and teaching is but another expression of this important truth.

In connection with this it is properly borne in mind that in Christian lands much of Gospel truth gets into men's minds and consciences indirectly. It is abroad in our common light, so as to be wholly unknown by few. The Holy Spirit may enter in through such truth—truth not at first hand or second, but in distant reflections and refractions from the general Christian atmosphere. But the normal means is the word of God, as preached, read, or taught in the education of the young (Matt. 28:19; 2 Tim. 3:15).

An *instrumental* connection of the ministry of the *Law* with that of the gospel, in the Holy Spirit's call to salvation must be recognized. The law, indeed, offers no salvation. Its principle: 'Do these things and thou shalt live,' is beyond application because of human corruption and guilt. "By the deeds of the law shall no flesh be justified" (Rom. 3:20). But St. Paul, whose self-effort at justification proved so thorough a failure, nevertheless assigned the law a close and important relation to the full force of the gospel opportunity and message. "By the law"—not the ceremonial but the moral— "is the knowledge of sin" (Rom. 3:20), which becomes a vision of despair. "I had not known sin but by the law," which "is holy, just, and good" (Rom. 7:7–12). "Wherefore the law was our schoolmaster to bring us to Christ" (Gal. 3:24). The vision of the law closes off a false hope, but impels to the true order of human salvation. Melanchthon's recognition of an auxiliary relation of the ministry of the law in connection with the call of the gospel is thoroughly just and important: "God terrifies by the law that there may be place for consolation and vivification, because hearts secure and not perceiving the wrath of God despise consolation." The recognized impossibility of justification through the law becomes motive for accepting it through the gracious atonement in Christ.

This co-operative use of the law in the gospel call is sustained by its more positive use after justification. The law is an expression of the holiness or righteousness of God, into whose image renewing and sanctifying grace is to restore man. God, viewed as to His moral Being, is ethical Law as well as Love. His immutable Nature is the absolute ground and necessity of all right and righteousness. Man's sin is the contradiction at once of God and His law. In this is found the guilt and misery of sin. The question of atonement turned on the possibility of forgiveness of it and recovery from it. Sinful man cannot be saved by the law, as he can neither keep it nor remove its condemnation. Under the provision of a gracious forgiveness, though he cannot be saved *by* the law, he can, and must be saved *to* it, to its holiness and righteousness. Only thus can he be saved *from* sin and sinning, and be recovered to the image of God, from which by disobedience humanity has lapsed. God's revelation of grace is also a revelation of righteousness—of God's essential righteousness, and Christ's righteousness *for* us; and also of that righteousness which we are to become *in* Him, as we die to sin and He lives in us, the life of our lives (Rom. 6:1–8, 22; 8:1–4; Gal. 2:20). The work of Christ was the supreme manifestation of both love and righteousness. There can be no place for "antinomianism" in our theology. The growing tendency toward elimination of law and juridical conceptions from the atonement is away from Scripture theology. Its naturalistic ethicalism fails to represent Christian Theism. Since God is Himself ethical Law and Righteousness, antinomianism becomes ungodliness and unrighteousness. And so, even after they have been brought to Christ and blessed with forgiveness of sins that are past, the continued ministry of the law as the divine guide to Christian conduct and character is an essential part of the process of saving men and making them Christ-like. The gospel is a gospel of salvation *from* sin, into the holiness to which *Holy* Love is seeking to bring us.

2. *It is both external and internal.* (a) The *external call* is the outward message of the gospel, as, in some form or other, it opens to view the prepared salvation, shows human need and opportunity, presents the appeal and promises of the divine love, and asks a consenting response and obedience. It is external, in that it comes from without man *to* him, to his intelligence and natural understanding. (b) The *internal* is the Holy Spirit's influence within the mind and heart through the word, as an internal agency or action on the soul. It marks the meeting point of the truth from without and the Spirit's use of it in constituting it His own call, divinely pressed upon the human spirit. (c) The *relation* between the external and internal has been differently viewed. Calvinistic theology has been wont to contrast them. (1) They are looked upon as so distinct as to be *separable*, the external possibly being without the internal. (2) The external as common to all hearing the gospel; the internal as peculiar to the elect. (3) The internal as with a real

intent to the predestinated conversion; the external as having no such real design. (4) The external as not only resistible, but without the internal, necessarily ineffectual; the internal irresistible, under predestinating grace. But our Lutheran theology recognizes no such separation. The external and internal are the two sides of one divine action or vocation, in the established order of grace under the Gospel—the inner call being always concurrent with the hearing of the word. He is "the Spirit of truth." He enters and calls *in* the truth. He is *immanent* in it. The word is not simply an instrument which He may use, or from which He may separate Himself or be absent, but the divinely appointed means in which He abides and works, so as to make *its* light the unfailing bearer of His own influence. Nor in the appointed order does the Spirit call apart from the word or gospel truth. It may, indeed, be lodged in the mind and resisted for a season, but come to effect when resistance is less.

3. *The call is general.* It is not restricted to any preordained individuals or classes, but is provided for *man-kind,* for *all* men, without limitation or distinction. This is certain from clear Scripture teaching. (*a*) From the comprehensive purpose in the atonement. "God so loved the world that He gave His Son" (John 3:16). The Son gave Himself to be "the propitiation for the sins of the whole world," and "tasted death for every man." (*b*) From the benevolent will of God in view of the needs of men. He desires that all men may come to the knowledge of the truth (1 Tim. 2:4; 2 Pet 3:9). (*c*) From the command of Christ (Matt. 28:19). From this it is rightly designated a universal call. But by such designation it is, of course, not meant to be asserted that all individuals of all nations and ages have been blessed with it, but only that the scope of provision is unrestricted, and the commission for preaching it contemplates man as a race universally. The human agency in the fulfillment of the commission of proclamation fails to work up to the given orders. The commission, however, expresses the obligation of the Church to make the actual universality correspond to the reach of the divine love.

4. *The call is sincere*—a true invitation to a provided and available salvation. The given vocation means all that it offers. Several considerations sustain this. (*a*) The Redeemer's work on the basis of which the Holy Spirit acts has made provision for all. That provision being real and full, the call is necessarily to be understood as meaning what it says. There is no room for thinking of the external call as an empty formality. (*b*) The Holy Spirit being "the Spirit of

truth" (John 16:13), cannot take the things of Christ and offer a redemption not actually competent or designed for those whom, through the word, He invites. From these truths, three conclusions are clear. (1) The call thus given is binding, creates *obligation*, on all to whom it is made. (2) To refuse to comply is a great sin, an aggravated sinning, not only against righteousness, but against unspeakable love. (3) The failure of salvation, in face of the redemptive provision of love, brings an increased condemnation. It is the sin for the forgiveness of which there is no atonement.

5. *The call is graciously efficacious, but not irresistible.* Several points will explicate this:

(*a*) As to the *positive* or graciously efficacious force. By this is meant that the call by the word and Spirit, whatever may be its actual result, has, *per se*, divine and sufficient power or efficacy to effect conversion and salvation, if not resisted. It furnishes an actual sufficiency of divine momenta for overcoming human inability and effecting salvation to the otherwise helpless. The intrinsic quality of the call, as well as the sincerity of its intention, constitutes all that is needed for the turning of the possibility of salvation into the reality for the submissive soul. This efficacy takes place in at least three ways:

(1) Through what is designated *illumination* by the Holy Spirit, *i.e.*, a carrying of light to the understanding through the truth as it is in Jesus and exhibiting Him—not without or apart from the truth, but yet in excess of what the truth *simply as truth* would effect. The truth is an instrumental factor, but the greater and effective factor is the Holy Spirit who is in the truth and uses it, adding the agency of His own divine office for taking the things of Christ and "showing" them. There is in the natural man a spiritual darkness in which he does not receive spiritual things or know them rightly (Eph. 4:18; 1 Cor. 2:14). Not the truth alone—that is Pelagianism—but the power of the Spirit *in* the truth must shed the necessary light into the darkness. The starting point for this illumination is the blindness of mind made by corrupt inclination, the obstructions of ignorance and error. The end to which it looks is a saving knowledge, the light of true life (2 Cor. 4:6). This teaching power of the Holy Spirit in the call, beyond the simple power of the truth as such, is implied in all the Scriptures which attribute the effect to Him, *e. g.*, John 16:8; 1 Cor 12:3; 1:18.

(2) Through a *quickening of the sense of the need* of a Savior, and the *obligation* to accept Him. This, too, is effected, not apart from the

truth, but through it, and with a force or power in excess of the truth alone. We must never count the power or operation of the Spirit a zero, or sink it in the simply natural effect of the truth, even though that truth be divine. Of course the truth here carried before the mind is that which exhibits the infinite love of God in the atoning work of Christ—truth in itself of the most impressive and subduing power. But to this the Holy Spirit adds a special divine influence, an incitement unique and supernatural. This is necessarily implied in all such passages as speak of Him as being resisted, grieved, quenched, etc. (Eph. 4:30; 1 Thess. 5:19); and such as make a distinction between the power of the word and that of the Spirit (1 Thess. 1:5; 2 Cor. 6:7).

(3) By *working faith* or *trust* in Christ. Faith is a result of the work of the Holy Spirit in the call, showing the things of Christ in such power as to enable not simply an understanding of them, but their acceptance. Saving faith, or the trust that surrenders the soul to the obedience of Christ, is beyond the spiritual ability of the natural man. The application of redemption is through "faith, that it might be by grace" (Rom. 4:16). "No man can say that Jesus is the Lord, but by the Holy Ghost" (1 Cor. 12:3). But the Holy Spirit, as the applier of the gospel, gives through it such a view of God's love in the redemptive work of Christ, as, with His own direct divine influence, to inspire and awaken faith. If the Spirit's grace is not resisted it is sufficient to work saving faith. Thus the call is through supernatural truth by a divine Agent, with a true purpose to save; and it cannot, with any fairness, be regarded in any case as a mere formal and empty offer.

(*b*) In its *negative* aspect, we note that the Holy Spirit's call is *not irresistible.* Even a casual reading of the New Testament, and much more a deep study of it, distinctly impresses the mind with the fact of human responsibility with respect to personal status before God and moral destiny. From its beginning to its close men are viewed as moral agents, with constitutional endowment of personal self-determination, and are called on to elect their attitude toward God and righteousness in view of the most solemn alternative issues of obedience or disobedience. The years of Christ's ministry were years of instruction in duty and faith and of persuasion to the true life. The great work of His atonement was a provision of grace under which man's broken spiritual nature would find *enablement* for that life. But the mind was kept clear of any idea that the gift of truth and the provision of grace in themselves constituted salvation. The demand was insistent for voluntary self-surrender to the truth as an essential condition of realizing its saving power. Everywhere it is kept plain that the issue of the gospel depends yet on the assent of obedient faith. And the Redeemer's picture of a final judgment is a picture of the bearing of human free-agency, in the outcome, that, despite the Savior's teaching and atoning sacrifice, some go away into everlasting punishment, as well as some into everlasting life. "He that believeth on Him is not condemned." "Ye will not come to Me that ye might have life" (John 3:18; 5:40). It is this truth of the *resistibleness* of the Holy Spirit's call that both theoretical and practical theology needs to fix in mind. The call may be prevented from becoming effectual by the perverse will of men. This is often emphasized: Acts 13:46; 24:25; Matt. 19:16–29; Acts 7:51; Eph. 4:30; 1 Thess. 5:19; Heb. 10:29. The sin against the Holy Ghost (Matt. 12:31), which has no forgiveness in this world or that to come, seems to have its ultimate, if not direct, explanation in this solemn truth. If the *last* and essential agency for the effective application of redemption is refused and dishonored, it must necessarily be fatal. For since Christ has made no atonement for the sin of rejecting His atonement, there is neither atonement to apply nor conditions for the application of any.

The words of Christ, "I would—ye would not," apply to His call through the Spirit as well as through His own lips.

In all this teaching concerning the Spirit's call, there is confessedly a wide divergence from the Calvinistic explanation. That holds, in harmony with its doctrine of absolute predestination, the external or common call through the word and ordinary influences of the Spirit as always inefficacious; but the *internal* call as necessarily effectual in all the "elect," because of the peculiar presence and pressure of the divine power. It is spoken of as "irresistible grace" (*gratia irresistibilis*). "It is irresistible," says Dr. H. B. Smith, "in the sense that it carries the will and the affections with it." In that type of theology an absolute election, "without any foresight of faith or good works, or a perseverance in either of them, or any other thing in the creature as conditions or causes moving Him [God] thereunto," leaves nothing contingent on the human will. Predestination determines the will and enforces faith irresistibly. With respect to the non-elect, faith remains an impossibility, under the formal external call. We do not find this view in the statements or logic of the Scriptures. The call, Scripturally viewed, is based on the universality of the atonement, and the sincerity of the divine desire to save all that consent and submit to the grace provided and offered. The Biblical teaching in regard to human depravity and man's helplessness, of himself, to accept or exercise saving faith, is thoroughly recognized, but also the truth that the requisite ability comes in and through the divine call and its prevenient grace as a gracious enabling by the Holy Spirit to all who do not refuse His work. This makes the saving work wholly of grace. But man can resist, as the Scriptures teach. While he has no power of his own nature to save himself, he has power to refuse salvation and destroy himself. So the Scriptures warn against resistance or neglect, and throw the responsibility for failure of life upon men themselves (Heb. 2:3; 10:28).

Milton Valentine

CHAPTER II
REPENTANCE AND FAITH

These stand in vital relation to the Holy Spirit's call through the message of the gospel. They integrate into each other. Neither is without some element of the other. They must be viewed in their coherence.

The New Testament term for repentance, μετάνοια, means a *change of mind*—not as intellect alone, but as also including the moral sensibilities and the will. It involves perception of past error or wrong, abhorrence of it, and a turning away from it. Theological analysis, therefore, recognizes three items in the full movement. The Augsburg Confession says: "Repentance properly consists of two parts: one is contrition, or terror on account of sin; the other is faith, which is conceived by the gospel, or absolution, and believes that for Christ's sake sins are forgiven, comforting the conscience and freeing from terrors. Then should follow good works, which are fruits of repentance." This seems to fail to incorporate the third element; but in the "Apology for the Confession," Melanchthon says: "We have ascribed to repentance these two parts, viz., contrition and faith. If any one desires to add a third, viz., fruits worthy of repentance, we do not make any opposition."[2] The term, therefore, expresses the whole inner consciousness of the soul under the grace of the Holy Spirit's call, as convinced of sin, trusting to forgiving love in Christ, and turning from sin into newness of life. These parts require study, both as to what they severally are in themselves and as to their inter-relations.

1. CONTRITION is a true and holy sorrow of heart, produced by the Holy Spirit through the word, on account of sin against God and righteousness.

1. When analyzed it is found to embrace: (*a*) A *true knowledge* of sin. The entrance of God into the moral and spiritual life of man is through the intellect, as the fundamental faculty in which moral personality is creatively constituted. If saved at all man must be saved in and through the essential faculty-endowments by which he

Christian Theology

has his moral responsibility—not by annulling them or setting them aside, but as the channels of access and moral influence. Hence the call, if it is to lead to repentance, must achieve its first success in the form of true knowledge of sin. We shall have occasion to refer to this principle in other relations, in which its obscuration has been to the great detriment of theological science. (*b*) *A sense of the divine* displeasure against sin. (*c*) *Self-condemnation*, compunction, under the rebuke of awakened conscience (Ezek. 36:31). (*d*) *Sincere confession* (Luke 18:13). (*e*) Genuine hatred of sin and a desire of deliverance from it (2 Cor. 7:9–11).

2. Concerning these parts of contrition, it is to be observed, (*a*) That while the knowledge of sin must be real and sufficient to assure an intellectual conviction, it can never become so complete as to cover all our sins, or the fullness of their evil. They are more than we can number and worse than we can perceive. (*b*) That, though true conviction is always required in saving repentance, there are degrees in its intensity and alarm. The emotional element may vary. (*c*) That its relation to pardon is decided neither by the quantity nor the ethical value of the contrition in itself, but solely by its actually taking us to Christ and His merits. We are not saved by the merit of the process through which grace leads us, but by the grace of the Redeemer to which it brings us.

3. The relative place of the *law* and the *gospel* in the Holy Spirit's agency of working contrition needs to be noted and defined. The law gives the standard of duty by which we "know sin." "By the law is the knowledge of sin" (Rom. 3:20; also 7:7). But while mere knowledge may come through the law, real repentance, melting, subduing sorrow for sin comes only in view of the redeeming love of God in Jesus Christ. The heart does not break into contrition in the presence of legal requirement, but under the constraining power of love that appeals from the saving cross (John 12:32; 16:8, 9).

II. FAITH, viewed as the second part of repentance or "change of mind," denotes a change *to*, as contrition does a change *from*—away from sin to Christ and His righteousness.

1. The relation of *contrition* to faith is very close. This, however, is not the positive or causal means of faith, but only the *privative* means. By it the indifference or self-satisfaction, in which no motive force is felt, is gone. A state of *receptiveness* is reached. An awful spiritual need is seen and felt; the remedy for the soul's woe and ruin is recognized as the essential necessity. *Desire* has room to spring up (2 Cor. 7:10). This 'desire,' thus awakened, has its roots

from the primal constitution of man as made in the divine image—made for fellowship with God and in want till He is found.

2. The relation of *faith* to the *true fruits* of contrition is also close. Only as faith lays hold of Christ does the sinner unite himself to the provided grace that can remit the guilt of sin, overthrow its power and restore communion with God. In faith the soul is carried across the chasm between the ruin of contrition and the new life of redemption.

3. *Constituents* of faith. Theology has well defined its essential elements as threefold. It consists, (*a*) Of *knowledge*. The principle of God's entrance, for salvation, into the soul through the faculty of intelligence, has normal and full force. The knowledge here is, of course, that body of redemptive truth used by the Holy Spirit in His call—taking the things of Christ and showing them. Without a knowledge of the essential truths of the gospel there can be no apprehension of Christ, no faith in Him—nothing to rest upon, nothing to appropriate. And so the Scriptures are explicit in making this the fundamental element. Christ declares: "This is life eternal, that they should know Thee, the only true God, and Jesus Christ whom Thou hast sent" (John 17:3). Of John the Baptist it was foretold: "Thou shalt go before the face of the Lord to prepare His ways, to give knowledge of salvation unto His people in the remission of their sins" (Luke 1:76, 77). See also Rom. 10:13–17; Eph. 4:18; Gal. 4:8, 9. (*b*) Of *assent, i.e.,* intellectual acceptance of the gospel teaching and promises as true. It is appropriately called "historical faith," intellectual belief, and recognition of the claims of Christianity and the truth of its doctrines. The gospel may be not only known, but *believed* in the way of general assent. It is an approving judgment of the knowing faculty, but attended as yet by an indifference that fails of personal and hearty self-surrender to Christ and His grace. With "knowledge," this "assent" is not yet saving faith. And yet it is an essential step or element in the movement that reaches the heart—the faith that realizes salvation. (*c*) The *third* or completing element of justifying faith is *confidence,* or self-surrendering *trust*—an act of the heart and the will resting on the grace of God, as provided in Christ, apprehending and appropriating all that is thus offered—atonement, forgiveness, and salvation. "This confidence is nothing else than the acceptance or apprehension of the merit of the God-man, appropriating it to ourselves individually" (John 1:12; Rom. 4:21; 10:10). Knowledge may

Christian Theology

exist without faith. Assent may be short of saving faith. But confidence or trust in and on the Savior is faith's completed reality.

This conclusion as to the completing element is abundantly sustained. In addition to the few Scriptures referred to, we may note (a) That the word faith (πίστις), from πείθω, to persuade, convince, make confident, assure, carries this conception. (b) It is distinctly called trust (πεποίθησις) (2 Cor. 3:4; Eph. 3:12; Heb. 2:13; Phil. 1:14). (c) In the nature of the case it must be so. Until there is a trusting of ourselves to the grace of God in Christ there can be no return to obedience and the life of holiness. This is the essential act of self-surrender. It thus accomplishes its sequent relation to contrition, the first part of repentance. While in contrition there is reached a state of *receptiveness* in the soul for the righteousness of Christ, faith, the second part, becomes its actual *reception*, apprehending and appropriating it. And it is important to observe that in faith's *totality* it exists in the three great constituent human faculties that form one's personality, the understanding, the sensibilities, and the will. These, as conjoined and united in divers acts, all moving to the same end and in a certain connected order, carry the whole spiritual personality into the new life of grace.

4. This faith is wrought in us by the Holy Spirit, through the word. It is not a product of our own natural ability. By reason of the depravity of human nature, its alienation from God and its bondage in sin, it cannot of itself exercise saving faith. The will is enslaved to indwelling corruption. So, with respect to this necessary function of faith, we are taught: "It is God that worketh in you both to will and to do" (Phil. 2:13). This working is that of "prevenient grace," by the Holy Spirit in His call through the message of the gospel. We are thus required to distinguish between the principal or efficient cause of faith, which is God, and its instrumental cause, the word. The faith, which it is impossible for man of himself alone to exercise, is made possible by the illumination and grace supernaturally given by the Spirit through the truth in Jesus. The Spirit thus reaches the understanding with knowledge, and the heart with contrition, and empowers the otherwise helpless will for faith. But this empowering is not an irresistible grace, as alleged in the Calvinistic teaching. It is not to be maintained that God works faith by compulsion, apart from or against the will—against an actively resisting or opposing will; and thus saves men by annulling or setting aside the human faculty of free choice and annihilating the crowning endowment of moral personality given by Him in the work of creation. He saves

man according to and through the faculties in which He made him in His own image. God respects His own creative work, and in His redemptive activity brings enabling grace for the right use of free will. The enabling comes as a gracious help or enfranchisement of the will, with ability for its free function. In itself, as we have seen, the natural human will is not free in spiritual things, but by quickening prevenient grace a free assent or acceptance of Christ is made possible. Men are not *purely passive* in conversion. They are measurably active in the incipient elements of faith—in "knowledge" or understanding of the truth, and in "assent" as formal belief of the truth, under the Spirit's call. And in "confidence," the self-surrender of sincere trust, the activity continues, under the progressive awakening and quickening. The whole movement is one in which God comes with enabling grace for man's acceptance of the prepared, but not yet actualized salvation. And the "assent" or acceptance is necessarily *man's act*, not God's—but man's, empowered by God's Spirit of grace. It is an act of the human *will.* God cannot believe *for* man; but, through the truth made potent by the Holy Spirit, He can make faith possible to the otherwise impotent human will. And so we find our Church theology recognizing the reality of an alternative choice in free will—not of the natural will as enslaved by sin, but of the will as *empowered* for a free and uncompelled acceptance. We find Lutheran writers, from Melanchthon down, writing of the will in the act of faith as *arbitrium liberatum,* "*will liberated,*" i. e., from its bondage and inability for its necessary office. Gerhard says: "It cannot be denied that in conversion the mind of man assents, and the will longs for grace.... Free-will is only susceptible of salvation. Only God is able to give it. Only free-will is able to accept it." This means that in conversion man is *not* "purely passive," but that by the prevenient grace, calling and preparing for faith, the before helpless will is so empowered by grace that it can exercise its *function of free election, either to consent to or refuse the call.* The applicatory grace of the call, while not irresistible, overpowering the will, yet makes salvation available to sin-disabled man by restoring to him the freedom of choice which he possesses in the sphere of the *natural* life, for the sphere and needs of the *spiritual* life. It is all of the divine working. There is no Pelagian taint in the doctrine. But it does keep clearly in view the great fact, so emphasized in the Scriptures, of human responsibility with respect to the issue of the provided redemption and gospel appeal. And it keeps in mind the truth that,

Christian Theology

correspondent to the divine "application" of Christ's work of redemption, there is, and must be, also an "appropriation," if men are to realize its saving purpose.

III. The third thing constitutive of true repentance appears in its fruitage—A NEW OBEDIENCE, THE CONVERTED LIFE. It is the sorrow for sin (2 Cor. 7:9-10), moving on, through sincere faith, into the spirit and conduct "meet for repentance" (Matt 3:8). This is of supreme importance as the test of its genuineness. If the fruit is not made good, how shall we know the tree made good? How shall we recognize the true work of the gospel if the law of God be not written again in the believer's mind and heart? (Jer. 31:33; Ezek. 11:19-20; Heb. 8:10). Unless the movement issues in this the contrition is not genuine, and the so-called faith is dead (Jas. 2:17-20). The new life of holy obedience lies already in the very essence of repentance and faith. The point of the fruitage is vital and needs special emphasis. The aim and goal of salvation is not simply remission of sin, but salvation from sin itself. The supreme purpose of God's saving love is human recovery to the life for which God made man in His own image, through a change of heart, issuing in true obedience and holy character. But we will come to this topic again, under another head.

Milton Valentine

CHAPTER III
JUSTIFICATION

In passing to the subject of justification, we reach the great truth in connection with which we discover the vital and central significance of "faith," whose characterizing features have already appeared in the grace of repentance, and whose essential action moves on in the saving process to its end. It is seen to become the living channel of the divine saving power into actual and abiding human experience.

In the Christo-centric theology of our Church, Christ, in His revelation of God and His atoning work, being the great reality about which *all* spiritual truth moves, *justification by faith* becomes the pivotal fact in the *application* of redemption. The Christo-centric principle, opening right doctrinal conception from the first, passes on in its determining force for doctrinal reality and significance, until, at the applicatory stage, it becomes not only "Christ *for* us," but "Christ *in* us the hope of glory." In the clearest sense Christ now becomes and *is* our salvation. Justification by faith, therefore, expresses more fully the very substance of the gospel than any other particular truth. For it exhibits the very meaning of the incarnation, the atonement, the whole scheme and work of grace. All looked to this—the salvation of men through faith in Christ. And salvation, thus conferred, sums up the aim of all. It was for this great truth the battle of the Reformation of the sixteenth century was waged, and *by* it, instrumentally, the Church was reformed. It was the "material principle" of the movement. Through its recovery from papal and scholastic misrepresentation, the channel for the life currents of Christ's grace was opened anew to the view of men. Around this all other parts of Christian doctrine come into harmony and unity. D'Aubigne has well said: "The powerful text, 'the just shall live by faith,' was a creative word for the Reformer and the Reformation." Luther has marked it as the doctrine by which the Church must stand or fall, *articulus stantis vel cadentis ecclesæ*.

The full significance of justification requires that it be viewed in both its negative and positive aspects. Only thus will we be led to appreciate the imperative human need for which the redemptive work has provided, and the historical facts which in the sixteenth century called for, and which perpetually vindicate, the great emphasis placed upon the doctrine.

1. THE IMPOSSIBILITY OF SELF-JUSTIFICATION
The confessional statement: "Our Churches teach that we cannot obtain forgiveness of sin and be justified before God by our own strength, merit, or works, presents the negative aspect of the question of the attainment of salvation. The integrity of the gospel system of grace allows no recognition of justification grounded in any degree on human innocence or merit. The Scripture teaching concerning original sin, and its disabling blight, has been already presented. But it is well to note here how this not only thoroughly implies but explicitly affirms the impossibility of reaching a state of acceptance before God on any other basis than that opened in the atonement and righteousness of Christ. It is implied in the very principle of the law, which is, "the man that doeth them shall live in them" (Gal. 3:12). Perfect obedience is made the legal condition of acceptance. That this is impossible with man is asserted in the harmonious voice of all the Scriptures. St. Paul declares: "We have proved both Jews and Gentiles under sin. There is none righteous, no, not one" (Rom. 3:9–10). "Now we know that what things soever the law saith, it saith to them that are under the law, that every mouth may be stopped, and all the world may become guilty before God. Therefore by the deeds of the law shall no flesh be justified in His sight. For all have sinned and come short of the glory of God" (verses 19, 20, 23). From this condition of sin and condemnation, in which every man is by nature, there is no escape by his own strength, obedience, or works. "The law worketh wrath" (Rom. 4:15). "No man is justified by the law" (Gal. 3:11). "If there had been a law given which could have given life, verily righteousness should have been by the law. But the Scripture hath concluded all under sin" (Gal. 3:21–22). All that the law can do toward forgiveness is by its revelation of sin and guilt, impelling to accept the forgiveness of grace. In view of the foregoing and other passages, reiterating this truth in multiplied forms and with earnest emphasis, believing theology is forbidden to concede any possibility of working out a saving righteousness by ethical obedience, good deeds, or any personal virtues. Under condemnation and blight of sin, the idea of *merit* as a claim for acceptance before God is a monstrous

contradiction. Hence the unequivocal declaration: "Ye are saved by grace, not of works, lest any man should boast" (Eph. 2:8–9). "And if by grace, then it is no more of works; otherwise grace is no more grace. But if it be of works, then it is no more grace; otherwise work is no more work" (Rom. 11:6). Not even the smallest claim to meriting the divine favor is conceded to men. Neither as supplementary of the work of Christ, nor in combination with it, do the Scriptures tolerate a notion of human good desert in the foundation of God's acceptance.

This teaching of the apostles, especially of St. Paul, by whom so many of the first congregations were planted or instructed, may justly be regarded as essentially marking the Gospel as established in the Church of the early centuries. It is illuminating to note this, and to understand how, in later periods, and through the Middle Ages, the Church's soteriological doctrine of atonement and justification became obscured. At the beginning Christian piety, realizing salvation through faith in Christ, was busied rather with practical duty than theoretical definitions and formulations—reaching these largely as heresies attacked essential truths, as in the case of the doctrines of the Trinity and the Person of Christ. The truth before us received general, quiet acquiescence. The Apostolic Fathers (A. D. ab. 92–150) clearly recognized the doctrine of the atonement and salvation through it, expressing it in Scripture phraseology, without attempting its *rationale*. The Church Fathers of the third and fourth centuries show continued recognition of it, with some tendency toward theoretic explanation, while guarding it against the implications of Ebionism and Gnosticism. Philosophic prepossessions, inherited from paganism, were not favorable to scientific elucidation of this great supernatural truth. Nevertheless it held ruling place in the heart of the Church. So, also, through the scholastic period. All professed to adopt it, and its explicit denial or rejection was a heresy.

A phenomenon of unhappy significance, however, began to appear in the fifth and sixth centuries, which must be noticed and sketched, if we are to understand the obscuration of the truth of justification at the opening of the sixteenth century. The religious life of the Church was undergoing a great change. It was lowered in tone, and the sense of sin was declining. Under the growing claims of priestly power and the hierarchical construction of the Church as an external organization, in alliance with the State, and its self-identification with the "kingdom of God," there came a loss of

Christian Theology

spiritual life and of conscious relation to the necessities of sinful humanity. It brought, on the one hand, a declining sense of the need of redemption and forgiveness by grace, and, on the other, a large use of human substitutes in the form of piacular masses, penances, indulgences, bodily mortifications, and special good works. Forgiveness of sins was made attainable through these means. The complete atonement, "made once for all," was practically discounted, and men were put upon the effort to work out a righteousness of their own. One root of this perverting development may be found already in Augustine's misleading statement: "God justifies the ungodly, not only by forgiving the sin he has done, but by giving him love, which turns him away from sin, and through the Holy Spirit makes him good." Augustine's name, like a royal stamp on a coin, gave currency to this representation. From his day the idea was developed, confounding justification with sanctification, and making it, not an objective divine act, but something subjective and constituting men internally and essentially righteous. It was interpreted as a *making righteous* by communication of the divine life. Possibly Augustine's aim was simply to safeguard against a merely nominal or dead faith, and to hold saving faith in undivorced connection with the new life of grace, as necessary to Christianity's quickening and transforming power. But his statement was used to represent justification as itself an internal regeneration, an act of interior ethical transformation. Most of the prominent schoolmen so taught, as Rome still does. Thomas Aquinas says: "Justification, primarily and properly, is a making just.... Justification as acquired is caused by works, but, as infused, it is by God Himself, through His grace."[2] In both conceptions it is thus made subjective; in one as a human work, in the other by a direct "infusion of grace." And when we recall the teaching of the times, asserting an *ex opere operato* action of the sacraments, we begin to see how the function of faith for justification, as set forth in the Scripture, was beclouded or vacated.

Two direct consequences of such teaching need special note:

1. Its corollary was the doctrine of *different degrees* of justification, according to the measure of the divine operation within the believer. Made to consist in a subjective holiness, of varied development, but always imperfect, no certain assurance of forgiveness and acceptance with God could ever be enjoyed. Instead of basing it on the objective perfect righteousness of the Divine Redeemer's work, the Christian was allowed to look only at the

partial measure of his inward holiness. Who could tell the minimum of infused righteousness that was necessary? No one could settle the degree of personal worthiness requisite before an infinitely holy God. No wonder that Luther could find no peace for his stricken soul till a truer view shed the divine light into his mind. No wonder that the Reformers so emphatically declare that the doctrine of Rome could give no relief and comfort to the sin-burdened conscience. The unhappy error stood in bold and self-condemning contrast with the declaration of St. Paul: "Being justified by faith, we have peace with God through our Lord Jesus Christ."

2. *An atoning and saving merit was attributed to good works.* These were included in the ground of justification, as influential in obtaining and advancing it. It is but just to say that the intention was not wholly to exclude the work of Christ from this ground. In underlying sense there was a continued recognition of His redeeming grace as entering into it. The human merit was represented as acting in *conjunction* with that of Christ—especially in the supposed *progressive* justification. But it all tended directly to misconception of the *nature* of justification and to undermine the believer's sense of dependence for it on the Redeemer's atonement and vicarious righteousness. And when Thomas Aquinas, the prince of the scholastic theologians, invented his subtle distinctions of kind and order in merit, the perverting and obscuring influence reached its fullness. His doctrine of *merit of congruity* (*meritum de congruo*), that is, of good deeds *before* conversion and independently of any gift of grace, which make it, not indeed necessary, but meet, fitting, and proper for God to recognize and reward; and of *merit of positive deservedness* (*meritum de condigno*), that is, of good works wrought by the new life of grace, as really meriting salvation and eternal life, taken in its entirety became the full doctrine of a salvation humanly merited and humanly wrought out. So seriously was the gospel of God's pure grace changed as to develop the consequent doctrine of Christian works of supererogation—works beyond the requirement of the principle of duty and more than were needed for self-salvation, constituting the accumulated treasury of the Church's grace, and used as the basis for the scandalous sale of indulgences. The gospel of grace was thus most darkly and damagingly obscured in a more than semi-Pelagian scheme of justification by human strength and good works. The vicarious work and righteousness of Christ were displaced from their sacred position as the one and all-

sufficient ground of the sinner's acceptance, and the way of grace was no more grace.

II. THE TRUE DOCTRINE OF JUSTIFICATION
A more concise, comprehensive, and vigorous statement of it could scarcely be framed than that given in the Augsburg Confession: "We obtain forgiveness of sins and are justified before God, by grace, for Christ's sake, through faith, if we believe that Christ suffered for our sake, and that our sins are remitted unto us for Christ's sake, who has made satisfaction for our transgressions by His death." This presents all the principal truths in the teaching of the Scriptures on the subject of justification, bringing to our attention the great and all-inclusive points: 1. *The nature of it:* "We obtain forgiveness of sins, righteousness, and eternal life"; 2. *The source of it:* "Grace"; 3. *The ground of it:* "For Christ's sake"; "Christ suffered for us, made satisfaction for our sins by His death"; 4. *The instrument of its reception:* "Through faith." These topics require special explication and orderly correlation.

1. *The Nature of Justification*
There are three essential elements which constitute and mark its nature, and which stand in clear opposition to the false teaching whose perverting influence has been mentioned.

(a) As an act of God (Rom. 8:33), it is *objective and judicial* in character. In this it disallows Augustine's representation of it as consisting, in part, of an infusion of love and purification of heart. That view, as we have seen, which confounded justification with sanctification, obscuring its very nature and basis, had sent its disturbing influence down into the scholastic period. Most of the schoolmen, conspicuously Thomas Aquinas, under the confusion, were led to teach *degrees* of justification, according to the extent of the internal sanctification and the measure of merit acquired by external works, ascetic practices, etc., turning faith away from the full atonement and free grace of God in Christ. But the proof of its external and forensic, and even *governmental*, nature becomes clear when looked at in the light of a few passages of the word of God. It is involved in the use of the word *to justify*. The Hebrew צדק, translated by the Seventy into the Greek words, δικαιοῦν, δικαιοῦσθαι, δίκαιον κρίνειν which are used in the New Testament to express this truth, conveys the idea of objective judicial acquittal Ex. 23:7, "I will not justify the wicked," refers to no inner change,

Milton Valentine

but to a relation to the law. In Prov. 17:15, "He that justifieth the wicked, and he that condemneth the innocent, are both an abomination in the sight of the Lord," the antithesis is between justification and condemnation, and both are objective in their character. In Matt. 12:37, "By thy words thou shalt be justified and by thy words thou shalt be condemned," there is no idea of an inner change, but a forensic decision. In Rom. 5:18–19, and throughout the chapter, the nature of this divine act is distinctly unfolded, and set forth in the clearest light as judicial and external. It is all wrapped up in legal terms and relations. The phraseology implies a judge, guilt before the law, and an acquittal, by virtue of "the righteousness of One" who has made an "atonement." The judgment is to condemnation, εἰς κατάκριμα, *i.e.*, really guilty; the grace is to justification, εἰς δικάιωσις. "Who shall lay anything to the charge of God's elect? It is God that justifieth" (Rom. 8:33). This involves a judicial accusation, and a free, divine absolution. Most plainly is this feature of justification included in the representation in 2 Cor. 5:19–21: "God was in Christ, reconciling the world unto Himself, not reckoning unto them their trespasses.... For He hath made Him to be sin for us, who knew no sin, that we might be made the righteousness of God in Him." A correspondence is thus traced between justification and the way in which Christ was "made sin for us." We are made "righteousness" in Christ in the same manner as He was made "sin" for us. But Christ was not made sin for us by actually becoming a sinner, but by bearing our sins imputatively. So we are justified, not by being made intrinsically righteous, or by an infusion, but only *actu forensi*. In short, the word to justify means, properly and generically, to pronounce righteous, either when man truly is so, or is really unrighteous. And it is to be remembered that in the justification of the believer, the person is in fact a sinner, and the act is not an affirmation of real moral character, but a "counting" or holding the truly guilty as acquitted for the sake of the vicarious sacrifice and righteousness of Jesus Christ.

(*b*) It consists primarily in *forgiveness of sin*. This is, in part, its *essence*, and accords with its external and forensic character. Being objective, it is a gracious pardon. Remission of sin and justification before God are used as interchangeable terms, though, as we shall see, justification involves a further objective feature. The Scriptures themselves use the *two* terms as designatives of the reality. St Paul, in describing justification (Rom. 4:7–8), quotes the Old Testament statement of it: "Blessed are they whose iniquities are forgiven, and

Christian Theology

whose sins are covered. Blessed is the man to whom the Lord will not reckon sin." So, too, in Acts 13:38–39: "Be it known unto you, therefore, men and brethren, that through this man is preached unto you the forgiveness of sins, and by Him all that believe are justified from all things, from which ye could not be justified by the law of Moses." On the basis of Christ's expiatory sacrifice for the sins of the race, God freely forgives the penitent and believing sinner all his transgressions. On the ground of the sufferings of the Just for the unjust, the unjust are graciously pardoned. It is a full absolution. There is now no *condemnation* to them that accept Him who made Himself the propitiation for human sin. This is the fundamental element of justification.

(c) It is completed in the *imputation of Christ's* righteousness. This meets the necessities of the sinner's case in a relation which reaches beyond the simple matter of pardon. Being forgiven, he is not left in the condition of a criminal merely released from punishment. He needs not only to be absolved from wrath, but counted as in an acceptable righteousness. His condition must not be negative, but one of positive restoration. Though absolved of his sins, being yet, however, in himself sinful and without holiness, he is not to be *counted* or held as miserable and poor and naked, but as clothed in spotless robe and made rich indeed. Apart from another and further gift of grace, in regeneration and sanctification, the *vicarious obedience of Christ under the law,* as truly as His atoning sufferings, goes to the benefit of those who take him as their Savior and salvation. The imputation of righteousness precedes the consequent divine work of renewal in character. But the imputation is no fiction. It is part of the grace organic in the representative relation in which the incarnation prepared Christ to act *for* man, not only formally but in divine *reality;* so that he who in faith takes Christ as his Redeemer takes Him in all that He *is* and *has done for man vicariously.* Hence, in the very act of justification, along with the non-imputation of his sins (Rom. 4:8), God imputes Christ's perfect righteousness. Thus, while pardon takes away from the sinner what he has, this imputation gives him what he had not. On the one side the penalty of his transgressions is removed, on the other the complete vicarious righteousness of the Redeemer is placed to his account. The two sides of his need are thus fully met in the substitutionary provision of saving grace. The accuracy and beauty of the language of the Augsburg Confession is thus clearly seen, when it marks two gifts in justification, forgiveness of sins and righteousness. "For God regards this faith, and imputes it as righteousness in His sight."

This is the great doctrine of the imputation of Christ's righteousness which stands so centrally in the faith of orthodox Protestantism. It presents with vigor the grand and comforting truth of the gospel, that the believer is "*complete* in Christ who is the Head of all principality and power." Able to work out for himself neither pardon nor righteousness, both are provided in the Savior's work, and already fully and freely bestowed in justification. There is such a thing as a "wedding garment" provided and given. "Christ is the end of the law for righteousness to every one that believeth" (Rom. 10:4). "For what saith the Scripture? Abraham believed God, and it was imputed to him for righteousness. Now to him that worketh is the reward not reckoned of grace, but of debt. But to him that worketh not, but believeth on Him that justifieth the ungodly, his faith is counted for righteousness. Even as David also describeth the blessedness of the man unto whom God imputeth righteousness without works" (Rom. 4:3–6). The fact that sometimes "the righteousness of Christ," and at other times our "faith" is said to be imputed to us, involves no contradiction. For faith is introduced merely as apprehending and appropriating the righteousness of Christ, which is then set to our account, because in Him made really ours. Moreover, in the distinction made between pardon and this imputation, we are not to suppose any real division of the act of justification. Though forgiveness of sins is based entirely on Christ's atoning work, and the imputation of His *righteousness* implies a reference to His whole active obedience for us, yet our acceptance of Christ secures the benefit of both, which are thus united in the same act of justification—even as His active and passive obedience were united in the atoning work. The one divine act of justification confers both forgiveness of past sins and Christ's vicarious righteousness. All this enables us to see clearly the truth already noted, that justification cannot be regarded as a judgment or decision as to the actual intrinsic character of the believing sinner, but must be held as objective and forensic, a gracious absolution and acceptance of the really guilty. While it *looks* to a final issue that shall, through regeneration and sanctification, make him in the end all that his justified status *counts* him to be, that transformation is not *wrought* in the *justifying act*, but only prepared for.

2. The Source of Justification
This, as already clear, is the pure "*grace of God.*" Technical theology rightly names it the "efficient cause" (*causa efficiens*) of justification (John 3:16; Rom. 8:33). "It is God that justifieth"—"justified freely by His grace" (Rom. 3:24). Even faith, however vitally involved in it, is in no sense its efficient cause. The term "grace," χαρίς (Hebrew, חֵן), traced in Scripture usage, designates not any divine act done for us nor any quality wrought within us, but the benevolence of God toward us in showing undeserved kindness. It is the divine Fountain that is the free Source of all that saves. And this source of justification and all other forms of grace must be referred to the whole Godhead, the Trinity in Unity. Hence our justification is interchangeably ascribed to the Father, the Son, and the Holy Spirit (John 3:16; Rom. 5:5; Gal. 2:20; Col. 3:13; 1 Cor. 6:11; Isa. 53:11). The connection of this truth with the use of the names of the Trinitarian Persons in the formula of baptism is obvious and suggestive.

3. The Ground of Justification
This, known as the "meritorious cause" (*causa meritoria*), is the whole work of Jesus Christ, by which He has atoned for human sin and wrought for us a complete and everlasting righteousness: "Justified freely by the grace of God, through the redemption that is in Christ Jesus, whom God has set forth to be a propitiation through faith in His blood" (Rom. 3:24–25). In this aggregate work of Christ has been laid the deep and secure foundation of acceptance with God. Three things must be re-called, adjusting the truth of the atonement to the truth of justification:

(*a*) Justification is to be viewed as based on the work of Christ as the *God-man.* Both before and since the Reformation the question was agitated whether Christ is our vicarious righteousness according to His divine nature or His human nature. The question is one of deep and vital significance for Christian doctrine, and a correct view becomes of great importance. The view which held that we are justified by Christ's righteousness alone according to His Divine nature, confounded the true, eternal righteousness of the Son of God, in His essential divinity, with that vicarious work which forms the meritorious righteousness redemptively provided for us in His obedience and death, and imputed to sinners; while the view which held that Christ is our righteousness according to His human nature alone failed to include what is indispensable to the merit, value, or sufficiency of His redeemiug work. Unless the Sacrifice were truly *Divine* also it would not be adequate. We are justified by Christ, as our righteousness, according to *both natures*, or on the ground of the atonement wrought by Him in His divine-human Person. And this is in accordance with the widely felt necessity of avoiding the false tendency to violate the inviolable unity of Christ's *Person*, and separate the different elements and aspects of His redeeming work, for the very accomplishment of which the incarnation took place and the union was formed. The spurious analysis has often run on till it has minimized and despoiled the *atonement*—say, by separating from it his whole course of *life*, and contracting it all into the few hours of His death and humiliation on the cross, seeing no "sacrifice" in the "self-emptying" of the "form of God" in taking the "form of a servant"; or by excluding His *Divinity* from these sufferings, and speaking only of human pain. Much rather should we see the atonement resting in the *unity* of the Redeemer's Person, acting according to both the natures brought into personal oneness in a *sacrifice* that reached from the throne, through the incarnation, on and on through all His righteous, suffering life, His expiatory death on the cross, His triumphant resurrection and ascension—all parts and aspects of the movement organically unified and mutually co-operative; so that Christ has become our sacrifice and atoning satisfaction *by all that He was and did and suffered and triumphed.* By pressing too much the analytic habit we are in danger of so specializing, contracting, and isolating the work of atonement as to fail to see how every element integrates in, and contributes to, its full consistent reality and efficacy. By guarding against this extreme tendency we do not lose the atonement, but get fresh vision of how it is the all-unifying heart of the wonderful manifestation of God in human flesh. "Christ is our righteousness neither according to His Divine nature alone, nor yet according to His human nature alone, but the *whole Christ* according to both natures, in or through that obedience which He, as God and man, rendered to the Father even unto death, by which He has merited for us forgiveness of sins and eternal life."

(b) Justification is based specially on Christ's *passive obedience*, or sufferings. The Scriptures give the highest prominence to this. It is made the central conception of the atonement. At the basis of justification, they place the great unparalled fact: "Christ suffered" for us—"whom God hath set forth a propitiation through faith in His blood, for the remission of sins." This "passive obedience" "unto

death" for us became, even on the lips of Christ, the synonym of the import of His incarnation (Matt. 20:28), and in the apostolic mind the inspiration: "God forbid that I should glory save in the cross of Christ." But this has already been set forth.

(c) It embraces also Christ's *active obedience* for us. His entire earthly work was vicarious. To act in our stead, He was "made under the law." His incarnation, in which is seen the initial act of His becoming "*our* righteousness," was preparatory not only to suffering for our sins, but to fulfillment of the law for us. As we have seen, more than the negative condition of being merely pardoned is necessary. For acceptance, we need to be counted "righteous" before God. The sinless, active obedience of the God-man was not simply a necessity for His efficaciously atoning death, but is itself part of the righteousness graciously imputed to us. This, too, has been already sufficiently explained. Its actual inclusion in justification is shown by a few passages of Scripture. In Rom. 5:19, St. Paul declares: "As by one man's disobedience many were made sinners, so by the obedience of One shall many be made righteous." The reference is admitted to be to the justification of the sinner through Christ. Were it based on His *death alone*, the use of the different and comprehensive terms, "obedience" and "disobedience," would be unaccountable. While the obedience may, and indeed must, be regarded as including "obedience unto death," or suffering, it expresses necessarily the whole work of satisfying the demands of the law. From the antithesis of the "obedience" of Christ to the "disobedience" of Adam, Christ's active obedience seems to be the prominent idea. Tholuck explains: "The entire holy life of our Savior is termed "obedience"(ὑπακόη), embracing in indivisible unity what the Church has termed the *obedienta activa* and *obedientia passiva*." In verse 18 the apostle expresses the same idea in a different form: "By the righteousness (δικαιώματος) of One the free gift came upon all men unto justification (δικαίωσιν) of life." In this passage the term "righteousness" seems to be the equivalent for "obedience" in verse 19. They are alike connected with justification, and are terms more comprehensive than seem natural for simple expression of Christ's death.

4. *The Relation of Faith to Justification*
This is the most vital point in the doctrine before us. And orthodox Protestantism, in all the evangelical branches of the Church, rightly

adheres to the essential features of the positive and exclusive relation of faith to justification, reached by the Reformation movement in freeing the Scripture truth from the perversions of Roman teaching. The great Protestant confessions have not relaxed their testimony on "justification by faith." It is true, indeed, that various aberrant forms of view appear in recent and current religious discussions, but they are not representative of the confessional standards of the Church. Rather they mark individual departures from loyalty to the authority of the Scriptures, repudiation of supernatural revelation and compounding with paganisms and monistic philosophies, either materialistic or pantheistic, labeled "new Christianity," or "Christianity for an age of science." These, in various ways having dropped faith in a supernatural redemption, atonement, and allied truths, have little or no place for this evangelical doctrine, and naturally turn off to trust in a simple divine Fatherhood, together with confidence in the merit of an ethical life, for reaching spiritual perfection and our destined immortality. But, deplorable as these aberrations are, they do not represent the creed of the Church.

The Augsburg Confession, the substance of whose teaching on the subject has been more or less exactly incorporated in all the great Protestant Confessions, declares that justification takes place "through faith," *per fidem, durch den Glauben.* These terms express the *instrumental cause,* or means of it. It is that through which justification is actualized, realized. The truth in question is of such vital importance, and lies so truly in the very heart of the gospel, as understood by the Church, that its meaning and relations cannot be too accurately and fully grasped. The very characterizing feature of the gospel is that it presents salvation as attained through faith. So fully does this express the essence of the system that "the faith" is made a synonym for Christianity. And the Reformation had as both its object and power the disclosure of the clear and indubitable relation of faith to the sinner's justification and salvation. As already stated, there are three elements in which its office and relations are seen, but their decisive bearing at this point calls for their restatement here.

(*a*) *Knowledge is implied.* This is the first element in which a definition of saving faith is constructed. It consists in part of knowledge, *notitia.* As man is a moral agent, his recovery to right relations to God must, if at all, be accomplished through the essential faculties that constitute him a man. The movement must begin through a gift of light in the understanding. The historical facts and doctrinal verities of the gospel must be known before the sinner can accept the hope and blessings they offer. Men must know the truth before it can be believed or make them free. "This is life eternal, that they might know Thee the only true God, and Jesus Christ whom Thou hast sent" (John 17:3). Yet however essential a knowledge of the objects of faith may be to its exercise, it is generically different from faith itself. It is rather a prerequisite to faith—the first element only in its total reality. "How shall they believe in Him of whom they have not heard"? (Romans 10:14). Though our Savior does speak of knowing (γυγνώσκειν) the true God and Jesus Christ as "eternal life," the eternal life is not the *immediate* product of the mere knowledge, but is attained through the knowledge as *leading to* faith, according to St. Paul's words to Timothy: "From a child thou hast known the Holy Scriptures, which are able to make thee wise unto salvation, *through faith which is in* Jesus Christ" (2 Tim. 3:15). Men may have theological knowledge, even in richest stores, without a particle of real justifying faith. Yet faith implies knowledge and establishes itself upon it.

(*b*) It involves also *assent* (*assensus*) of the understanding. The truths of the gospel, besides being known, must be recognized as real verities. This is what may accurately be designated *historical* or *intellectual* faith. It is the judgment's consent to the contents of the mind. But, as with respect to knowledge, this "assent" is rather a prerequisite to saving faith than faith itself. "It is not enough for us to know and believe that Christ was born, that He suffered and rose from the dead." It is a belief which devils may have, without any moral or spiritual return to God. The assent of reason, simply, to the truth, divinity, and reliableness of the remedial scheme of grace, though essential as a preliminary basis for the act of appropriating the offer of salvation, in which the cardinal essence of faith consists, must be regarded as inadequate. It represents the state of the masses in Christian lands, who, intellectually, consent to the truth and excellence of Christianity, but live in utter indifference and neglect of Christ and salvation. The reason of the inadequacy of this merely assenting judgment of the mind is plain. It moves altogether in the sphere of the natural. It is only the same kind of mental assent as is given to any other historical or scientific truths. It includes no personal submission of heart and life to the offered divine grace, no surrender to the direction and will of Christ.

(*c*) Its completing element is *trust* or *confidence* (*fiducia*). Not until the soul, in heart and will, obediently accepts and trustfully takes Christ as its Savior from sin, is true saving faith reached. It is a confidence that reposes on the grace of God as revealed in Christ the Redeemer. It is essentially an act of self-surrender along with voluntary appropriation of the purchased and offered redemption. While the "knowledge" and "assent" belong wholly to the logical understanding, this surrender to Christ, in trust and reliance, embraces the action of the will and conscience. Hence St. Paul declares, with striking definiteness and force: "*With the heart man believeth unto righteousness.*" We must not fail to understand that this faith makes a real appropriation of the merit and righteousness of Christ. It truly "puts on Christ" (Rom. 13:14). His whole obedience, even unto death, is imputed to us. "This is the record, that God hath given to us eternal life, and this life is in His Son" (1 John 5:11). Hence it is that "He that hath the Son hath life, and he that hath not the Son of God hath not life" (1 John 5:12).

The relation of faith to justification has its significance, therefore, in the fact that it marks the point in human experience where God's graciously provided offer of salvation meets man's enabled freedom, with its momentous opportunity of securing it. It exhibits the necessary human act, through which, if at all, the Divine grace can make its aim effective. Justification is *through* faith. Forgiveness of sins and Christ's righteousness are not appropriated in unbelief. Unbelief negatives their reception. Faith is necessarily man's act. God does not and cannot believe *for* him. Through His truth and the Holy Spirit *in* the truth He can and does *enable* faith; but *human faith* is contingent on man's exercise of the enabling power. The power is of God's "prevenient," preparing grace, illuminating and quickening the mind and heart through the Gospel and the Spirit But it does not directly give to men the act of faith itself;—it only enables *them* truly to believe and accept Christ, or make receptive response to the divine offer of forgiveness. The clear Scripture teaching, not only that the gospel needs to be divinely "applied" to the minds and hearts of men, but has to be "*appropriated*" by faith, is direct proof that man is *not* merely "passive," but also active in its saving reception. For man, to whom the offer and duty are divinely presented through the word of the gospel, is *held responsible* for non-reception. Under enabling grace (*liberum liberatum*) he can either believe or refuse.

Christian Theology

A few other points, definitive of faith's relation to justification, need notice:

(1) Faith *alone* is its *instrumental* cause or condition. As the merits of Christ are the *alone ground*, so this is the alone condition—"only believe." The faith that rests on Christ's work and righteousness needs nothing else to supplement it for "justification." It is impossible for corrupt man to satisfy God's perfect law. St. Paul assures that by "the deeds of the law no flesh can be justified in His sight," and "that a man is justified by faith without the deeds of the law" (Rom. 3:20-28). The Reformation recovery of the pure gospel doctrine of justification by faith required and forever requires the exclusion of everything or anything as co-operating with faith for justification. The word "alone" (*sola*), known as the *particula exclusive*, properly stands over against admitting anything before, after, or alongside of Christ, simply apprehended by faith. Though the faith must be true and vital, so as to issue in regeneration and sanctification, it is not the regeneration or sanctification that "justifies," or is the instrumental cause of justification, but alone the faith that takes Christ in His provided grace and righteousness. Justification *precedes* regeneration and sanctification.

(2) Faith justifies, not by reason of what it *is*, but by what it embraces—not by its own ethical quality or merit, but by its reception of Christ's atoning righteousness. Faith is, indeed, in itself right, an action of soul eternally good and holy. It is forever, *per se*, a sacred duty; but when by grace we feebly meet the duty, it cannot be regarded as earning remission of all sins. It justifies, not as a virtue or intrinsic state of the soul, but simply as holding in its embrace Christ Himself in all His redeeming work. The idea of a meritoriousness of faith needs to be rigorously excluded. Because of its instrumental relation to our acceptance before God, there has been a tendency to look upon it as saving by its intrinsic worthiness. But the only merit or worthiness is in Christ; and faith, being itself God's gift, is only the hand that receives the blessing of reconciliation. "Faith does not justify us before God, as though it were itself our work, but solely because it receives the grace promised and offered without merit, and presented out of the rich treasure of mercy." Though faith be accepted and imputed for righteousness, it is still, like every other grace in man, defective and incomplete, and therefore cannot in its own virtue become a foundation of confidence. So soon as the believer would trust to the worthiness of his faith, he would trust to something wrought within

him, and deny Christ as the only foundation. "Faith alone justifies, not because it is the root, or is meritorious, but because it lays hold of Christ, for whose sake we are accepted."

(3) This faith, through which God justifies, now becomes prevenient and preparatory to the *further* divine action in *regeneration and sanctification*. We must keep the distinction clear, as the Scriptures do, between justification and these consequent and different works of God. However closely related, justification logically and necessarily *precedes* regeneration. They cannot be identified, and they must not be confounded. Justification is "objective and forensic," viz., forgiveness of sins and crediting the forgiven sinner with the righteousness of Christ, a *status* of acceptance before God. Regeneration is the *inner or subjective* spiritual change, initiating the renewal and sanctification of the fallen and sinful nature—to be progressively carried on through purification from sin, so as to make "meet" for the heavenly kingdom. The meaning of the renewing and sanctifying grace is to actualize, in the personal life of believers, the purity and righteousness of character which are already credited to them in justification. And the deep philosophy of justification as leading to regeneration is seen when we remember that only when the accepted sinner can look up into the face of God as a forgiving and reconciled Father can the heart go up in gratitude and purifying love, in hatred of sin, and aspiration to be transformed into the Redeemer's likeness.

(4) Bearing thus in mind the distinction and difference between justification and regeneration, we are also to remember that they are inseparably *connected* with each other in the real and normal movement that is to complete the full salvation from sin. In its essential nature the first is adapted to issue in the second, and the second will infallibly appear. If regeneration fails to appear, it is because the professed "faith" is not *true*, living faith—has not really received Christ. St. James teaches us, and the history of the Church confirms it, that there is sometimes what is called faith that is not true faith, and is without either justifying or regenerating power. It is "dead," is no living reality. There is no conflict between St. Paul and St. James. Interpreted in their meanings, St. Paul assures: 'Faith alone justifies,' and St. James explains that this saving faith must have a vitality that is truly fruit-bearing, a spiritual reality that moves into the new life. When faith is genuine and really "justifies," then regeneration, in its renewing and sanctifying power, will

appear, exhibiting the on-moving progress of personal salvation, carrying it forward, beyond its first stage of forgiveness, into purification from sin itself. It is the very nature of faith to set a man to *doings, to obedience.* To "believe" is itself a doing of what God requires, in view of His own offer of provided pardon. To *do nothing* in response to the gospel call is to remain unsaved. But the very *act* of faith, as graciously empowered, is the beginning of doing God's will, starting the spiritual activity of obedience that carries, as well as promises, life from the dead. Faith itself, therefore, initiates a life-energy for obedience, accepting Christ, doing His will, and *working out all* the gracious movement that God works *within* the soul through the needful regeneration and sanctification. Neither this faith, indeed, nor any of its obedient activities, as of the undeserved working of God within believers, can justify as of *merit* or *desert*, but, as we have seen, are simply God's gracious way of starting in men the life powers of confidence, duty, and holy love. The faith that saves is a living, quickening, working, transforming spiritual power.

(5) Though justification by faith is a common doctrine of all orthodox Protestantism, it becomes modified in some branches of the Church by shaping it to fit peculiar confessional teachings upon other but related doctrines. Looked at from the angles of such peculiar teachings, this common doctrine presents a somewhat changed significance. For instance, when adjusted to a Pelagianized anthropology, with its denial of "original sin" and its claim for large natural ability in spiritual things, the divine *grace* in the act of justification is diminished, and self-complacent, unscriptural notions of human merit are fostered. On the other hand, in the scheme of absolute predestination, justification by faith, instead of being central and determinative in the economy of salvation, is forced into a merely subordinate place. It does not present the pivotal point on which the sinner's free and gracious salvation really turns, or where God's grace, meeting the human will, enables that will with strength either to "believe" and accept salvation, or to refuse the gracious provision and counsel of God. In that scheme God's secret *decrees*, unchangeably, from eternity, fore-ordaining whatsoever is to come to pass, leave no alternative choice to human freedom with respect to the question of personal salvation. By the eternal "election" the destiny of every soul of the race is fixed, some chosen to life, the rest passed by or reprobated, without any foresight of faith or good works, or perseverance in either of them, or any other thing in the

creature, as conditions or causes, moving God thereto—the men thus predestinated being particularly and unchangeably designed, and their number so certain and definite, that it cannot be either increased or diminished. According to this, the offer of the gospel is not the presentation of an open and real opportunity for all men to be saved, but only the ordained step of a sovereign actualizing of the salvation of the elect, whose faith has no determinative relation to their election. Their "election" settled everything. They are justified, *i.e.*, elected, chosen, immutably, from eternity—justified by predestination. There is no open door to salvation for the rest of mankind. It is to be regretted that the authors of the Form of Concord, by an unhappy admission of Flacius' extreme and misleading statement of original sin, have provided the occasion for some holders of that Symbol being led into the Augustinian doctrine of absolute predestination, at variance with the Church's pure doctrine of justification by faith.

Christian Theology

Milton Valentine

CHAPTER IV
REGENERATION AND CONVERSION

As we have seen, the divine saving work must extend beyond justification. Unless the forgiveness of sins and imputation of Christ's righteousness be followed by an internal renewal of heart, correcting the corruption of our nature, the work would fall short of the necessary salvation. The deepest and most calamitous woe of man is that his very nature is fallen and sinful beyond self-recovery. It is in deadly moral disorder. He needs healing as well as forgiveness—restoration to holiness as well as pardon of sin. He must be recovered to true *inner life*, the life of personal righteousness, love, and goodness, if he is ever to be again the high, blessed being he was created to be, "in the image and likeness of God," happy and ennobled in real "fellowship" with God. Only when his heart is brought into musical rhythm with the Divine Will is he fully, perfectly saved. This work must, therefore, progress from the grace of justification, through the further grace of regeneration, conversion, and sanctification. We unite the consideration of regeneration and conversion under one head for the sake of clearness with respect to both.

I. DEFINITION OF REGENERATION. Preliminarily, regeneration may be stated as a work wrought by God through the Holy Spirit, in which He quickens the soul with power and inclination to live a new spiritual life; or so changes the heart as to recover it to the love of God and holiness. But specific definitions have not always been the same, nor of equal import. Like those of justification, they have not exhibited the same inclusions and limitations. Especially has the line of difference between this and justification not been kept clear and uniform. For instance, as already mentioned, St. Augustine confused the distinction between them and opened the way to subsequent doctrinal misconceptions that so obscured the gospel of grace as to call for the Reformation. The definite distinction required, however, by the gospel teaching and established by the Reformation, came only gradually into general use. The lingering diversities found in a few cases, along with a general agreement, have made it necessary to fix the exact definition demanded by the principle of justification by faith.

Under this principle and the determining position Scripturally given it in our Reformation theology, Regeneration is accurately defined: '*The action of grace, by which the Holy Spirit, in and through saving faith, bestows the power by which the soul is quickened and made capable of a new and holy life, in love to God and spiritual things.*' This at once expresses not only its own intrinsic reality, but at the same time fixes the relations of the other forms of associated grace integrated in the whole movement of the order of salvation. The part of the definition essential for its exact correctness and fullness is the clause "in and through saving faith"—in order to relate regeneration rightly to faith, and preclude the error that *it precedes* faith. It is a definition which accords with the theology of Luther, Melanchthon, and our Confessions, but from which some later dogmaticians diverged somewhat. It actualizes to thought not only the literal affirmations of the Scripture teaching, but also the figurative expressions, such as "new birth," "new creation," "new man," etc., which are found employed to indicate the greatness of this change in the inward character of the true believer.

II. THE NECESSITY OF THE CHANGE. This is absolute and universal. All men are sinful, and helplessly so in themselves. They are not saved by forgiveness of guilt and imputation of Christ's righteousness alone, or if left in the sinfulness, blight, and wreck of their ethical constitution. They are not fully saved till saved from sinning and from their natural alienation from God. Without this change, they are unprepared for fellowship in the divine order of the world, or for the enjoyment of the heavenly life. Their intrinsic character is unadjusted to the essential conditions of blessedness. The apostle gives the philosophy of the necessity: "To be carnally-minded is death; but to be spiritually-minded is life and peace. Because the carnal mind is enmity against God; for it is not subject to the law of God, neither, indeed, can be" (Rom. 8:6–7). And the conclusion is emphasized by Christ Himself: "Verily, verily, I say unto thee, except a man be born again, he cannot see the kingdom of God" (John 3:3).

This absolute necessity of regeneration is naturally an unwelcome truth to men. The sinful bent of their desires, united with their self-esteem, makes them averse to its recognition. The immense activity of our times in scientific speculation, especially in different forms of cosmic evolutionism, has been made the occasion of increased tendency to question or deny this necessity. Effort is made to *justify* the denial. The implied lapse of humanity into sin is replaced by an asserted natural and necessary "ascent" into ethical life. The Christian theism of a personal God, above nature as well as immanent in it, is displaced by a view of nature that excludes the *supernaturalism* involved in a redemptive regeneration. The inclination toward denial of "original sin," or toward minimizing its disabling significance, seems to be obtaining larger sway. But the radical depravity of human nature and its incapability of self-purification, have lost none of their proofs. The teachings of Christianity have not been overthrown. Nor has the increasing denial or doubt of the unwelcome truth shown any tendency to promote the sway of virtue or piety in actual personal, domestic, or business life. The repudiation of belief in depravity has not been the disappearance of the fact. The offered gospel of an unfallen humanity, with the call simply to cultivate it into piety and regnant virtue, is not proving itself either true or divine by any better *fruits* in the way of sinless living, purity of heart or thought, holy love, righteousness, and unselfish goodness. They are not diminishing the number or enormity of impieties, wrongs, vices, crimes, lusts, atrocities, barbarities, and innumerable depravities whose record increasingly burdens the daily newspaper and horrifies the conscience. Natural science, invention, art, human learning, and literary culture are neither voiding the abysmal reality nor proving themselves regenerative from it. They are by no means confuting Christianity's assertion of the necessity of a supernatural regeneration.

Reply may, indeed, be offered to the force of these facts that they are found, at the same time, in the presence of the Christian teaching and the provided remedy. But the reply is a mere sophism. For the relations of the two teachings are not parallel with respect to the point in question, *i. e.*, as evidence of an enthralling depravity and the need of a supernatural recovery. Christianity *accounts* for the horrible and persistent wickedness, in a universal depravity of human nature. The new teaching, while equally compelled to recognize the condition and its unethical quality, *fails* to account for it, save in the mere freedom of an *unimpaired*, capable, and self-perfecting humanity. It makes its only appeal to this supposed capable humanity and its intrinsic resources. Compare the two doctrines as to results. The gospel comes declaring man's self-helpless thralldom in sinfulness and providing not only a gracious forgiveness of past sins, but also an actual redemptive renewal into spiritual life—the true spiritual manhood of purity, righteousness, and love. It distinctly assures to obedient faith the divine grace of regeneration. In Christ God's love makes mighty and successful appeal to the human soul. The naturalism of evolutionist science, discrediting the truth of a lapsed state of thralldom to sin, simply calls to self-culture in native virtue. It sees no necessity to be met; it turns away from the supernatural provision. The question is: Which teaching is showing itself the more successful and divine by its fruits? It is safe to say, as indubitably certain, that the Christian gospel, which sets forth the need of spiritual renewal and the supernatural grace to meet it, has presented sufficient testimony of its regenerative power in its work of nineteen centuries to assure its reality and its incomparable benediction to men and nations. Its divine power has been certified in countless millions of cases, as, in widening range over the earth, it has been creating souls anew, quickening them out of sin into a new life of love to God and man, into spiritual purity, unselfish goodness, self-sacrificing service, Christ-like manhood. And through the regenerate mind of believers and the onward working of its message and mission, it has given the world new and advancing *civilizations*, whose distinctive type and transcendence of all pagan products are perpetual demonstration of a supernatural regenerative power working in Christianity. Is it not "scientific" to say: "By their fruits ye shall know them"? Is the naturalistic thought of our day, in repudiating the idea of supernatural divine action in the moral world, in teaching that the present life of man is *normal* in its inherent aptitudes, and that men are not to look to God for other help, but to address themselves solely to self-care and culture, a type of thought more *effective* for conversion from the manifold shocking and degrading immoralities to which we have referred, or for the quickening of conscientiousness, or the renovation of character into righteousness, purity, holy love, and all the unselfish goodness and nobility of soul which have marked the regenerate life of the Church? To ask this question is to answer it to minds that have candor enough to confess the manifest ethical loss that marks every wave of lapse of faith in Christianity's redemptive gospel and its inspiring view of the love and saving purpose of God. Christianity's millions, actually transformed through experienced forgiveness of sin and renewal into a victorious piety and virtue, showing an advancing fellowship with God in a supernatural type of spiritual life, are a certifying signature of divine worth, a sign that cannot be cut off.

III. IT IS GOD'S WORK—NOT OURS. We have seen how truly justification is God's work. "It is God that justifieth." That, however, is *objective*—an outward *status* of forgiveness and acceptance before God. This also, though *within* the believer, is a product of God's working. It is a result of His action, impossible of human accomplishment. God enters into the soul through the truth and call of the gospel, convincing of sin, and through His Holy Spirit working an enabled faith which discerns and appropriates this forgiveness, based in Christ's vicarious righteousness. But the saving work cannot stop here. Besides and beyond this *status* of pardon and accredited righteousness graciously bestowed upon the believer, his very nature must be recovered from its sinfulness and corruption into its true spiritual life of love and obedience. This is the great change *within* the *soul* to which justification looks and which realizes its radical and full meaning This, as well as forgiveness, the Scriptures explicitly declare to be thoroughly a product of God's work. Christ's own statement is unequivocal and emphatic: "Verily, verily, I say unto thee, except a man be born again he cannot see the kingdom of God," etc. (John 3:3–7). The emphasis, of varied form and iteration, in this declaration, makes it impossible to question either Christ's reference here to this spiritual change or His affirmation of it as a divine gift or work. It is a regeneration "from above," "of God." Its source is not in the life derived from natural generation ("born of the flesh"), but in the grace of the Holy Spirit ("born of the Spirit"). The apostles, taking up at once the Savior's teaching and explaining His redeeming work, began and continued to reaffirm this truth as fundamental in the doctrine of the order or way of salvation. It necessarily includes this spiritual renewal of the believer's nature, the recovery of its love to God and holiness. And it is observable, that while they explain in various places the great change in literal terms (Rom. 8:2–11, 20–39), they continue also to apply the figurative terminology in which Christ's own statements primarily shaped it. John 1:12–13: "As many as received Him to them gave He power to become children of God, even to them that believe on His name; which were born not of blood nor of the will of the flesh, nor of the will of man, but of God." Jas. 1:18: "Of His own will begat He us through the word of truth." 1 John 3:9: "Whosoever is born of God doth not commit sin." 1 Pet 1:23: "Being born again, not of corruptible seed, but of incorruptible, by the word of God,

Christian Theology

which liveth and abideth forever." Tit 3:5–6: "Not by works of righteousness which we have done, but according to His mercy He saved us by the washing of regeneration." Eph. 2:10: "For we are His workmanship, created in Christ Jesus unto good works." Also 1 John 4:7; 5:4.

The problem of harmonizing the human personality with this divine working, so as not to annul but preserve and secure the elemental functions of each, often thought to involve contradiction, needs only a just representation. It might, indeed, seem that, as regeneration lies in the realm of ethics in which personal freedom is the pre-supposition and fundamental principle, to introduce the thought of a *divine* working as concerned in the change must be to bring together mutually repugnant conceptions. But that is to misconceive the nature of the divine action. It is not to be imagined as wrought by setting aside the human endowment of free faculties, but through God's entrance into them in adapted truth and spiritual motives. He has specially prepared these. The whole reality of the redemptive work in and through the incarnate Son and teaching Spirit expresses these additional truths and moral influences. The recovery of the human powers or life from their depraved action in sin, through these truths, is exactly adjusted to the soul's normal endowments, reaching into blessed issue through freedom and love. Regeneration is degraded out of its divine reality whenever conceived in the mode of the necessitation which belongs to physical change, the dreams of magic, or the mere passivity of "block" or "stone." For man is not a "stone" or "stock," but a personality, moving by and in choices, and spiritually moved through them, and saved, if saved at all, according to the constituent endowments which make him a man. God acts on him as a free agent and he becomes a new creature through the consent of his own will. He is not and cannot be treated as a block or stone, but as capable of being led to become a consenting and active subject of the saving influence. Unquestionably, as we have seen, revelation assures us that the corruption of human nature is such that the higher endowments and adaptation are in helpless captivity to evil. The *faculties* of lofty, holy choice and personality are there; but in their relative enfeeblement by ignorance and sinfulness, they are in themselves incapable for the office of the Godward choice. The abnormality of the "carnal mind," the habitude of the natural man, is even "enmity against God," not subject to His law, nor capable, unhelped, of self-subjection (Rom. 8:7–8). But aided through gifts of divine truth thrown into the intellect and appealing to it and to the conscience and the sensibilities or desire of welfare, the "will" as the faculty of choice, *can*, thus enfranchised, either *consent* to or *refuse* the appeal—can *accept* in the faith of self-surrender, or *deny* the new motives and continue in the service of sin. In this "prevenient" grace of the "call" of the Holy Spirit through the gospel, the illumination of the understanding and the persuasive force of the spiritual motives for the choice, there is a divine enablement for the possibility of the will's free action either way—the sublime point of the meeting of God's grace and the personal responsibility of man for salvation, the two great, supreme realities that *must* be preserved according to the fundamental conceptions of a moral universe. The regeneration that is reached through justification by faith is thus wholly of grace, by God's working; and no one is "cast out" that willingly comes or yields to Him in faith.

IV. Making this truth specific in Trinitarian theology, we are to note that the work is to be directly predicated of the *Holy Spirit*. He regenerates. The scholastic theology used the designation "*efficient cause*" to express this. In the Trinitarian redemptive economy, as we have found, the Father "gave the Son"; the Son "gave Himself" to the incarnation and propitiatory self-sacrifice for reconciliation; and the Holy Spirit is sent and proceeds from the Father and the Son, to take the redemptory provisions and bring them into the possible acceptance and experience of men. It is He, as at once the Spirit of the Father and of the Son, who takes the message of the prepared salvation ("the things of Christ"), and with it, as already explained, enters into the minds and hearts of men, and through the faith thus enabled and begotten, brings the heart into the love of God and of His holy will. Thus, the Holy Spirit is the efficient Cause of regeneration and the new life.

V. And further, specifically, as thus becomes evident, this divine work by the Holy Spirit is not accomplished directly or without means, but mediately through the truth, the word of the Gospel. Only through this, either in the form of preaching or sacramental administration received in faith, does the Holy Spirit's regenerating power pass into the soul or life of believers (Jas. 1:18; 1 Pet 1:23; Rom. 10:14–17).

One of the most important necessities for doctrinal clearness is the exclusion from the conception of this great spiritual change of the still repeated notion that it is, or may be, wrought apart from the instrumentality of the divine truth as believed and yielded to under the influence of the Holy Spirit. Under the impulse of ideas drawn from pagan incantations and magic or from priestly arrogations of functional powers gradually creeping into ecclesiastical theology and obscuring the pure teachings of Christ and the apostles, certain mystic or magical, or *ex opere operato* processes long ago obtained recognition in the Church, whose perverting disturbance is still felt. Sacramental forms or exhibitions of the saving truths, efficacious through *faith* in the truths exhibited, were viewed as efficacious irrespective of faith on the part of the recipient. Instead of the conception of Irenæus: "Where the Spirit of God is, there is the Church and all grace," a priestly and hierarchical Church set up its formal manipulations, subjecting the soul to human mediators and requirements, and obscured the directness and fullness in the divine order of the Holy Spirit's saving work through the living Word made regenerative in believing hearts. Multiplied rites and ceremonies, trading in indulgences out of fictitious ecclesiastical treasures of grace, hid from view the divine Spirit and His means of grace for both forgiveness of sins and the new life of faith. This obscuration of the Holy Spirit's office in salvation has long and widely disclosed itself in the invention of, and emphasis upon, sacramental ceremonies, on the one hand; and, on the other, in fanatical claims of the Spirit's *direct* and perfect regeneration *apart from the divine power of God's word* in the heart of faith and love. And though Protestantism has long been preaching the great truth of both justification and regeneration by the Holy Spirit through "faith" in the redemption provided by God in the Gospel of His Son, the harmful obscuration still beclouds many minds. In the divine order, the Holy Spirit, through the ministry of the "word," takes the great soul-stirring truths of the prepared reconciliation and salvation, enforcing them upon the mind, heart, and will, securing understanding, conviction, assent, the trust of faith, with love to God and the obedience of righteousness. It is all a work of God for a necessary ethical renewal or spiritual regeneration, for which both the agency and the means are perfectly and fully adapted, in inherent forces—the only conceivable way to reach and win the concurrence of the constitutional faculties of the human soul made, in the essence of its being, personal, after the image of God. God neither ignores nor sets aside His own creative work in saving. Through the Son and Spirit, the Father "draws" men (John 6:44; 12:32); but He draws successfully only those that are willing. "How often would I have drawn thy children together, and ye would not" (Matt 23:37).

VI. Regeneration is *not an irresistible* divine work. Like the call of the Gospel, it is always an *efficacious* work on the divine side, *i. e.*, has intrinsic energy potential for actual accomplishment of the spiritual change; but the divine working is not compulsory or resistless. The desire of the divine love may be withstood by depravity and willfulness. In Calvinism, with its absolute predestination of salvation to all the elect, there is, indeed, place for the idea of irresistible grace, to take away all contingency in their case. Hence its dogma of *irresistible grace*. But such a scheme of irresistibility is inapplicable in a Gospel of universal atonement and a call that distinctly conditions realization of the provided salvation on faith's actual acceptance of Christ, with incessant warnings against the possibility of neglecting or rejecting so great salvation, and the increased condemnation and guilt of so sinning against both Christ and the Spirit. Whether Mark 16:16 belongs to the evangelist's original text or not, the statement: "He that believeth and is baptized shall be saved, but he that believeth not shall be condemned," expresses the teaching of the New Testament on this point. It is another expression of the Protestant exegesis of the whole gospel as to the only provided way of salvation: "justification and the new life *through faith*," which is of necessity an act of man, inspired by the Holy Spirit through the word.

VII. The change is not to be characterized as "*instantaneous.*" It has sometimes been represented under this idea, either as marking the very beginning of the new life, or as confounding it with "justification." The notion is aided by pressing too far the analogy in the figurative expression, "new birth." But rather are we to hold the change as necessarily gradual, because it is accomplished through means with an intelligent moral agent. The "deadness in sin," which the new life is to replace, is a depraved disposition and action of our living faculties. The beginning of the spiritual life is the beginning of their right action under the light, help, and purity of grace. The change is from false into the true principles of living, in God and righteousness. The divine influences of the Spirit through the truth act for recovery and renewal gradually and progressively. As regeneration depends on the conduct of man in respect to influences exerted upon him, its progress will be retarded or hastened as resistance is greater or less, or as faith accepts the Spirit's guidance and quickening power. Our dogmaticians differ in their representations, but show a large tendency to hold regeneration as gradually and progressively accomplished, while prevalently declaring it to be instantaneous in the case of infants.² The Form of Concord asserts: "In this life we receive only the first fruits of the Spirit, and the new birth is not complete, but only begun in us." As will hereafter appear, there is even *less* reason for thinking it instantaneous in the case of infants. For the very "faculties" for understanding and reception of the "word," which is the Holy Spirit's means of regeneration, are *not yet functionally in existence*, for immediate and full upspringing of love of God and righteousness. The conception of Dr. W. F. Gess is better: "This [regeneration] may possibly be done gradually by God from the time of baptism, so that the Spirit gains power in us imperceptibly, as Tersteegen says,

> " 'As flowers their opening leaves display,
> And glad drink in the solar fire.' "

The *nature* of *the change* in regeneration thus comes into distinct view. Let the defining points be recalled: *(a)* God does not set aside the constitutional faculties of the soul, by virtue of which man is a self-determining free agent, but enters them through His truth and Spirit with enabling light and motive for their right use and exercise. Without this the soul is helplessly in the servitude of sin. *(b)* It is no change of the "*substance*" of the soul, either as an addition or a subtraction or transmutation. It neither gives nor blots out any constitutional faculty. The contention of *Flacius Illyricus* (1567) that sin is the very substance of fallen human nature, and that in this renewal God creates from nothing a new essence of soul in the believer, was a gross error. Linked with this was the kindred error that the "new man "is thereby made a "new" or *other personality*. But the personality constituted through the first or natural birth is immortal—the consciousness of personal self-identity persisting *through* the change, and the memory of the saved in the future world still carrying that identity in their ceaseless gratitude for redemption (Rev. 7:9–10, 14–15). The change means not another *person*, but renewal of the sinful person into the true ethical life and character for which God created him. *(c)* Positively and specifically stated, therefore, it consists in a change in the free *action* of our constitutional faculties and powers, of thought, affection, and will, recovering them from sin into their right life in piety, obedience, and holiness. Here the old rule holds good, that "grace does not destroy but heals nature." Martensen well says: "Regeneration is not a metamorphosis, a transubstantiation of human nature; the *ego* in man, his personal identity, is the same in essence after regeneration as before, but by regeneration the essential principle of the *ego* is realized, and it becomes the free instrument of divine grace." The intellect becomes receptive of the truth, the heart is induced to trust God and love Him, and the will to obey Him in Jesus Christ. The *sinfulness* of human nature is brought to yield by the grace or influence of the Holy Spirit, and ability is given to begin to live and act in gratitude and happy service.

VIII. A distinction needs to be noticed between regeneration and *conversion*, if we are to adhere exactly to theological definitions—though the two terms are often found used synonymously. In the Scriptures they are employed to designate the same great change, but they do so with a difference. There are various features in the difference: (*a*) Regeneration, designating the beginning of the new life, primarily and necessarily views the great change from the *divine side;* conversion designates it as viewed from the human side, or as seen and exhibited in men. (*b*) Regeneration, because it *initiates* the change, makes emphatic the truth that it is wholly of the Divine efficiency, leaving nothing for man but to suffer it or "assent"; while conversion fixes the view primarily upon the objective human change of character and conduct, the person freely turning from sin to obedience and pious living, (*c*) Regeneration fastens attention upon the divine, internal, secret work of the Holy Spirit, as the explanation how men dead in sin may and do pass into new life of the soul, implying, of course, the liberation of the human will for exercise of faith and the appearance of its fruits of outward conduct; while in conversion the outward conduct is declared as the living evidence of the divine creation of life within. The term conversion, therefore, as a form of representation of the change, expresses it not so directly and positively as a work of the Holy Spirit within man; but as a manifestation of that work in the fruits of the liberated human will, bringing it and the other regenerated inner faculties into forms of holy thought, feeling, and life.

IX. The specific and essential features in the saving work under the Holy Spirit being thus traced and brought into distinct view, as the Scriptures clearly define and describe them, it remains yet that their logical and actual *order*, or inter-relation in the movement, be also traced and made explicit. For only when we apprehend these inter-relations and their inter-action do we obtain the real spiritual theology of the work as a divine total. Without a clear recognition of the *ordo salutis*—the divine order of the process—we cannot rightly understand and appreciate either the full significance of each part of the movement, or the coherent integrity and perfection of the whole issue.

We find this divine *ordo salutis* only in the light of the great all-determinative truth as to the way of salvation, recognized as "the material principle of Protestantism": "Justification by faith alone." It was this truth, as we have seen, that the Reformers discerned to be the truth of a "standing or falling Church," whose logical application overthrew the misleading errors of Romanism in its *ex opere operato* sacraments, doctrine of penances, good works, and human merit, hiding from view the all-sufficiency of the grace of Christ and the Holy Spirit. Luther's deep and clear experience of salvation led him early to distinct recognition of the divine order of the work, as so definitely put in his Preface to Romans: "Faith alone justifies us and fulfills the law. Faith is a divine work in us, which changes and regenerates us; it slays the old Adam, makes us new creatures in heart, disposition, and spiritual strength, and brings with it the Holy Ghost. Faith is a living, active, powerful principle; it is impossible that it should not always be producing good fruits." In his Smalcald Articles he wrote: "What I have hitherto and constantly taught concerning this I cannot in the least change, viz.: That by faith (as St. Peter says) we acquire a new and clean heart." Similarly, Melanchthon, that wonder of spiritual and logical consistency, affirms and reaffirms this order in varied and most explicit forms, declaring justification as immediately given to faith, and regeneration as reached *through* forgiveness of sins. "When we have been justified by faith, and regenerated, we begin to love God, give thanks and praise Him.... There is now, through the Spirit of Christ, a new heart and spirit within." "These things cannot occur until we have been justified and regenerated." "Faith brings the Holy Spirit and produces a new life in the heart" In his "Loci" he says: "With faith terrified minds are comforted, at the same time the Holy Spirit is given and brings forth a new life in the heart, in harmony with the law of God." The Augsburg Confession itself brings us his testimony: "By faith alone is apprehended remission of sins and grace. And because the Holy Spirit is received by faith, our hearts are now renewed, and so put on new affections, so that they are able to bring forth good works." The Form of Concord, though guarding against viewing justification as a mere process or means of conversion, nevertheless makes the Holy Spirit's indwelling and renewing work follow justification by faith. It is explicit and minute in stating this—defining the "order of causes and effects, of antecedents and consequences," affirming that "faith alone, without works, justifies, but yet it is never and at no time alone." "Faith lays hold of God's grace in Christ, whereby the person is justified. Then when the person is justified, he is renewed and sanctified by the Holy Spirit."

This, as the logical and real order of the Holy Spirit's working the power of redemption into the life of men through a divinely wrought or enabled faith, conferring forgiveness or justification as its first gift, regeneration as a necessary sequence, and moving on through sanctification into full salvation, thus taught by the Reformers and in the Confessions, was continued by our oldest theologians, as Chemnitz, Haffenreffer, Hutter, and Gerhard, till Calovius and others began to put *regeneration* before justification, displacing the latter from its crucial and ruling significance, lapsing, perhaps unintentionally, into alliance with the rejected error of Osiander who had asserted the dependence of justification on the new heart of the believer. As an example of the original and only consistent Lutheran teaching, we quote Gerhard: "That change whereby a man, justified before God, becomes a new man, through which the Holy Spirit awakens new motions in a man, this does not pertain to the act of justification, but is a certain effect following the act of justification." 'Only he whose heart has learned the need of forgiveness has learned, therein, also the need of cleansing.'

But though Calovius and the seventeenth century dogmaticians, influenced seemingly by the condition of infants, usually inverted the place and relations of justification and regeneration, the change failed to satisfy either the teaching of Scripture or the logic of theology. For if we assume that in infant baptism regeneration must be given first, then we are compelled to accept the monstrous incongruity of holding that there might be regenerate persons without either faith or justification. Vain attempts were made to conceal the incongruity by interpreting regeneration to mean no more than a mere restoration of "capacity" for faith (the *arbitrium liberatum*). But such a dilution of the vital truth of regeneration is unscriptural, and suited to efface the difference between nature and grace; for a state without faith or justification would not be in compliance with the requirement to believe on Christ nor hold its recreative power. Lutheran pietism was right in reasserting and maintaining the stricter significance of regeneration.

That the aberration through Calovius is scripturally and theologically untenable is evident in the return of Lutheran theology of the recent period to the Reformation order. The point is of such vital moment in evangelical doctrine as to justify quotations from our leading theologians. Thomasius, whose eminent standing is well known, says: "As faith is a new life in the heart, it cannot remain inactive; inasmuch as it is the experience of the prevenient love of God, it enkindles a reciprocal love, and the manifestation of this feeling is good works." "As it is on the one hand an operation of the Spirit of God through the Word, so it is itself, on the other hand, 'a new light and life, an active, divine force which renews heart, mind, and spirit, and makes a person a changed man, a new creature,' as the Apology expresses it, and as Luther says in his famous words of his Preface to the Epistle to the Romans." "And this radical renovation is not to be reckoned only as one of the fruits of faith; it belongs to the essence of faith; it inheres in it as its ethical principle." Martensen: "This believing appropriation of the *crucified* Savior brings with it actual fellowship of life with the *risen* Savior in His Church; a fellowship in which the believer possesses the righteousness of Christ, not only outwardly, but inwardly, as a creative principle for a new development of life. Christ dwells in the heart of the man by faith, yea, faith is itself the living bond, the secret point of union between Christ and the individual soul, *unio mystica*" (Gal. 2:20). "A man cannot be a partaker of the new life unless he have a good conscience, purified from the sense of guilt and of God's displeasure (Heb. 10:22), and in like manner the forgiveness of sins and the cleansing of the conscience cannot exist without a real and living fellowship with Christ, His fullness and righteousness being the animating principle of individual life.... Faith is like the grain of mustard-seed, a small, insignificant, but fructifying seed-corn, which contains within it the fullness of the whole future." "It contains within itself a mighty germinating power which must necessarily beget a holy development of life." Nitsch (Carl Immanuel) says: "We have to consider faith under a threefold relation, as the reception of salvation. It is, in the first place, the good in the varied relations of those to whom the gospel is announced, and thus, in contrast with unbelief, is good conduct towards grace in the Divine Word. In the second place, in contrast with all καύχησις which consoles itself with works, it is the reception of Divine pardon for sin through Christ, and as such, is the mediate gift of calling grace, whilst the peace of God and the purified conscience are immediate gifts of the Holy Spirit. Finally, in the third place, it is the reception of a higher vital power, and the principle of the new life itself, in so far as the latter cannot be imparted to us otherwise than through communion with Christ."

Gustav L. Plitt, one of the best of the recent Lutheran scholars of Germany, has explained it thus: "Thou canst receive Christ only with the heart. That thou doest when thou dost open thy heart and speak to Him with the heart, 'Yea, I believe it is so.' Behold, thus through the gospel He enters by the ears into thy heart and dwells there by faith. Then thou art pure and righteous, not through thine own act, but by means of the Guest whom thou hast received into thy heart by faith. When we believe we lay hold of Christ, and with Him we receive two things, viz.: His righteousness and His fulfillment of the Divine Will. Faith, as Luther says, is a spiritual appropriation in the conscience, and, in addition, the soul receives Christ and all His righteousness, confides and rests itself thereon, just as if it had itself done and merited it. Such a reception is a spiritual appropriation. Such is the character and nature of true faith. Christ is assuredly given to us in such a way that what He has and is, is accounted to us, just as if it were our own. And whoever believes this actually realizes. We embrace the righteousness of Christ, and God imputes it to us for the sake of Christ, and reckons it to us as our own. *This is justification.* We are freed from all the debt of the law; our person is acceptable before God as righteous; we are the children of God, heirs of salvation and eternal life. But we see also a second thing through faith. As Luther says: 'When such a faith is in thee, and thou hast Christ in the heart, thou darest not think that He comes alone and poor. He brings with Him His life, Spirit, and everything that He is, has, and effects. Therefore, St. Paul says that the Spirit is given, not on account of thy work, but on account of this gospel. When the gospel comes it brings Christ; Christ brings with Him His Spirit. *Then the man becomes new* and holy; all which he then does is acceptable.' The person of the believer is not only acceptable before God on account of Christ and His righteousness, but he is renewed through Christ and is changed. But this renewal, which takes place gradually and reveals itself in the good works of the new man contributes nothing to justification."

Dr. Ernst Sartorius, professor at Dorpat, and Super-intendent-General of Prussia, declares: "The new birth, no less than the natural, presupposes generation, which in the wider sense forms part of its notion; while in the narrower, justification is that which generates, and sanctification, as the new life, that which is born.... Without this faith there is no regeneration, no new creature, but everything remains in the selfish state of the old Adam."

Dr. Christoph Ernst Luthardt teaches: "*In and with faith* the Holy Spirit becomes the principle of a new life in regeneration and a bond of real inner-life fellowship with the Trinity in the mystical union. In Scripture teaching, faith begins a new life through the power of the Holy Spirit. The divine entrance of this life is designated in Scripture as regeneration: John 3:3, 'born from above'; 5:5, 'of water and the Spirit' Tit. 3:5 connects it with baptism; 1 Pet. 1:3, 23, with the word, 'begotten again through the word,' and Jas. 1:18, 'of His own will begat He us with the word of truth.' As to the teaching of the Church: Here first of all belongs what was formerly taught concerning baptism, which was directly designated by this name, cf. already Justin Martyr, 'Apol.,' p. 61. Here later, in the middle ages, the idea of justification as a *transmutatio*, through the infusion of grace, or as grace making acceptable, through which man is himself united with God (Thomas Aquinas). The mixing of truth and error in this was corrected through Luther's doctrine of *faith* and its twofold operation, viz., to *justify* and to *renew*, and indeed, so that the second of these follows upon the first. First, 'we in Christ,' after that 'Christ in us.' First, faith that through the blood of Christ we are redeemed from sin and have forgiveness; secondly, if we have faith, that we shall afterwards become different men and walk in new life. The chief good of salvation I must have first. If, however, my sins are forgiven, etc., then I say, one is to be pious, etc. While according to Luther and the Confessions, justification precedes regeneration, the dogmaticians after Calovius placed justification after regeneration.... Through this different usage of terms, the form of the doctrine is modified among the dogmaticians."

F. A. Philippi, recognized as a learned and able vindicator of strict Lutheranism, in discussing the effort of some dogmaticians to connect the gift of regeneration specially with baptism, while that of justification is given to faith through the word, says: "This view is prominently antagonistic to the evangelical doctrine of the order of salvation. Justification and regeneration are here torn asunder, and faith, which *experiences all operations of salvation* is apprehended only as the medium of justification. But rather there is always given through justification by faith, *eo ipso*, the gift of the Holy Spirit, which is ever the Spirit of regeneration and renewal of the inner man. The indissoluble causal connection of justification and regeneration is here broken through, and only a mere *post hoc* of regeneration in relation to justification is asserted, which notwithstanding is always a *propter hoc*. Accordingly, in agreement with their theory there can be in the case of adults a justification without regeneration, so, on the contrary, in the case of infants, a regeneration through baptism before justification. With them justification appears as a mere *post hoc* in relation to regeneration. But if children of wrath, how can God standing over against them as Judge approach them as the God of salvation with the gift of regeneration before His wrath-judgment over them be removed, and they through faith have become partakers of the forgiveness of sins; out of children of wrath have become children of God and made heirs of eternal life? Even in the case of adults, there appears—torn loose from the justifying effect of the word, and independent of it, self-dependently following it—the operation of salvation, the completed effect of baptism, occurring as *ex opere operato* consisting in *gratia infusa;* and it cannot be denied that this doctrine, notwithstanding that with it faith and justification are in themselves evangelically determined, yet so far as the sacramental conception is concerned, leans toward the Romish side."

X. The only other point to be noted in this connection is the old question of *synergism*, or whether conversion is wholly God's work, or there is in any degree a concurrence of man's work in it. For the long controversies on the subject we can only refer to the Histories of Doctrine. It will be enough to mark out the essential truth as presented by the Scriptures and logically required in the psychological necessities and relations of the human soul in the change. A recapitulation of the truths thus far assured will throw explaining light on this long contested question. The following points are involved:

1. The entire divine *schema* or purpose, making redemptive provision for forgiveness of sin and renewal into holy life, is purely of God's love and working—the love that created man turned his recovery to true life and blessedness. It has been wholly God's work. "God so loved the world that He sent His only begotten Son." "For by grace are ye saved, through faith, not of works." Without this free work of love, the way and the powers for reconciliation would not exist.

Christian Theology

2. As to the appropriation or application of the redemptive provision, man's natural state of mind, by reason of self-alienation from God and lapse into sin, is one of aversion and helpless weakness, wholly incapable, in and of himself, of effectively desiring or willing the purification of his nature and a life of love and holiness. "No man can come unto Me except the Father which hath sent Me draw him" (John 6:44); "except it were given unto him of My Father" (John 6:65).

3. In this situation God, in *prevenient* grace, comes to men before they come to Him, in His message and means of love and reconciliation, entering into their minds in the truth of His redemptive provision and will, that truth being the Holy Spirit's means of calling and winning assent and acceptance of forgiving love and new life, thus securing willingness and overcoming the natural inability to exercise faith. This gracious action is a *divine enablement* to meet the fundamental human condition of faith or self-surrender, for pardon and acceptance with God. The human will is thus set free for its divinely-meant function of free choice and spiritual obedience. Apart from this man can and will do nothing. In and under it he can yield *assent* as a moral agent. This is *God's working* through prevenient grace. Yet the *faith* thus divinely secured is man's act. God does not and cannot believe *for* him—only enables him to exercise the faith to which he is divinely urged. Because this faith is the product of the prevenient grace, it is to be credited to God's free love, and not as man's *merit*. It is all and wholly "of grace." Hence the saving process thus far is usually termed "monergistic." It is surely not the "synergism "of Pelagianism or Socinianism, which meant man's co-operation, even initiative, of his own natural ability. Yet this primary exercise of faith in truth and fact presents the human will in concurrent action with the divine grace. Sartorius well says: "Nothing but want of judgment could here say that if conversion is no work of man, he only occupies the relation of dead material to it, and that it cannot be required of him. It is not required of him that he should *do* it [regenerate himself], but it is that he should *suffer* it, that he should not close himself against the Spirit of God, but should let Him produce a new life in him by the divine Word (Rom. 10:17; Gal. 3:2). It is indeed one thing to receive life and quite another thing to give it; but to say that he who receives life is to occupy only the relation of dead material, which is neither susceptible of life nor receives it, is foolish and presupposes a deficiency of thought concerning the

Milton Valentine

relation of receptivity and spontaneity in the province of life.... *God works that man may work*, says Augustine. God does not work that man may *not* work, but that he may work aright in the strength of God, in whom he can do all things that he could not do of himself" (2 Cor. 3:5; Phil. 4:13). And Kahnis explains: "The proposition that the rejecting of salvation has its ground in man neutralizes not only the conception of predestination, but also the conception of grace contained in the Form of Concord. This proposition demands, according to invincible logic, that the man who can refuse salvation be not passive *(willenlos)* in laying hold of the same. For he who can oppose and does not oppose, wills not to oppose. And he who wills not to oppose just wills to receive." But this so-called "monergism" in Lutheran theology, this precedence of God's work and dependence of man on it for ability to believe and attain life, does not form the absolute monergism of the Calvinistic doctrine, and must not be confounded with it. For the latter rests in absolute predestination and "*irresistible* grace," and is in strife with the vital principle of moral agency and human responsibility with respect to the call of the gospel, which Lutheran understanding recognizes as fundamental.

4. The exercise of this initial faith, thus *enabled* by the prevenient grace and influence of the Holy Spirit, and the consequent experience of Christ in the fullness of his atoning and forgiving love, bring into operation the *regenerating* principle which inheres in the state of justification, the quickening and upspringing of love, gratitude and the new life of obedience and righteousness, by the same Spirit. And when the Holy Spirit's prevenient work, which has thus enabled the "consent," or reality of accepting faith, has further, through that same faith and its gift of forgiveness of sin, given also the regenerate *life, then* this new life, itself a work of God, *can*, through the power of the Holy Spirit, *co-operate* in its development and advance. Such co-operation is required as *duty*— not as a meritorious earning of salvation or reward. The entire movement of salvation is of God's pure grace. And the whole conception of the new life is our giving God's will and holiness free action and control within us and our lives. This realizes salvation, blessedness, heaven. "Work out your own salvation with fear and trembling. For it is God that worketh in you both to will and to do of His good pleasure" (Phil. 2:12–13). "When ye have done all those things which are commanded you, say, We are unprofitable

servants; we have done that which was our duty to do" (Luke 17:10–11).

It thus appears that the free cessation of human resistance and the positive consent, on man's part, to the call of the gospel, is itself a product of divine grace. The energy of free-will in which acceptance of Christ takes place, is by the enabling influence of the Holy Spirit God comes to men first, and His work is the efficient cause of their coming to Him and their conversion.

5. At the same time, the *failure* of salvation in the case of those to whom the gospel has been brought and offered, is the fault of men, because they *refuse* to exercise the grace which has come to them. *Chemnitz*'s statement may be accepted: "This then is the import of what has been tanght concerning prevenient, preparatory, and operating grace, that not our part is the first in conversion, but that God anticipates us with the word and the divine afflatus, moving and urging the will. But after this emotion of the will, divinely occasioned, the human will is not purely passive, but moved and assisted by the Holy Spirit, does not resist, but assents and becomes a co-worker with God."

Milton Valentine

CHAPTER V
SANCTIFICATION

Sanctification, sometimes called renovation, is technically employed to express the continuation of the divine work begun in regeneration, whereby the power of the new life is steadily increased and depravity and sin are more and more overcome in both heart and life (1 Thess. 4:3; 5:23; 1 Cor. 1:30; Col. 2:6; 2 Cor. 7:1).

1. Some distinctions are to be noted: (1) It is distinguished from *justification, (a)* in that justification is objective, an act of God without us, pardoning and counting us righteous, while sanctification is a work wrought *within* us. The first absolves from the guilt of sin; this cleanses from sin itself. *(b)* Justification is complete at once, while sanctification is a progressive work, and never reaches a point in this life beyond which there is no room or demand for improvement (Rom. 7:22–24; Phil. 3:10–14). (2) It is to be distinguished from *regeneration,* in that while regeneration conveys the power and reality of the new life, this is a progressive *increase* of actual holiness day by day, to its completion in the "eternal life." (3) It differs from *both justification* and *regeneration,* in that while these are wholly and purely God's work, sanctification involves man's own concurrence and co-operation. It includes, as plainly meant, a real *synergism*—that the true believer must "work out" into manifest fruitage of holy living and righteous, loving character, the possibilities which grace has put into the whole redemptive provision (Phil. 2:12–13). The *new life,* divinely inaugurated, must be actually and actively *lived, into personal victory* over evil and into goodness, if salvation is to be consummated. The justified and regenerate man becomes a "co-laborer with God" (1 Cor. 3:9; Rom. 2:7), a secondary cause subordinated and enabled by God, so that he may not only renew himself daily by the power received from above, but instrumentally co-operate in the progress of the Redeemer's kingdom.

2. Though important to make and maintain these distinctions for the sake of theological exactness in definition, according to real

peculiarities and relations, it is equally so to note and remember that they cohere in a unity that is inseparable. They cannot be separated in normal Christian experience, so that we may have one without the others. The theological tendency to trace out differences and distinctions in the parts which constitute the process of actualizing personal salvation is in danger of obscuring their essential unity or organic integration. What to some may seem pedantic distinctions must necessarily be made and maintained, but the certainty of the distinctions must be attended with even greater emphasis upon their *indispensable* co-action in the life of Christian experience. *Regeneration* must appear in that experience, if one is really "justified" through the faith whose very principle is spiritually vitalizing—the reception of Christ into his heart and life. It is not "justifying faith" if it be "dead" or non-vitalizing. So *sanctification* must follow regeneration—the *advance* of the given life, in more or less distinct measure, being the indispensable condition and indeed the very *reality* of the saving force and movement. It is the law of "life" to advance in the direction of its own governing principle. The normal Christian life must therefore progress—exhibit its adaptation to consummate in recovered holiness. The reality of justification marks not only the beginning of grace, but also the principle of the further grace of the new life—actually giving that life in initial movement which sanctification is to carry forward to completion. But never, to the end of his earthly life, is man's "justification" other than at first, *i. e.*, *forgiveness* and acceptance on account of Christ's propitiation and imputed righteousness. For he is never "justified" on the ground of his own sinlessness. And the "regenerate state" into which he comes through justification and the Spirit's quickening, as it is only a progressive reaching of the new life, must be carried forward by *sanctification*, in which God, through the believer's own co-operation, consummates the complete salvation from sin and restored holiness. Sanctification is, in truth, only the co-operative stage of the regenerating movement on to its completion. Both justification and regeneration continue and move forward through sanctification to the final salvation. The distinctive forms of work, therefore, which enter successively into the movement of personal salvation, present a unity upon which the success of the whole saving effort depends. Only in the real progression of Christ "*for*" us in justification into Christ "*in*" us of regeneration and advancing sanctification, is Christ made in final realization the power of "an eternal life." Only thus is the principle

Milton Valentine

or law of holiness, righteousness, and love restored to the life of the human soul, expressed as the writing of the law in the heart of man. Antinomianism, which resolves the process of salvation into repeal or lowering of the standard of moral law or ethical excellence, has no place in the theology of the Scriptures or in the Christian life. "The law is holy, just, and good." Redemption is the divine movement for overthrow of moral evil, Love's triumph for the supremacy of ethical law (Matt 5:17-48; Rom. 3:31; 8:3-4).

3. Its *efficient cause*. (*a*) Its total aim is effectuated in the saving work of the Trinity (1 Thess. 5:23). (*b*) The work of Christ enters as a power and provision for its accomplishment (1 Cor. 1:30). (*c*) Especially the Holy Spirit as applying the redemption provided in God's grace and truth (John 14:16-17; Rom. 15:16; 2 Cor. 3:18; Tit. 3:5; Gal. 5:22).

4. Its *instrumental cause*. It is not effected directly, but through appointed means, the word and sacraments (John 17:17; Eph. 5:26).

5. Though progressive, it is never perfect in this life (Phil. 3:12-14; 1 John 1:8-10). It nevertheless forms the completing process in the spiritual recovery of the soul, and in its consummation makes the ransomed "meet for the inheritance of the saints in light" (Eph. 5:26; 1 Thess. 5:23).

THE MYSTICAL UNION

As involved in God's gaining entrance thus, through His truth and Holy Spirit, into the human mind, effecting spiritual renewal and purification, there is formed a peculiar, vital relation that has been not inaptly designated the Mystical Union. This is not to be confounded with what is historically known as "Mysticism," which in its different types is allied with pantheism or breaks with the evangelical teaching of redemption. But the Mystical Union takes account of the evangelical reality which Mysticism failed to apprehend, and in whose place it wove its transcendent and pantheistic dreams and pieties. We must clearly discriminate this deep and essential reality from the theological musings of historical mysticism.

The chief Scriptures asserting it are the following: John 14:23; 15:1-7; 1 Cor. 3:16-17; Gal. 2:20; Eph. 5:30. The natural and necessary interpretation of these Scriptures, in the light of the divine working through the word and Spirit in the mind and heart of believers, justifies us in affirming of this union: (1) It is not simply the common immanent presence of God, by virtue of which He is in everything, according to the truth: "In Him we live and move and have our being" (Acts 17:28). This divine immanence in all nature, whatever it may be, is not itself the redemptory benediction promised in the gospel as the saving indwelling and working. (2) It is not a mere figure of speech, a word of ideal stimulation, but most true and real. (3) It is not a making into one substance or essence the essences of God and of the believer, or a realization of any pantheistic idealism. It stands apart from all the forms of varied monistic unifications of God and man in the theosophic philosophies of our day. (4) But it is the special presence, or indwelling, which God, the Father, Son, and Holy Spirit, gives to the believer, by which He really abides in him, accomplishing within him the work of grace, comfort, joy, and purification. It is St. Paul's experienced reality: "I live, yet not I, but Christ liveth in me: and the life which I now live in the flesh I live by the faith of the Son of God who loved me and gave Himself for me" (Gal. 2:20); and the fulfillment of the promise: "If a man love Me, he will keep My words, and My Father will love him, and we will come unto him and make our abode with him" (John 14:23). Sartorius well expresses it: "God dwells, Christ dwells, in man, and man in Him by love, not as though any mingling or identification of the Divine and human natures took place, for this would not be love, whose essence consists always in the union of the distinct; they remain diverse and essentially different as the created and the uncreated, and yet are made like and united in the fervor of love and its return. It is not from afar, but as indwelliug (immanent) that the Holy Spirit of the Father and the Son bears witness to our spirit that we are the children of God."

Viewing thus the gospel of salvation in its whole aim and mode, in its redemptory provision and applicatory process, it is luminously clear in divine adaptations, both as an impressive and touching appeal of self-sacrificing Love, and as an exact correspondence to the constitutional faculties of the human race, for the recovery of free personalities from the error and bondage of sin into which they had lapsed. Its appeal and means, if rightly traced, are found to reveal the perfect philosophy of Absolute Wisdom and Goodness, forming a distinct and impressive seal of its divinity.

Milton Valentine

DIVISION III
THE MEANS OF APPLYING REDEMPTION

In accomplishing the saving work in the movement we have traced, the Holy Spirit operates through provided and clearly marked *means* or instrumentalities. While He Himself is the "efficient cause" (*causa efficiens*) of the spiritual result, He employs these means as "instrumental causes" (*causæ instrumentales*). In the light of the Scriptures we are not permitted to separate His saving work from these means. They are indispensable. They are the Word of God, the Sacraments, and, in modified sense, the Church. Only through the illumination of the truth in that Word, in these Sacraments and the Church, entering into the mind, impressing the conscience and guiding the will, do the free spiritual changes of personal choice, conduct, and character in conversion become conceivable. Without the gospel message, showing the spiritual need, the provision, and the way of its realization, the necessary change could not be wrought. Hence, it has justly been regarded as a test of the genuineness of the saving work of the Holy Spirit, whether it is found to be also a product and fulfillment of the redemptive truth. The suggestion of a *direct, immediate* (without medium of the truth) working of the Spirit, by miraculous impact on the substance of the soul, or guiding thought, love, and will apart from the actual divine reality of things in the prepared salvation, is simply an illusion of fanaticism or the result of ignorance—whether the suggestion come from uninstructed spiritualism or from the dreamings of monistic philosophies. The Holy Spirit takes the realities of redemptive love and provision—'showing the things of Christ.' "Ye shall know the truth, and the the truth"—through the Spirit's working—"shall make you free."

The relation of the Church in this connection is very peculiar. The Holy Spirit creates the Church through "the means of grace," primarily and distinctively so called; but then the Church, the organized body of believers, itself becomes instrumental for the administration of the word and sacraments, and a means of God's approach to men and the application of redemption to their experience. Nitsch is fully justified in saying: "In one point of view the Church is a continual means of grace for the redemptive ministry of our exalted Redeemer, and no one can be in and live in Christ, unless he be guided in some way by the vital ministry of the Church."

We must discriminate the distinct sense in which the designation "means of grace" is employed in theology. There is a proper non-technical use of it, to express in the broadest way all instrumentalities, exercises, services, opportunities which prove helpful to the Christian life, beginning with those above named, but including then also faith, prayer, Christian fellowship, endurance of afflictions, benevolent activity, etc.

> "All common things, each day's events,
> That with the hour begin and end,
> Our pleasures and our discontents,
> Are rounds by which we may ascend."

In a certain and true sense all these things become means by which we may exercise and develop the Christian life. But in systematic theology the term is restricted to the word and sacraments, because of a real distinction between these and the other things named. The distinction is twofold: (1) Between what is *subjective* and what is *objective*—the word and sacraments being external; faith, prayer, meditation, and the exercises of grace in general being internal. The difference is between the means created by God and proffered for our utilization and a resulting activity within us. (2) Between what is *God's means toward us*, and what is our means toward Him. In theological science the designation, "The means of grace" has in great degree been restricted to the former. The restriction is legitimate because the inquiry in the case is in connection with the *divine* application of redemption *to* men. It might, however, be a question whether it would not have been better to make the designation include *all* the means on both the divine and human sides, with a proper distinction between the two classes. Some dogmaticians call "faith" a means of salvation. They do this because they distinguish between the means of salvation on the part of God, δοτίκα, those offering salvation (the word and the sacraments), and the means of salvation on our part, ληπτίκα, those apprehending or receptive of the offered salvation (faith in the merits of Christ). Along with faith, such writers treat of the experiences of eschatology, such as death, resurrection, etc., inasmuch as these things are means in a general or executive sense.

We restrict our discussion, however, to the means of grace in the limited sense. As already said, these are *necessary* in the normal movement of Christian progress. They have been *appointed* to this end. Of the 'word' of knowledge of Christ's work and doctrine, He has Himself declared: "The Comforter, the Holy Ghost, whom the Father will send in My name, He shall teach you all things and bring all things to your remembrance, whatsoever I have said unto you" (John 14:26; see also Luke 24:46–49); "Go ye, teach all nations, teaching them to observe all things whatsoever I have commanded you" (Matt 28:19–20). This teaching is "the gospel of Christ," which "is the power of God unto salvation," the preaching of which is necessary everywhere, that men may believe (Rom. 1:16; 10:13–14; 1 Cor. 1:21). As to the sacraments, we have the establishment of Baptism and the Lord's Supper (John 3:5; Matt 28:19; Tit 3:5; Luke 22:19–20; Matt 26:26–27; Mark 14:22–25; 1 Cor. 11:23–29). We are informed of no way of application of salvation apart from these means. The Form of Concord teaches that the Father will draw none unto Himself without means, but He employs the word and the sacraments as the ordinary means.' We know of a Christian spiritual movement certainly as of God only when wrought through these means, in more or less direct way. A distinct consideration of each means is necessary.

Christian Theology

Milton Valentine

CHAPTER I
THE WORD

As a means of grace, it designates the gospel message as presenting the truth and call of God to salvation through the provided redemption in Jesus Christ—whether the presentation be oral or otherwise. Besides the teaching or preaching ministry appointed in the Church, there are manifold ways and channels through which this truth becomes clearly and responsibly known to men. Through the reading of the Scriptures or Christian literature the light has come to pervade the intellectual atmosphere, and it could not well be wholly excluded from the mind. Not any particular way of its becoming known gives this truth of the gospel the character of a means of saving grace, but the content and nature of the truth or Word itself. It belongs to the realities it reveals and their intrinsic bearing on men's relations to God and righteousness.

Regarding this means a number of points need to be fixed in our view: (1) The Word is the *primary or leading* means of grace. It ranks first, and is the fundamental and essential means, without which there is no other. "How shall they believe on Him of whom they have not heard?" (Rom. 10:14–17). (2) It is the *comprehensive means*—not as making the others useless or unnecessary, but as *constitutive* for them. These can have no existence except in and through the Word. Theology, following Augustine, rightly designates the "sacraments" a "visible Word." "The Word is joined to the element and it becomes a sacrament, truly a visible Word." "Baptism is not mere water, but that water which the Word of God enjoins and is connected with God's Word." So the Lord's Supper becomes such only in the use of the Word, and thus a visible expression of Christ's propitiatory death. Without the Word, it would be but a mute and unmeaning physical action. The sacramental action is in fact but another and specific form of the administration of the Word. (3) In the order of grace, the Word has been endowed with a real efficacy for enlightenment, regeneration, and sanctification. It has this efficacy, not in the way of magic, incantation, or automatic

Christian Theology

necessity, but by virtue both of the adaptation of its truths to the intellect and moral suasion of the human soul, and by the indwelling presence and influence of the Holy Spirit working through these truths with enlightening, convincing, and moving power. Beyond the innate suitableness and tendency in the supernatural truths of redemptive love, provision, and appeal, to convince of sin, turn from it and create the faith that accepts the provided salvation, we rightly count the Spirit's influence through them as a positive force for efficacy. So "the engrafted (implanted) Word is able to save souls" (James 1:21); is that "which effectually worketh in you that believe" (1 Thess. 2:13); is "quick and powerful" (Heb. 4:12); is "the power of God unto salvation" (Rom. 1:16). And thus the products of grace in men are credited at once to both the Word and Holy Spirit, as: "Of His own will begat He us with the Word of truth" (James 1:18); "Sanctify them through Thy truth; Thy Word is truth" (John 17:17). (4) This presence or union of the Holy Spirit in and with the Word ought to be conceived of as *constant;* for the message of gospel truth has been provided as the very means of His divine working of salvation. He is always in it, so that when its direction and plea are resisted, He and His call are resisted. When the Word is to produce its effect, the Spirit must not come to it from without, but is inseparably operative in and through it. (5) This union is to be regarded as resulting in a unity of *energy and operation energy and operation.* "The Holy Spirit does not do something by Himself and the Word by itself something else, in the conversion of men, but they produce the one effect by one and the same action." (6) While the Word is always efficacious, *i.e.,* has an inherent power for producing its appropriate effects, it is *not irresistible. Per se* it is always a power, but it may be withstood and the proper effect thwarted. This defeat by resistance turns into an occasion and ground of condemnation (2 Cor. 2:16). (7) Both the *law* and the *gospel* are included under the term Word, in their respective relations, viz.: *(a)* The moral Law, summarized in the decalogue, as it presents the duty of man as to right life and character, for all ages, everywhere, is to be preached both for conviction of sin and guidance in holiness. To this belongs the Sabbatic law. The moral law is, of course, to be distinguished from the ceremonial, *i. e.,* all the regulations concerning sacrifices, rites, and forms of the Jewish typical service; and from the Jewish civil law, or regulations for the Jews as a State—all of which were temporary and have passed away. *(b)* The Gospel, as the whole message and doctrine of salvation, and as chiefly efficacious for contrition, faith, justification, renewal, and sanctification. (8) The Word is the *chief* and most important means of grace, because it, as noted, is constitutive of the rest, and comprehends them—the sacraments being a "visible Word." The Scriptures lay the chief stress upon it, attributing to it, under the Holy Spirit, each and everything involved in saving men; e. g., illumination (2 Pet 1:19; 2 Tim. 3:15); faith (Rom. 10:17); regeneration (1 Pet 1:23; James 1:18); sanctification (John 17:17); salvation (Rom. 1:16).

That the Word is the chief or most important means of grace is the common teaching of Protestantism as against Rome's sacramentalism, which asserts that saving grace is actually conferred only by the sacraments. It has been emphasized by the Lutheran Church from the first.

Luther, in "Preface to the German Mass," 1526, says: "In the divine service the greatest and most important part is the preaching and teaching of the Word." In his "Commentary on Daniel," chapter 8: "The gospel is the sole, purest, chief sign of the Church, much more certain than baptism and the bread, because alone through the gospel are these conceived, made, developed, born, clothed, strengthened, and kept. In a word, the whole life and essence of the Church stand in the Word of God, as Christ says: 'Man shall live by every word that proceedeth out of the mouth of God' (Matt 9:4)." He tells us: "Upon any one upon whom the office of preaching is laid, is laid the highest office in Christendom. He may then also baptize, administer the Lord's Supper, and have all pastoral care; or if he wishes otherwise, he may abide in preaching alone and leave to others baptism and other subordinate offices, as did Christ and Paul and all the apostles (Acts 7)." In his comment on Psalm 68:26, he writes: "Thus we see that more stress is laid on preaching than on the Lord's Supper; for the prophet here teaches that in the congregation preaching is the praise of God, and nothing is said about the Lord's Supper, unless it be implied in the word "congregation," for the Lord's Supper has no value in a crowd without the Word of God." In the Smalcald Articles he declares: "In those things which concern the spoken, outward Word, we must firmly hold that God grants His Spirit or grace to no one, except through or with the preceding outward Word." Thomasius well says: "To Luther the Word is the primary means of grace. It also conditions the nature and operations of the sacraments, for without the Word they would be nothing but a 'mere hull,' 'like a body

Christian Theology

without a soul,' 'a letter without a spirit,' 'a scabbard without a blade.' "[1] Melanchthon, in the "Apology," affirms: "God cannot be treated with, God cannot be apprehended, except through the Word. Accordingly, justification occurs through the Word, just as Paul says, 'The gospel is the power of God unto salvation to every one that believeth.' Likewise 'faith cometh by hearing.' " "We are regenerated, as Paul says, 'in the knowledge of God,' and 'beholding the glory of the Lord, are changed into the same image.' "[3]

Dr. Luthardt, of Leipzic, has well summed up the truth here: "The chief means of grace in the Church is the Word of preaching, which, through its testimony in regard to sin (the law) and grace (the gospel) is fitted to work penitent obedience of faith and to serve the Holy Spirit to this end in proportion as it is a true expression of the salvation in Christ, *i. e.*, is scriptural. In the Scriptures, the Word has fundamental significance. Already in the Old Testament, all progress in the history of salvation rests on the Word and faith. And also in the New Testament is the Word from the very beginning the form of revelation (see Heb. 2:3); and the historical facts of salvation clothe themselves in the Word of apostolic preaching, as the necessary means of faith (Rom. 10:14–17, ἡ πίστις ἐξ ἀκοῆς). Therefore, Jesus Himself points this out as the calling of the apostles (μαρτυρεῖν, κηρύσσειν), and promises them the Holy Spirit. Preaching is the first activity of the newly-founded Church. *It is more important than baptizing* (1 Cor. 1:17). At the very beginning it was performed by the officially called, yet its efficiency does not depend upon this (see Acts 8:4, seq., 11, 19; 18:26), nor upon the state of the heart of the preachers (see Phil. 1:15, seq.), provided it is true, *i.e.*, Scriptural preaching, or in harmony with the Old Testament Scriptures (2 Tim. 3:14, seq.), and with the fuller New Testament facts of salvation. As to the practice of the Church—although preaching was rhetorically developed in the Greek Church, in the Church of the middle ages was used with great success by a few celebrated preachers, and in the Roman Church after Trent was brought into greater prominence in the cultus; yet here it fell decidedly into the background as compared with the sacraments. On the contrary, the Reformation placed the Word, both of Scripture and of preaching by the Church, into the foreground. Luther exalts it above everything as an 'almighty power, so powerful a thing that it can do and perform everything'; 'it accomplishes all things'; 'it brings forgiveness of sins,' etc, etc 'It brings Christ with it; therefore, whoever embraces and holds it embraces and holds Christ, and thus through the Word has eternal deliverance from death.'"

Von Zeschwitz, of Erlangen, expresses the judgment: "Luther's greatest merit is not only that he restored preaching to its original purpose, as a true and fruitful explanation and application of the Holy Scripture, but much more, that he set it in the center of the whole evangelical worship.... 'Faith comes by preaching, and preaching from the Word of God.' Hence, preaching and the Word of God enter into the controlling central point in the evangelical worship."

Dr. J. L. Funk, in his "Church Orders of the Evangelical Lutheran Church of Germany in its One Hundred Years," says: The apostle Paul (Rom. 10.) explains preaching as "the audible voice of the gospel, as the way to living faith, the knowledge of God and Jesus Christ, with eternal life. Wherefore, the Evangelical Church restored preaching not only into use, but to the highest and most important place in Church worship, to the highest and central position."

Dr. Theodosius Harnack, of Dorpat, whose evangelical standpoint is well remembered, states: "The Word of God claims central, all-dominating place in Christian worship."

Dr. Ernest Christian Achelis, of Marburg, perhaps the most distinguished living professor of practical theology in Germany, writing historically of Luther's teaching, testifies: "The congregational service has its climax and culmination in preaching.... Preaching is the chief part, which rules the whole service."

As to the truth in question, viewed both Scripturally and historically, there can be no more doubt in the correctly informed Lutheran mind, than there is as to the fact that justification by faith is the chief or determining doctrine concerning the way of salvation. And the *rationale* of it becomes easily manifest in the explaining light of the following facts and relations: (*a*) So far as the grace conferred is concerned, this being the same in both Word and sacrament, in this respect the Word and sacraments are equal. (*b*) The Word being the constitutive factor for the sacraments, the sacraments are dependent upon the Word for their existence as means of grace. (*c*) The sacraments are dependent on the Word also for their *efficacy*, inasmuch as they work only *through* the Word— the Word of the gospel received before, the Word of promise present in the administration, and the same Word of direction and promise held fast in faith also after the sacramental action. (*d*) The Word is

Christian Theology

universal in its application, while the sacraments are limited in this respect—baptism in the case of adults being applicable only to such as have already accepted Christ in faith begotten by the Word and who therefore are already justified and regenerated; and in case of infants by the limitation which requires already existiug faith in parents, or birth-status within the Church. The Lord's Supper is limited to those who have already been made believers by the Word. The sacraments are not an equal necessity with the Word for saving faith and entrance into the state of justification and regeneration. (*e*) As the Word, under the Holy Spirit, administers grace for all parts of salvation, the grace of illumination, contrition, faith, justification, and sanctification, and that administered by the sacraments is conferred *through* the Word, the sacraments manifestly become only a secondary and auxiliary form of means for the same grace, in tributary relation. All Christian theology, save that of Romanism and the Greek Church, agrees that men may be saved without the sacraments, but not without the Word.

The emphasis thus given this truth is called for by its bearing on proper maintenance of other truths that form the cardinal doctrines of salvation, to which the life and order of the Church should be consistently conformed. For example, it is needed in order to preserve in its purity the fundamental and vital doctrine which forms the material and guiding principle of the way of salvation—justification through faith alone. For the Council of Trent sets forth the dogma for the Church of Rome that the grace of justification is conferred only through administration of the sacrament, for the reception of which and its gift of justification a positive faith in the Word of divine promise is not necessary, but simply that no obstacle be offered—the well-known dogma of *ex opere operato* efficacy of the sacraments, *i. e.*, efficaciousness without faith. The sacrament is put above the Word, as not working its grace through the Word, but as directly efficacious in the peculiarity of its sacramental power, even apart from the recipient's faith. The great Romanist theologian, Bellarmin, interprets the doctrine: "The Catholic faith does not allow the grace of justification to be apprehended by faith alone and applied to men, but wills that the sacraments also be necessarily required to this end, so that if faith exists in any one, even in the highest degree, it will nevertheless not justify unless the sacrament is received in fact or in desire; yea, the sacrament is more requisite than faith." This beclouds the Scripture teaching of the way of salvation. Thus Rome's continued denial of the gospel of justification by faith alone by her unscriptural sacerdotal exaltation of sacramental administrations, requires the distinct maintenance of the truth we have been considering. And the importance of such distinct maintenance is augmented by the fact that this unevangelical and priestly exaltation of sacramentalism, passing into the Church cultus, is given a teaching force through a symbolism of church architecture and ceremony, centralizing and making the sacramental feature conspicuous and ruling, and lowering and pushing aside the preaching of the Word. The sacrament is exalted to the subordination of the Word. It is thus exalted as the *grace-conferring medium*, under priestly administration. The Word is placed aside, as conferring no grace, but simply showing the need of grace. The teaching force of this cultus symbolism, obscuring the pure doctrine of justification, regeneration, and sanctification, through the Word—*always by the Word*, whether alone or in sacramental action—demands the emphatic and perpetual safeguarding of the Christian mind against the specious and misleading error.

Christian Theology

Milton Valentine

CHAPTER II
THE SACRAMENTS

The word Sacrament (Latin, *sacramentum*, from *sacrare*, to consecrate), means something sacred, some divine reality. The Latin term was applied to the soldier's oath, employed to establish and set forth his military obligation. It is not strictly a Scripture term, but was introduced by Jerome into the Vulgate version, as a translation in various places—eight times out of twenty-seven—of the Greek μυστήριον, "mystery," as, for instance, in Eph 1:9; 3:3–9; 1 Tim. 3:16; Rev. 1:20. It is not, however, there found applied to either baptism or the Lord's Supper. It was introduced into theological usage by Tertullian at the close of the second century and the beginning of the third. It was at first loosely employed, after the manner of μυστήριον, for any sacred doctrine or rite. But subsequently it was applied more particularly to Baptism and the Lord's Supper, and a few other solemn rites connected with worship. The story of later Roman Catholic sacramental development and misleading error must be left to the history of doctrine.

1. *Definition.* A Sacrament is a sacred rite, appointed by God, uniting the Word, especially the Word of institution and promise, with an external element or elements, through which saving grace is offered and conferred. This fulfills the universally accepted explanation of Augustine, that the adding of the Word to the element constitutes a Sacrament, which thus becomes a "visible Word." It agrees, too, with Melanchthon's explanation: "A ceremony or action in which God holds out to us that which the promise annexed to the rite offers." A Sacrament is composite. This is its distinguishing feature. Apart from the Word included in its constitution, the ceremony could carry no saving significance or grace to the soul, but through the Word the elements and action become impressively luminous with great vital truth for the quickening of faith and love and life.

2. *The number of Sacraments.* The number is determined by the definition. As the term is not original in the Scriptures, and the manifold "mysteries" of redemption are not each and all embodied in ceremonial action, the number is rightly limited to specific

Christian Theology

ordinances of direct divine institution. There are but two such ceremonial institutions, directly appointed by Christ and recognized in practice by His apostles: the Lord's Supper and Baptism. The churches of Protestant Christendom are thus fully warranted, both in accepting this number and restricting sacramental claims to these two forms of ceremonial action. The institution of Baptism by Christ is assured in the solemn commission to evangelize all nations through preaching the gospel and administering the church-forming and covenant-sealing rite—'making disciples, baptizing them.' The baptizing on the day of Pentecost was in obedience to an already given and accepted order of Christian evangelizing procedure as appointed by the risen Savior. The ordinance and rite stand recognized in the church life of the apostolic day (Rom. 6:3-4; Col. 2:12; Eph. 5:26; Tit. 3:5). Whether or not Mark 16:16 is part of the original text, it marks a practice that followed immediately on our Lord's ascension. As to the Lord's Supper, though prominent writers of our time have questioned whether Christ really intended to appoint a permanent ordinance in the Church, His purpose to do so remains indubitably clear in His own language, and is witnessed to in the understanding of the apostles and the usage of the apostolic Church.

The multiplication of Sacraments in the Roman and Greek Churches adds five others to Baptism and the Lord's Supper, viz.: Confirmation, Absolution or Penance, Extreme Unction, Ordination, and Matrimony. This inclusion is made on a less specific and less determinative definition of a Sacrament, especially with respect to the points of explicit divine appointment, and of prescribed external elements and conjunction of the Word, which we regard essential to the New Testament Sacraments. The added five must be held as of merely ecclesiastical institution, and lacking in their elemental constitution the external signs in connection with which the words of institution form the divinely-appointed Sacraments. They neither rest upon equal authority nor contain a like combination of parts as a means of grace for the generic application of redemption under the Holy Spirit. Whatever value some of them may have as ecclesiastical forms, e. g., confirmation or ordination, their use rests only in their appropriateness and actual utility. But the Roman and Greek emphasis on sacramental administration, as compared with that given to the preached Word, taken in connection with a priestly rather than teaching ministry, manifestly tends to obscure and pervert the pure gospel way of salvation through faith in the Lord

Milton Valentine

Jesus Christ, leading to dependence on priestly ceremonies of *ex opere operato* Sacraments—vacating thus the force of both Baptism and the Lord's Supper; of the first by adding the sacrament of penance for atonement of sins after Baptism, and of the latter by turning the Lord's Supper into the Mass as a propitiatory sacrifice. These facts explain the ground upon which the Reformation retained only Baptism and the Lord's Supper as true New Testament Sacraments. They explain also the historic reason of the Council of Trent's reaffirmation of them all and its anathema against all dissent.

3. *General Doctrine of the Sacraments*. While specific peculiarities will appear in the discussion of each, the essential truths involved come into view in the following points:

(*a*) Being of direct, divine appointment, they are of binding, perpetual, and universal authority. They are for the observance, in their true place and relations, of all believers. The Quaker contention has been too obviously variant from the import of the Scripture records and interpretation of the Church to sustain itself.

(*b*) The two things requisite to constitute a Sacrament are the spoken divine Word and the visible material element or elements. The latter are the water in Baptism and the bread and wine in the Supper, and by the Word is meant the first divine instituting declaration and command, through which the element is appropriated to its sacred use, together with the promise involved.

(*c*) The two things thus united are not of equal force or virtue for the giving of sacramental character to the rite, but the *effective* cause (ἄιτεον ποιητίκον) for this is the Word; i.e., the Holy Spirit, who is ever in the Word and acts through it, causes these two essential parts to become a Sacrament. The spiritual force moves not from the physical part or side, but from the spiritual reality of gospel truth and power, to the production of a divine Sacrament. The words of institution are thus of permanent force.

(*d*) The Sacraments are means or bearers of grace to believing recipients. This seems necessary to explain and justify their appointment. The creation of them implies their instrumentality for a unique service in conveying the grace of the gospel to our experience. We cannot regard them as mere memorials of events or truths, to form a decorous commemoration in religion, as a fourth of July in patriotism. Even on this low conception, they would indeed be illuminating and quickening to spiritual interest and strength, and so in an inferior degree a means of grace. But not only their specific appointment, but their actual constitution as created by God through the Word, itself a positive means, requires that they be held as fully means of grace. And yet not in an *exclusive sense*—as excluding the communication of the same grace through the Word preached. Here we must avoid the manifest error of the Council of Trent, already mentioned, which so exalts sacramental grace as to credit it alone as the means of justification and renewal—reducing the Word from its office as a communicating means to that of simply making known the grace of salvation needed. The irrefutable truth is that the Word and the Sacraments confer the same grace. Strictly speaking there is but one means of salvation, distinguishable as the audible and visible Word, through which the same and all grace is imparted to men, at one time in the form of the Word alone, at another in the form of sacramental action, in which the Word is the constitutive reality. The Holy Spirit is in, and works through, the saving truth. "As the word enters the ear that it may reach the heart, so the external rite strikes the eye that it may move the heart. It is, as it were, a picture of the Word, signifying the same thing as the Word. Wherefore the effect is the same." Is forgiveness of sin through Baptism; it is also through the Word of the gospel. Is regeneration through it; it is also through the Word. Is strengthening of faith through the Lord's Supper; it is also through the Word otherwise received. As, according to this, the Sacraments effect the same grace as the Word, the question arises, why has God employed a twofold means to this end? The answer has been well given: "God, who is rich in mercy desires to present His grace to us not only in one way, through the Word, but also to help our infirmity by suitable aids, through impressive rites, in which His promise is repeated and reassured. And the Sacraments have a peculiar impressiveness, because of their administration to each individual believer. While Christ does not give something specially contained in them which cannot be had otherwise, this individualizing administration gives them the force of a sealing certification to faith. Still it remains true that 'far more depends upon the words or the promise than upon the signs [visible elements]; for we can do without the signs, but we cannot dispense with the words; for faith cannot exist without the divine Word. God's words are His letter, His signs are the stamp and seal of the letter.' " The teaching of our theologians is thus fully justified, that under the Holy Spirit, the Sacraments work the grace of which they are real means through the Word of the gospel which creates them, and which they reiterate and impress.

(*e*) The assertion, further, by some of our dogmaticians, of a *heavenly material* (*res* or *materia cœlestis*) as an essential constituent is not to be maintained as a necessary part of the generic doctrine of the Sacraments. The claim has been made that besides the Word and the elements, there is a third necessary something as the real bearer of the communicated grace—as, for example, the "body and blood of Christ" in the eucharist. This *materia cœlestis* is viewed as antithetic, though correspondent, to the *materia terrena* or visible element. There is more than sufficient reason for not pressing this conception. (1) In the earlier Lutheran period, down to 1586, or after the Form of Concord, no such doctrine was formulated. Not only so, but the formulation was such as, impliedly, to exclude it. Luther, in the Smalcald Articles, says: "Baptism is nothing else than the Word of God, in the water, commanded by His institution, as Paul says, 'a washing in the Word.' " In the Large Catechism, he makes the water itself, by reason of its union with the the Word, the divine or sacred bearer of grace, a "divine, heavenly, holy, and blessed water." In his Postils, he calls it "water of God by reason of the Word." The confusion in the effort to determine the *res cœlestis* in Baptism discredits the assertion of its being a generic sacramental reality. The dogmaticians disagree, some holding it to be the Holy Spirit, some the blood of Christ, some the Holy Trinity. It is conceded, of course, that the Holy Spirit is in the Sacrament since He is in the Word which is joined with the sensible element; but He is certainly not there in the form of an elemental *means* of grace, but as the *Giver* of grace through the sacramental means. It is singularly inept to lower His *personal office* through the means into the place of a medium of His work. And even with respect to finding such a *materia cœlestis* in the "body and blood of Christ," it would be difficult to show that the interpretation of these into a third sacramental supersensible *materia*, would not militate against the very purpose of the Savior in constituting bread and wine as a real *visible* sacramental means of conferring His grace. The consecrated bread remains bread and the consecrated wine remains wine, not at all transubstantiated into body and blood; but would it not seem a vacating of the very service for which they have been divinely chosen and set apart, if we maintain that they do not actually serve for this, and predicate *invisible* elements as the administrative media of grace? The present Christ in the Supper is the personal Source of

Christian Theology

grace, in His glorified indivisible divine-human nature. Moreover, the theory destroys the analogical consistency between the Word and the Sacraments, according to which, in the first case, grace is communicated by the Word alone, and in the second, by the Sacrament in which the Word is constitutive, the Holy Spirit being operative for the result in both cases. Accordingly, these difficulties and the confusions to which they lead have developed a tendency, beginning with Baier, to drop the claim of *materia cœlestis* as a generic essential to sacramental constitution, and to be satisfied with the earlier and simpler definitions. (*f*) The *Form* of a Sacrament is the whole external action, consisting of the administration of the visible element, with the divine words of institution and promise. A consecratory rite, preceding the administration and preparatory for it, setting the element or elements apart to their sacramental use, seems eminently proper, at least in the case of one Sacrament. But, as we shall see hereafter, this rite needs to be carefully safeguarded from the conception that it is absolutely essential, and especially from the notion of its effecting a change in the elements, or transubstantiation. But of this, more later on. While sacramental character is effected by the union of the Word *in and with the administration itself,* such formal rite serves as an impressive reminder of the service to which God Himself is appropriating the given elements. This so-called "consecratory" rite for setting them apart has its efficiency for this in the simple reciting of the words of institution, connecting the Word with the elements. It is but a formal placing together what God has chosen and Himself unites.

(*g*) As the content and service of the Sacraments are only what God makes them, their *efficacy* is not dependent on the character or holiness of the person by whom they are administered. They are efficacious under the Holy Spirit in and through the Word. They are sometimes administered by ungodly men, always by only incompletely sanctified men, but believing and sincere recipients are not thereby excluded from the grace they offer. The ministrant ought to be holy, but the Sacraments are constituted by God, not by the ministrant's character. Neither does their efficacy depend on the *intention* of the minister, any further than intention is necessary to perform the action of administration. Rome's teaching, that the priest's "intention" to confer the grace as provided and lodged in the Church's Sacraments, is requisite when he dispenses them, is not sustained by any Scripture doctrine. Though the asserted necessity tends to exalt the priestly powers claimed for a hierarchical ministry, the assertion of it is thoroughly variant from the Biblical teaching as to the constitution and import of the Sacraments.

(*h*) The Sacraments are not to be viewed as efficacious *ex opere operato, i. e.*, by the mere performance of the rite, without *faith* on the part of recipients. Though their *validity, content* or *intrinsic essence* is not made by the recipient's faith, the actual reception of the grace provided and presented *is* dependent on his faith. All saving grace, justification, regeneration, sanctification, is conditioned on faith. Without the believing heart and desire, the offered grace is not appropriated, the blessing is not taken into the soul and life. The Sacraments are appeals to faith and for its quickening; and apart from faith there is no recipiency for the divine provision. "By grace are ye saved," says an apostle, "*through faith*" (Eph. 2:8). The absence or refusal of this leaves the saving power of grace unreceived. It is the danger of obscuring this solemn truth that justifies Protestantism in its constant opposition to Rome's encouragement of dependence on *ex opere operato* administration and reception of the Sacraments, a leaning upon the external ceremonial and priestly intention and power, with a relative neglect to foster direct personal trust in the Lord Jesus Christ and bring the soul into immediate love to and confidence in Him. For, the faith for right reception of sacramental grace should, manifestly, not rest on the effectiveness of the sacramental action itself, but through it lay hold upon the gracious Redeemer and Savior Himself, and the special promises of grace belonging to the particular Sacrament received. Only thus does the soul realize itself as brought into living and conscious communion with the Redeemer.

(*i*) We rightly maintain that the *dispensation* of the Sacraments has been divinely committed to the *Church*, the community or body of believers, united or organized for fellowship and worship; and not, as an exclusive function, to a priestly class, a hierarchical order or office. It was to the twelve (or eleven) as "*disciples*" that Jesus, in instituting the Supper, after having *given* the elements and directed *them to eat* and *drink*, added, "as often as ye shall thus do," *i.e.*, eat and drink (not administer to others) "do it in remembrance of Me." There is nothing in Jesus' action or words to suggest a function of *apostolic* or even *official* administration, but of loving and grateful fellowship in *reception* of the eucharistic commemorative and grace-bestowing meal. After His death, resurrection, and ascension, the instituted rite of fellowship passed into the frequent use of the disciples in the breaking of bread. Paul's reference to this in 1 Cor.

Christian Theology

11. shows plainly that it was practiced as a congregational or Church possession for fellowship in remembrance of the Savior's atoning work and grace. The same is true of Baptism, as the Sacrament of reception into Church communion. Manifestly, therefore, and in logical sequence, the Church, as the organized body of believers in fellowship, entrusts these sacramental administrations to its properly called and ordained ministry. This is a necessity for good order. This ministry represents the Church, and acts for it, in maintaining its proper sacramental dispensations as well as that of the preached Word.

(j) The Sacraments are an ordinary necessity to salvation. This is involved in the fact of their divine institution. They were meant to supply a real and important need, and the Church cannot rightly fail in their use and administration. They have a fixed place and function that cannot, without disobedience to the divine order, be set aside or neglected. The Augsburg Confession, in Latin copy, says: "Our churches teach that Baptism is necessary to salvation." In the German it simply says: "It is necessary" (*nöthig sei*). But the necessity is not to be understood as absolute, *i. e.*, that the grace of salvation cannot possibly be given apart from them. Doubtless God can and does save by means of the Word alone. Even in the Sacraments, as we have seen, it is in and through the Word that the Holy Spirit works the sacramental grace—the same grace, too, by which through faith we are regenerated and sanctified. This is certified scripturally by the instances of the dying thief on the cross, and of Cornelius to whom was given the Holy Spirit with His saving gifts *before* any sacramental administration. Protestant theological interpretation has consentiently accepted this truth. Luther argues that as Jewish children dying before circumcision were not lost, neither are Christian children dying before Baptism. In reference to such of them as die before Baptism, he says: "The holy and merciful God will think kindly of them. What He will do with them He has revealed to no one, that Baptism may not be despised, but has reserved it to His own mercy. God does wrong to no man." The line that distinguishes the necessity of the Sacraments from being absolute is in the principle that "not privation, but contempt of them, condemns." It is an *ordinate* or *ordinary* necessity, arising from divine *institution and precept*, for the proper and right order, to which obedience is due and needful for full realization of the power of saving grace in the Church and the believer.

Milton Valentine

BAPTISM

A few preliminary facts will bring the rite of Baptism rightly before our view for a just consideration of the main aspects under which theology is specifically concerned to understand it.

1. As already noted, Christ Himself instituted it (Matt. 28:19), though as a religious rite Baptism already had been in use among the Jews, both in proselyte Baptism and that of John. In its ceremonial and meaning it had already an initial spiritual import to fit it to be taken up by the Savior, and by Him given divine institutional place in the completed endowment of the Church. He made it, however, a new reality by filling the rite with the full import of the saving gospel and the grace of the new life, and so superseding the earlier ceremonial. The apostolic use of it on the day of Pentecost inaugurates its new divinely-given place and function as an institution for the Church.

2. It has been appointed as the formal act of establishing the covenant of grace in every individual. This is clear from the place Christ gave it in the very terms of instituting it, viz.: "making disciples, baptizing them." Its pentecostal use recognizes this fact, as employed in connection with the reception into the fellowship of the Church, or body of believers, of the thousands who gladly received the word of salvation. As a means of grace, it thus becomes a church-forming Sacrament.

3. It corresponds to, and takes the place of, circumcision in the Old Testament as the formal establishing act for the covenant of salvation. Through circumcision Abraham and his seed came under formal covenant as God's people. Baptism was made the sealing rite for entrance of believers in Christ into covenant status. The spiritual force of both was and is far more than a formal outward relation. The reality signified and properly realized was the inner life of grace and love in the soul. St. Paul joins with Deut. 30:6 in magnifying the deep spiritual significance of circumcision, when he declares that the circumcision which made the true Jew was not that "which was outward in the flesh," or a formality without the obedience of faith, but "that of the heart, in the spirit, not in the letter" (Rom. 2:28–29). And he distinctly places Baptism in the room and stead of the Old Testament covenant seal, when he explains to the Colossian Christians: "Ye were also circumcised with a circumcision not made with hands, in the putting off of the body of the flesh, in the circumcision of Christ, buried with Him in baptism." This will

Christian Theology

explain its initiatory relation and use as faith's covenant with God in entering the fellowship of His people.

THE PROPER SUBJECTS OF BAPTISM

There are two classes of these: *First, adults,* who through the Word have been brought to repentance and faith. The teaching of the Holy Spirit on Pentecost guided the apostolic administration along the line of this rule (Acts 2:41; 8:12, 36–39, even apart from the disputed verse 37; 10:44–48; 16:14–15, 31–33; 19:3–6). This limitation to only *believing* adults is involved in, as well as grounded upon, the fundamental principle of the gospel, that no saving grace can be received, even through the Word, without faith. Though the Sacrament, in itself valid, should be administered, the receptive faculty and function are wanting. There is no appropriating heart— only a heart of unbelief. Only to faith Baptism conveys its assuring and sealing grace of salvation. Believing adults are therefore proper subjects. *Secondly, the infant children of believers.* This is strangely disputed. But the proof leaves no ground for doubt. It rests in the unquestionable fact that from the first God directly and fully instituted infant membership in His Church, on the basis of the parental relation. The specific facts are the following:

1. Under the Old Testament dispensation God established the covenant of faith and obedience for His people with Abraham. It distinctly included the children of believers as members of the Jewish Church. God said to him: "I will establish My covenant between Me and thee, and thy seed after thee in their generations, for an everlasting covenant, to be a God to thee and thy seed after thee" (Gen. 17:7). "In thee shall all the families of the earth be blessed" (Gen. 12:3). This was the covenant basis of the Church of the Old Testament, the door of which, in Christ and His endowment with redemptive grace, was to be opened to the Gentiles. St. Paul, writing to the Galatians about the extension of the blessings of the Church to the Gentiles expressly calls this covenant "the covenant that was confirmed before of God in Christ." He even says: "The Scriptures foreseeing that God would justify the heathen through faith, preached the *gospel* before unto Abraham, saying, In thee shall all nations be blessed" (Gal. 3:8). In the covenant in which God built the Church of the Old Testament, and which in Christ opened its gates to the Gentile world, He said: "I am *thy* God; I am the God of thy *children.*"

Milton Valentine

In adding a seal to the covenant, He explicitly and emphatically included the *children* with the parents. "This," says He, "is My covenant which ye shall keep: Every male child among you shall be circumcised." "He that is born in thy house and he that is bought with thy money must needs be circumcised, and My covenant shall be in your flesh for an everlasting covenant" "He that is eight days old shall be circumcised." "And the uncircumcised man-child—that soul shall be cut off from his people; he hath broken My covenant" (Gen. 17:10-14). This rite of circumcision, St. Paul tells us, was a "seal of the righteousness of faith" (Rom. 4:11). It ratified the covenant of faith on the human side. "I am thy God," runs the covenant—hence Abraham was circumcised. "I am the God of thy children"—hence their circumcision was required, that the righteousness of faith might be imputed to them also. Circumcision was the divinely-appointed recognition of the Church relation of the infant children. In receiving the parents the Church possesses the children. In circumcision God bound up the believing parent under most solemn responsibilities, to recognize this infant membership. No difficulty was raised to this seal of the righteousness of faith, on the ground that children eight days old could not believe. Faith was then, as now, the essential thing for a living Church. Yet of this principle of spiritual life was circumcision the seal to infants. How? Plainly on the ground of the organic oneness of the family, its unity of life and faith. The faith of the parents was to descend and be perpetuated in the children. The offspring were at once viewed as believers, because their spiritual life was as yet embraced in the life and formative direction of the family. So God planted them in the Church, with their parents, to grow there into the life of the Church and of God.

This order was the law for the Church down to the coming of Christ. Moses incorporated it into Levitical rule (Deut. 29:10-13). Joshua included the "little ones," in renewal of the covenant. Isaiah, picturing the coming of the Messiah as a Shepherd, represents Him as carrying "the lambs of the flock in His arms and in His bosom" (40:11). When Christ came infant membership was in full force. John was circumcised. Jesus was circumcised.

2. In the New Testament dispensation the question is, have the right and obligation to infant membership been withdrawn? Let incontestable facts be recalled. (1) The New Testament Church is a larger and richer development of grace than the Old (Heb. 8:1-12; 10:16-17; 2 Cor. 3:6-10). It would hardly diminish the privileges of

the covenant. (2) Only God can repeal His own positive statutes; and if He has not distinctly repealed this, or unless it expires by necessary limitation, the law of infant membership is and must be in full force. There is not a single word of such repeal in the New Testament. No new command to include children is needed. It is enough that the New Testament simply assumes, as it does, that the law continues to hold. That it has been so *meant* to continue, there is positive evidence. It is found: (*a*) In the fundamental oneness of the Church in the two dispensations. The Church passes through different dispensations without losing its identity. "The forms of dispensation affect not the substance of the things dispensed." The old priesthood may give place to the Christian ministry, circumcision to Baptism, the passover to the Lord's Supper, but the covenant is the same everlasting covenant, through which all nations are to be blessed (Rom. 4:13; Gal. 3:29; John 8:56; Rom. 15:8; 11:20–24). The grafting into the Christian Church of believing Jews is "into their own olive tree" (Rom. 11:17–24). (*b*) Christ emphatically vindicated the right of the children to place and recognition in His kingdom (Matt. 19:14). (*c*) The commission to make disciples of all nations includes them in its necessary scope. For to Jewish thought, from the law of circumcision, the sealing of Jewish converts by Baptism could not but be understood as taking the little ones along with converted parents. St. Peter, under the Spirit, gave it this scope by bringing the order of the new rite under the old rule of application: "The promise is to you and your children." The apostolic household baptisms are the consistent illustrations of the rule. St. Paul declares a believing half-parentage "sanctifies" the children, *i. e.*, makes them ecclesiastically "holy," as entitled to the same covenant seal as belongs to the believing parent (1 Cor. 7:14). The fact that the Jews, intent on seeing grounds of complaint, never raised objection to Christianity as annulling the covenant privileges of children, confirms the truth that there was no exclusion, (*d*) All these facts have their consistent outcome in the *practice of infant baptism in the early Church*. This is historically certified beyond question. Justin Martyr (about A. D. 138) wrote: "Many, both men and women, remain who were made disciples to Christ (ἐμαθητεύθησαν τῷ Χριστῷ) from their childhood." Irenæus (A. D. 125–190) "He came to save all by means of Himself, all, I say, who through Him are born again to God (*renascuntur in Deum*), infants and children, and boys and youths, and old men." That "*renascuntur in Deum*" refers to Baptism becomes clear from Book

III., xvii. 1. Origen (A. D. 185–253): "According to the usage of the Church baptism is given even to infants." "For the Church has received a tradition from the apostles to give baptism to infants." Tertullian (A. D. 160–240) opposed it on several grounds, but his opposition recognized the existence of the custom. Cyprian (A. D. 200–258) maintained, not as a new decree, but as keeping firmly the faith of the Church, that the baptism of infants need not be delayed till their eighth day. The Council of Carthage (A. D. 252) unanimously condemned the opinion that it ought to be delayed to the eighth day. Thus infant baptism is irrefutably accredited.

THE MODE OF BAPTISM

The mode or form of administration is not a vital matter—except in so far as it consists in the application of water, joined with the divine Word, to a proper subject, by an authorized person in the divine Name. As a ceremonial feature our Church does not hold any one specific form of it as essential to validity. While admitting that valid Baptism may take the form of "immersion," its universal practice has been "affusion" or "sprinkling," as both most convenient and appropriate. It resists the Baptist claim on Scriptural and practical grounds. So also do nearly all the Protestant Churches of Christendom. Luther, indeed, employed immersion phraseology in discussing the Sacrament, but assented to the different practice, evidently, like Calvin, considering the mode a matter of indifference. While immersion soon became the rule in the early Church, it was not an exclusive form. For the writer of "The Teaching of the Twelve Apostles" (about A. D. 150), presenting his understanding of their doctrine, prescribes an alternate form in "pouring water upon the head thrice, in the name of the Father and Son and Holy Spirit." Immersion, however, long held sway, except in case of the sick (*clinic* baptism), till in the thirteenth and fourteenth centuries choice was allowed between it and sprinkling. Thomas Aquinas thought it might be safer to baptize by immersion, yet sprinkling or pouring was allowable. These came into common use at the close of the thirteenth century, and are the present practice of the Roman Church. In the Greek Church immersion is insisted on as essential.

The word βαπτίζω, from root βάπτω, does not itself define the mode, since its meaning, beginning with "to dip," "immerse," "overwhelm," "bathe," varies into "to wash" or make clean with water, with increasing reference to the generic aim of "purification"

Christian Theology

or cleansing, so as in its Christian application to mean, "*to administer the rite of ablution,*" *i. e.*, washing or cleansing without respect to the form. Baptism is, accordingly, a generic term, and is determinable neither in its essence nor form by the way the element, water, is applied, but by the divine *service* of cleansing from sin. It is distinctively the Sacrament of *spiritual purification,* through both forgiveness and renewal. It sets forth this work of God's grace.

The proper mode of the ordinance is best perceived and settled in the light of the general tenor of the Biblical acts of purification, which New Testament Baptism sums up. The facts are impressively significant. All through the Old Testament the purifying rites fell prevailingly, if not entirely, under the forms of pouring and sprinkling—mostly in connection with the shedding of blood as an atonement and return to right life. For instance: (1) In circumcision, the Old Testament sign of the covenant till Baptism was divinely put in its place, a rite indicating dedication to inward purification, "circumcision of the heart" (Deut. 30:6; Rom. 4:11), the rite was by the shedding of blood. Nothing in it suggested immersion or pointed forward to it. (2) In the Passover, also a sign and assurance of grace (Ex. 12:22), besides the shedding of blood, was prescribed the sprinkling of the blood, as saving from the destroying angel, or judgment, and this was perpetuated in the Old Testament Church as a rite emblematic of the saving blood of Christ and of His cleansing grace (Acts 22:16). (3) So in the Levitical sacrifices (Ex. 24:6–8; Lev. 1:5, 11; 4:25, 30; Heb. 9:19–22; 12:24; 10:22; 1 Pet. 1:22). In nearly all the sacrifices we find the priest took part of the blood and sprinkled it round the altar and on the people, and poured the rest down at the foot of the altar. In all the various sacrifices for cleansing from sin, we never hear of immersion. Everywhere the atoning grace is emblemized by sprinkling and pouring. Between immersion and remission or cleansing from sin no such connection was ever formed. (4) The old ceremonial purifications, as in Lev. 14:7; Num. 19:17–18, referred to in the New Testament as "baptism," "divers baptisms," face the same way. For while some of them, as baptism of "clothes," "cups and pots and brazen vessels" (Mark 7:4), may have been by immersion, when the subjects of purification were *persons* the law of direction prescribed sprinkling or pouring, as may be seen in Lev. 14:7; Num. 19:13, 18–19. (5) The consecration of priests and kings, a setting apart to the service of God in these special relations, was done by the sprinkling of blood and the pouring of oil (Ex. 29:21; Lev. 8:30; 1 Sam. 16:1, 13). (6) The prophecies of the grace of

Milton Valentine

Christ's day represent that grace under the conceptions of sprinkling and pouring. Always the pardoning and purifying grace of the Redeemer is foretold through the symbols of affusion or sprinkling—never by that of immersion (Isa. 32:15; 44:3; 52:15; Ezek. 36:25). No prophetic figure pointing to the new dispensation would ever suggest such a mode of Baptism. These facts from the Old Testament ritual of forgiving and sanctifying grace are of direct and immense significance and force as to the proper form of Baptism.

When we pass to the New Testament facts, we find these to accord best with the modes thus established in all the purifying and consecratory rites and symbols in the Old Testament order. (1) The baptism of John, though not identical with Christian Baptism, may be noted as suggestive of baptismal mode. Was it by immersion, as sometimes asserted? In the absence of positive historical affirmation, it is exceedingly improbable. For immersion would have violated all the types referring to the new dispensation which John announced and have left the act without normal significance. Further, the administration, "when there went out unto him all the land of Judea and they of Jerusalem, and were all baptized of him" (ever under a most modified import of the language as to the multitude), would have been to him an impossible task. We have no right to invoke a miracle here. (2) When we add the baptism of Christ by the Baptist, the idea of immersion is further precluded. This baptism marks the presentation of Jesus to the public, marks His open assumption of His Messianic offices, as He was about to enter upon His ministry. In the light of Jewish order this rite providentially became His self-chosen consecration to His offices of Priest and King. Such consecration was always by *sprinkling* and *pouring*—never by immersion. The use of the latter would have left it a strange anomaly, violative of Jewish symbolism. And there is no need to suppose or assume immersion because baptized at or even "in" the river Jordan. The instinct of Christian art is far more logically interpretative of the Scripture record than is immersionist exegesis, when it has sent down from the early Church its picture of Jesus and John standing in the margin of the Jordan and the Baptist pouring the living water on the Messiah's head. (3) Very pertinent in this connection is the narrative of the Baptism by the Holy Spirit on Pentecost (Acts 1:5; 2:16–18, compare with Matt. 3:2; Luke 24:49; John 14:16, 26). There is no immersion there. When God baptizes His people, with great effectual Baptism, it is by "pouring out" of His Spirit. Is it to be supposed that God has meant that the Church shall make the form of water Baptism violate the form of the divine Baptism? (4) All the cases of Baptism by the apostles are best explained as by this mode, as family baptisms at home or in prison, of the eunuch, Cornelius, etc., where the water or conditions for immersion are hardly conceivable.

But answer must be made to the appearance of immersion in Rom. 6:3-5. Though often plausibly claimed for that mode, the passage, if looked at carefully, furnishes no proof of it whatever. For there is no allusion to the *mode* of the Sacrament in the language. The comparison refers to the true effects of it, in the spiritual purification from the world and sin. The design evidently was to show that by the solemn profession made at Baptism, the baptized persons had become *dead* to sin as Christ was dead to the living world ("died unto sin") when He was buried; and that as He was raised up anew to life, so *they* should also walk in the new life. The comparison or parallel is as to effects, not the mode. Proof of this is clear in the fact that the apostle immediately changes the figure and calls it "planting"—a planting (still by Baptism) "together in the likeness of His death."

THE EFFECTS OF BAPTISM

Prefatory to this inquiry and as preparing for correct conclusions, it is proper to recall some fundamental truths already settled. (*a*) That by the fall and original sin man has lost none of his essential psychical faculties or components of his personal constitution. His misuse of them is not their extinction, but a perversion of their ethical intent and right direction. (*b*) Original sin or depravity is not substantial, or, as Flacius blunderingly represented, "of the substance of the soul." Sin consists in the state or action of the constitutional faculties, as an enslaving propensity or tendency to moral evil or unrighteousness, out of true and needful harmony with God and the requirements of ethical well-being. (*c*) The inner work of salvation and renewal is not to create new faculties or change the soul into another substance, but to recover man's state of soul, and the trend and action of his faculties to health, order, and holiness, in the love of God and righteousness. The saving work effects its purpose, not by setting aside the constituent personal faculties, by which man is man, but by acting *in, upon, and through* them, with divine truth, for a free consent to return to life in God and duty. (*d*) Therefore all statements or forms of expression which present it in either physical or magical terms, as the planting of a "seed" or "germ," the creation of a "new personality," if taken literally, are misleading. True, the "word of God" is mentioned as "seed" sown in the mind and heart But this "Word," as the great "means" of grace, used by the Spirit, must not be confounded with the "*effects*" of that "means." We find no such expressions in our Confessions, but they are not unknown in dogmatics. A "seed" or "germ" expresses "substance and attribute," or a substance with its attributes. But the saving change through the means of grace allows only a correcting of the sinful state and activity of the soul, a change of personal *character*. The human personality, psychologically viewed, the personal ego or soul, is self-identical from its origin all through this life and in eternity. Apocalyptic disclosure represents the purified saints in their heavenly state as having carried their consciousness of personal self-identity from their lost condition in sin into complete holiness and blessedness through the cleansing of the blood of the Lamb. In the light of these principles we shall be able to trace the effects or benefits of Baptism.

1. With Respect to Proper Adult Subjects
1. As clearly taught by the Scriptures, it formally *establishes, seals, and sets forth the believer's status of direct and vital relation to God through faith in Jesus Christ*. The Baptism ratifies, on both the divine and human sides, the covenant of grace and salvation. The person has come to it as a believer, whom the prevenient working of the Holy Spirit has brought to faith, and *through* faith to forgiveness or justification, and the first desires for the new life; and he personally binds himself to the grace which promises the full salvation. It brings the force and benefit of a personally sealed covenant, certifying to the generic gospel promise, "As many of you as have been baptized into Christ, have put on Christ" (Gal. 3:27). "Buried with Him by baptism into death, that like as Christ was raised up from the dead by the glory of the Father, even so we also should walk in newness of life" (Rom. 6:4). Nothing merely external and formal can be meant by the relation thus formed, but a real, spiritual connection, grafting into Christ, with saving efficacy and development.
2. Baptism, being further and distinctly the sacrament of cleansing, exhibits and administers *regenerating and sanctifying grace*, as well as justifying. Through the Holy Spirit it is made a

Christian Theology

means of the renewal in which the true believer becomes a "new creature." We are surely entitled to hold the appointment of this ordinance in direct connection with Christ's reference to water, in affirming the necessity of the new birth (John 3:5), and the apostle's recognition of a "washing of regeneration" (Tit 3:5). It is true, the proper subject of adult baptism, as already a believer, is thus already justified and initially regenerate. The "Word" being the chief and comprehensive means of grace, the means in these means, has, in the case of adults, precedence, and through it the Holy Spirit works both faith and renewal. But faith is to grow, and regeneration is a progressive work and is never perfect in this life. Regenerating grace is always needed. And the Sacrament, being a visible Word, confers this grace in administration and gives covenant assurance of it unto perfect sanctification.

3. It also forms and manifests a fellowship relation and union with the Church of God. It is, as we have seen, a Church-forming Sacrament. This union is part of the proper "confession" of the Savior, and vitally essential to the development of the new life. It is an unspeakable benefit thus given—fellowship in the perpetual use of the means of grace, the communion of saints in spiritual worship, service, Christian obedience. Because of the social constitution of humanity, no one can develop his true ethical life in isolation. The altruistic intent marks its loftiest excellence and blessedness, and this fellowship of brotherhood and service is of supreme moment in the counsels and order of redemptory training. Hence, the order starts with organizing the new subject of grace into the community of mutual love and of co-work with God's world-saving aims.

4. We must observe, further, from these three points, that Baptism is not a means whose effects are at once all accomplished at the time and in the act of administration, but the establishment of a relation of perpetual spiritual forces and fruitage. The established covenant takes up, binds, and consecrates the whole life to its close. It is, on the part of the person, the surrender and pledge of it all to God's redemptive will and order; on the part of God a covenant for forgiveness and purification to the full measure of faith's recipiency and appropriation. According to the believer's faith and co-operation will the baptismal benefits be turned continuously into actual spiritual life. Without faith at Baptism, though the Sacrament was a valid offer of grace, none was appropriated. The human side failed to take it. But God's provision and covenant are forever true and available. Repentance and faith may claim them. Luther's

direction is fully in place: "If you have not believed, believe now." The church member's advance is intertwined with the obligations, responsibilities, and realizations of the baptismal covenant. He is never done with the privileges, promises, and appropriations till the full consummation of saving grace is reached. He is never done with his Baptism. From all errors through blindness or lapses through weakness, he needs, not a repetition of the Sacrament, but to step back upon God's given, accepted, and abiding covenant

II. With Respect to Infant Baptism
The peculiarity in this case, calling for special consideration is in the fact that infants cannot yet believe or exercise faith. Though wrought by God, faith is an *act* of the soul; and every definition of true faith makes it include knowledge in the intellect and trust in the heart and will. No intelligible conception of "faith" in an infant has even been given, either as a condition for Baptism or as an instantaneous result, at an age when not yet a single faculty of knowledge or intelligent confidence is possible. Exegesis is utterly forced when it assumes to find Scripture for it in Matt. 18:6; Mark 9:42. Though infant baptism was practiced in the Church from apostolic days, in the early centuries, middle ages, and down to the Reformation, it was not connected with any claim for infant faith. On the contrary, it was positively and universally repudiated. This fact appears historically in two forms. *First*, in the form of *exegesis, i. e.*, of the only passages (Matt. 18:6; Mark 9:42), which some modern dogmaticians have used to teach it From Clement of Rome, down through the centuries, the Christian writers apply the "little ones which believe," not at all to infants, but to adult members of the Church. *Secondly*, in positive disclaimer of infant faith. It is distinctly and uniformly rejected as something outside of the possibilities of the infant period. Abundant testimony is borne to infant baptism and infant salvation through Baptism, but they were based in other considerations than assumption of personal faith in the infant. In all its characteristics of reality, it was held as not predicable until the period of understanding is reached. The very conception of faith made it impossible to credit it to unconscious babes. Examination of Bail's *Summa Conciliorum Omnium* discloses no acts of Church Councils teaching or suggesting infant faith. We have to sum up that from the apostles down to the sixteenth century, such faith was not recognized by either theologians or any creed of the Church.

Christian Theology

The exegetical mind discovered no such doctrine in the Scriptures, and the confession-making councils of the Church formulated none. Yet infant baptism and infant salvation through baptismal grace were steadily maintained.

The initiation of the claim for infant faith is due to Luther. It grew out of the intense stress—yet none too much—which he placed upon the fundamental truth of justification by faith, as the essential, all-determining principle in the order of salvation. Without faith, saving grace through neither Word nor Sacrament could be received or appropriated. Being thus a necessity, Luther conceived and represented it as wrought by God's prevenient grace in the unconscious child. At his first breaking away from Rome, with its *opus operatum* sacraments, he turned to the view of Thomas Aquinas, that the faith of the *Church* vicariously represented the child, and taught that God, in answer to the prayers of parents or the Church, wrought faith in the infant itself for believing reception of Baptism. By this he, indeed, avoided the Roman Catholic doctrine of an *ex opere operato* infusion of faith *by* the Sacrament, and kept in harmony with the principle: *non sacramentum, sed fides sacramenti justificat*. But this first explanation proved discordant. It collided with: "Faith cometh by hearing, and hearing by the word of God," which in no practical or intelligible sense could be predicated with respect to the infant. It still inverted the order of relation between the gifts of grace and the means of grace, assuming the bestowment of the great gift of faith before any means were used—the all-embracing saving grace conferred *without* means. It confused the conception of faith itself by emptying it of the very elements of knowledge and intelligent trust which had been set forth as its constituents. It was not a consistent working explanation, and does not represent Luther's final ground for infant baptism.

His work as a reformer was progressive, and continually developed the necessity for new adjustments of doctrinal details under the recovered view of the way of salvation and the fundamental positions of Protestantism. It was a profoundly reconstructive movement, advancing, in a deeply agitated period, through ever fresh emergencies calling for quick solution of many complex theological and ecclesiastical problems. So his advance could not stop in this first explanation. Under stress of the serious and insurmountable difficulties which it involved, as already indicated, and its further assumption of an almost infallible efficacy for vicarious prayers, attributing to them a kind of *ex opere operato*

Milton Valentine

force, Luther modified his position so far as to "turn over to the doctors the question whether the infant personally believes before or in Baptism, and to declare: We do not baptize upon that, but solely upon the command of God." He surrendered the idea that unless we can prove that the child has faith, we should not baptize it, and that its baptism cannot benefit. Baptism has its place, authority, and validity by virtue of Christ's command. So "Baptism is genuine though faith be wanting." "Therefore, let it be decided that Baptism always remains true, retains its full nature, even though a person should be baptized and yet not truly believe." Though the child may not believe at the time, Baptism, nevertheless, establishes God's own covenant of faith and grace, for the use of faith whenever it is awakened through the Word and Holy Spirit, and abides in its validity and force as a means of grace through the whole Christian life. This modification is of paramount significance. It frees the administration of infant baptism from the demand that the child shall be regarded as a believer before its reception. It turns the view away from that question and rests it on God's word of command. Baptism is thus recognized as a means of grace rightly administered, as we have already seen, under the terms of the "everlasting covenant"—to the believer and his "seed"—in harmony with the essential faith of the Church in the past. Sartorius states the truth correctly: "We baptize, not because there is faith [in the infant] but that there may be faith."

Though some Lutheran dogmaticians have chosen to accept Luther's earlier teaching, infant-faith, either as a pre-condition for Baptism or as an immediately produced effect of its administration, forms no essential or even consistent part of Lutheran confessional theology, and has been increasingly disappearing from the teaching of its theologians. The full proportions of the negative judgment deserve to be understood. For fifteen centuries of Christianity the doctrine found no place in the creeds or conciliar deliverances of the Roman or Greek Church, and their exegesis was against it. It is not in any of the Protestant Confessions. It is not in the Augsburg Confession, nor in the Apology, the Small Catechism, the Smalcald Articles, nor the Form of Concord. It is only in the Large Catechism, and there only in such a way as places it outside of confessional requirement and surrenders it as the basis of the administration of the Sacrament. Dr. Plitt, of Erlangen, an authority on confessional theology, says: "Child-faith is not a symbolical doctrine." The master dogmatician, Gerhard, wrote: "Infants do not by birth bring with

Christian Theology

them faith to Baptism."[3] Dr. Frank, of Erlangen: "It is foolish to inquire for a faith which children must bring with them to Baptism, which, perchance, might be bestowed upon them through the word or through the prayers of the sponsors or the intercessions of the Church. All such things are figments, arising from a false application of a correct principle." The late Dr. Luthardt, of Leipzig, so strenuous a confessional theologian, says: "When our children are baptized they know nothing of the transaction; for their mental life is still lying in that dreary slumber from which it only gradually awakens. They have no consciousness of what takes place at their Baptism, for they have as yet no consciousness at all."[2] This expresses what has come to be the prevalent view as to pre-baptismal infant faith.

And further, a supposed infant faith as the immediate product of the Sacrament's administration is equally at strife with the psychological possibilities and theological consistency. For the psychological incompetence is the same. The subject is still an unconscious babe. This fact was the sole basis for the long centuries of the Church's denial of such faith. By very reason of the infant's unconscious condition it was unable to "believe unto righteousness," or to believe anything—whether before Baptism or immediately after. In their whole manner of writing of the matter the theologians of the Church never for a moment limited the recognized impossibility to the period before Baptism. For it is still true that faith must have an object, a truth discerned, a promise understood, a Savior apprehended. To credit this intelligent apprehension to infants in Baptism is too absurd to be thought of when not a single faculty of the understanding has yet awakened; when, by consent of all, they know nothing of what has been done to them. Faith, indeed, "comes by hearing"; but the nursling does not hear in the sense of any mental or moral act; and to imply, as has been done, that the mere resounding vibrations of air on the ears, without any more meaning to its mind than the murmurings of the forest winds or the noise of the cataract, is efficient as a faith-begetting hearing, is a degradation of the whole working to the absurdity of magic or incantation. To suppose that the Holy Spirit uses the "Word"—whether "audible or visible"—in that way, is without the least warrant of Scripture. It was through Timothy's "knowledge of the Scriptures" from his childhood that the faith of his grandmother was wrought in his heart. The attempt thus to apply the Protestant principle of the Spirit's working "faith through the Word" wholly

Milton Valentine

misses the mark. This failure throws the doctrine back into the rejected and blighting Roman invention of the *opus operation* action of sacramental administration, with the added peculiarity of incredibility that the *opus operatum* effects a human *act*—for the exercise of faith *is* such—and one whose constituents are knowledge, assent, and voluntary trust It is, indeed, a surprising feature in this contention for infant-faith, that it is ready to fall back on the discarded Romish *opus operatum*. And still further, in many writers it has dislocated the order of salvation, and placed "regeneration" before "justification." For it is to "baptismal *regeneration*" that they have turned for an explanation of the divine work that creates the supposed faith—a work which, it is thus assumed, *regenerates*, not only before justification, but before faith, and in order to confer faith. This order thus clashes with the primacy of faith and justification with respect to regeneration, as unmistakably fixed and held controlling in the theology of Luther, Melanchthon, and the Confessions. Because of these and other inconsistencies, it is no wonder that a large proportion of our modern conservative and confessional theologians have rejected this claim of infant-faith, and hold that while Baptism rightly belongs to children of believers, and seals to them the covenant of faith, the beginning of actual personal faith comes later, when the developed faculties of understanding and consent make the Spirit's working of it possible through the Word.

1. Clearly, then, under this view of their Baptism, its first effect is to give them the status of accepted subjects of grace, a state of sealed acceptance with God in and through Jesus Christ. This is a state of *forgiveness*, of being taken into the divine favor, as provided in the vicarious atonement and perfect righteousness of Jesus Christ, and under the influence of the grace of the Holy Spirit. It confers what theology defines as "justification "and adoption. It thus assures the safety or salvation of its subject should death call hence before the period of personal responsibility is reached. Nevertheless, it has a normal significance looking especially to the full realization of the grace of personal faith and the regenerate life of piety and holiness of adult years.

2. Further, it effects *membership in the Church*, identifies with the body of believers, gives a place within the fellowship of faith and Christian obedience. This is of deep and vast import. For it has vital relations that explain and justify it. The birth of the children from Christian parentage constitutes them naturally, or ac cording to divine order, a part of the *Church's population*, life of its life, to be

Christian Theology

carefully and formally recognized and made participant in its covenant blessings. This is the explaining philosophy of infant baptism to which normally the offspring of believers alone have access. And its peculiar office is to unify the family life, as well as the Church organism, and to hold the Church's infant population true to its inheritance of faith and give effective training into it. It is an infinitely wise and beneficent order for holding the Church's own children within the fellowship of salvation and nurture in the Gospel, which is the Holy Spirit's means for saving faith and all the fruits of the new life.

3. As still further explanatory, answer needs to be given to several questions:

(*a*) May the child be said to be *regenerated* by the act of Baptism? We may properly answer, Yes; but only in the sense that the established vital and grace-conveying relation, under imputed righteousness and the Holy Spirit, may be said to hold, in its provisions and forces, the final covenanted development. The given relation, if not broken, insures the covenanted effect. But, often on the human side it is wretchedly broken. Thus, since the Baptism marks, not as yet the final issue, but rather the point from which the divine grace *begins* to act for the whole Christian life, the human breaking of the covenant—by failure of the pledged teaching and nurture, or by refusal of the baptized, when grown, to accept Christ—results, as experience sadly proves, in complete failure of the regenerate life. Regeneration is fully provided for, but the actuality can come only in the time and order of the ongoing process—the personal faith coming only by hearing the word of the Gospel and the acceptance of the provided enabling grace and new life. The faith and regeneration are there at first in the *potency* of established means, to be realized in the future—*putatively* made the child's by its covenant state. If the full regeneration of adults is admitted to be "necessarily gradual and progressive," from the impediments to be overcome, with what reason can we deny the necessity of waiting, in unconscious infants, for faith and its fruits of love and sanctification?

(*b*) Should we speak, then, of *regenerating* children by Baptism? We must answer, No; for though there is thus a sense in which such expression may stand for truth—and even the phrase "baptismal regeneration"—it is almost inevitably misleading to the common mind. For to the popular understanding the word means no such modified conception, but the actual change of heart, through faith.

Milton Valentine

We believe it to be a serious error, perverting the doctrine of the Scriptures and our Church when some dogmaticians, despite disclaimer of *opus operatum* doctrine, assert regeneration unqualifiedly as a *fait accompli* by the act of Baptism, instead of regarding it as establishing the covenant relations and forces from which the actual renewal and the whole Christian life proceeds, according to the means and order of grace. The representation is sometimes shaped into physical and magical conceptions irreconcilable with all that the Scriptures teach of the mode in which God acts on rational natures and moral agents for faith and obedience—leading to gross conceptions, as the implantation of a germ, a magical alteration of the substance of the soul or a direct "infusion "of a "*habitude*," akin to the Roman claim. The misguiding and blighting consequence under this idea that the regenerating change has already been effected, has been and is that the *teaching* of the saving truth, the requisite "nurture and admonition of the Lord "which furnish the Holy Spirit's means of working faith and regeneration, are neglected, and the Church's children never come to conversion. Later Lutheran theology has been justly protesting against this immediacy of baptismal faith and renewal as untrue to the real doctrine of the Church—an element alien to its fundamental principles. Dr. C P. Krauth, referring to the common understanding of baptismal regeneration, says that" such baptismal regeneration is not the teaching of our Church."

(c) Are the baptized children to be accounted as believers and members of the Church? Their membership in the visible Church is at once real and complete; and they are accordingly to be numbered as believers (*fideles*) sealed by the Sacrament of faith. They are certainly not "without" (1 Cor. 5:12) but *in* the fellowship of the Church's life, whatever that may be. As to counting them as "believers," this follows from the fact that the Church is properly "the congregation of believers," of which they are members. But the counting must still be under reservation of the truth that there may be some members, both adults and children, falling below the spiritual import of the Church covenant.

As this subject is one of great practical importance, it seems best to conclude its presentation with a brief epitome of the determining features of the doctrine as clearly reflected from the Scriptures.

1. The explaining basis of infant baptism is found in the light of the divine covenant of faith and salvation, which, from its very beginning, included children equally with their parents. Dr. Krauth

Christian Theology

has well said: "Divine covenants do not require consciousness and intelligence on the part of all whom they embrace. On the contrary, they embrace not only infants, but prospectively generations unborn, as, for example, the covenant with Abraham and his seed after him, sealed by the sacrament of circumcision," This original covenant is the very one under which Baptism, taking the place of circumcision, is administered to children now. It is the "everlasting covenant" for the unification and fellowship of God's people (Rom. 4:1-17; Gal. 3:6-9; Col. 2:10-12; Acts 2:39). It is the Church's charter for infant membership and the application of its sealing Sacrament.

2. This covenant, being a covenant of grace, makes the reach of that grace include also the believer's off spring during the whole unconscious period, or until developed into capacity for intelligence, choice, and responsibility. To faith, the covenant assures not simply the individual parent's salvation, but the safety in covenant adoption of his children: "The promise is to you and your children"—at least until these children refuse and break the gracious relation. God has organized the family in unity, and adjusted the scope and powers of covenant grace to this unity. He respects the solidarity of the family life, as He Himself has constituted it—not a number of individuals cast together, but an organic circle of life, at basis physical, but also moral and spiritual. And the grace of the covenant comprehends not simply the parents but the children also. The great error and wrong of many on this whole subject is in a one-sided individualism, their utter obliviousness of the divinely-constituted solidarity of the family. They disrupt and destroy the oneness of the family organization, obliterate its principles of cohesion, order, duty, and responsibility.

3. Infants, though unconscious of anything done to them, are not baptized in disregard of the *principle of faith*, or its necessity in the order of covenant grace and salvation. If the teaching of Protestantism is that "not the Sacrament, but the faith of the Sacrament justifies," it is met in the fact that the parental faith is by the covenant reality the faith of the *family organism*. The family life is held in its unity till childhood emerges into distinct personal self-direction; and the *faith* also of that family unity acts for it, and is required to act for it through that period. The parental faith, as in the Old Testament sacrament of circumcision, brings the child to Baptism, and represents it there, not as a fiction but in sacred reality. As to the child's physical preservation and development the parental life is in full charge, with solemn responsibility. As to its spiritual

life and development the same law holds. This life and development God submits to the care and guidance of the faith that dwells in the parental life. The matrix of the parental life and faith holds the whole infant life and development till the age of independent, self-determining personality is reached. And when the parental faith brings the child to Baptism, it is not baptized without the very faith which has been, in the Church's charter, divinely empowered and charged to act for it, and through which grace comes to it. The child is not, indeed, in spiritual reality a child of God by natural birth, but passes into this position or relation by virtue of the sealed covenant, and the scope over which the parental *faith* is empowered to act for it; and thus it becomes a sealed "heir according to the promise." God covenants with and for the child through the parental life.

4. While the child is thus not baptized "without faith," it is yet not baptized indefinitely on "the faith of another." It is not after the notion of a common "vicarious faith," *i. e.*, of "an other," in unqualified sense. The "other" is definite, restricted, *parental*—to which, on the basis of the unity of the family constitution, God gives peculiar office and responsibilities. It is distinctly to *this* faith that God commits the charge and keeping of the children, and demands the sealing of covenant grace. This is God's gracious plan for the spiritual life and salvation of the children of the Church. It is well put by Dr. Kurtz, the Lutheran historian, of Dorpat: "The will of the parents is unconditionally the will of the young child. And the faith of the parents is the faith of the child which has not yet come to self-conscious independent personality."

5. The design of this order of the covenant is not simply that God may hold as His own the unconscious little ones of His Church, under sealed acceptance and adoption in Christ, but also and especially insure to them faithful teaching of the full gospel of salvation, the appointed "nurture and admonition of the Lord," that under the Holy Spirit through the Word, they may come, in due time and fully, to true personal faith and the regenerate life. This descent of the parental faith into the child's faith is thus sacramentally provided for, exhibiting both the supreme divine purpose of the Sacrament and its practical adaptations and significance.

THE LORD'S SUPPER

Of the two Sacraments instituted by Christ this was the first appointed, though it follows Baptism in the order of its use. A

Christian Theology

proper understanding of it requires distinct consideration of three things: its Form, Design, and Theoretic Doctrine.

THE FORM OF IT

In generic designation, the Lord's Supper is that Sacrament or rite in which by the institution and word of Christ, bread and wine are made to believers the "communion of His body and blood" and a memorial and pledge of His redeeming love. Besides the designation, "Lord's Supper" (1 Cor. 11:20), it is called "The Lord's Table" (1 Cor. 10:21), "The Communion" (1 Cor. 10:16), and in ecclesiastical terminology also the "Eucharist," and "Sacrament of the Altar." Its complete form involves:

1. *The elements of bread and wine.* No particular condition of either is specified. Though the bread used at the institution was unleavened, no word of limitation to this, as an incidental feature in the Passover table, appears in any Scripture. On the contrary, the accounts of its apostolic-day observance (Acts 2:42; 20:7; 1 Cor. 10:16–17; 11:20–29) rather suggest ordinary bread. By general consent, unleavened bread is not necessary. With respect to the wine, the Scriptures make no specification as to any particular state or quality of it, simply designating it as "the fruit of the vine" (το γενήμα τῆς αμπελου) (Matt. 26:29), and by use of the "cup" indicating it as the *liquor* of the grape. The question whether it be fermented or unfermented is not vital. The fact determining this is that, in the Biblical use, the fresh or only slightly fermented juice of the grape is truly "wine," as well as the fermented. This is proved by the application of the Hebrew word *Tirosh* in the Old Testament, and its translation by the Seventy in the Septuagint. This word is found employed thirty-eight times. As an agricultural term, its use is closely connected with the field and the vintage. *Tirosh* is represented in all stages, in the cluster, gathering, trodden in wine-vat, bursting out in overflow, put in store-house, tithed in first fruits as "new wine." It cannot be positively proved, in a single instance, to designate intoxicating wine, though one passage is claimed to do so. In liquid form it was the fresh juice of the grape. That in Biblical sense and usage it was "wine," is rendered unquestionable by the very best authority to which exegesis can appeal—the Septuagint translation. This was made about two hundred years before Christ by Hellenist Jews, masters alike of both the Hebrew and Greek, knowing both what *Tirosh* meant and the proper Greek term to

Milton Valentine

express it—early enough in Jewish history to assure the Hebrew usage, and late enough to connect that usage with Christ's own day. To the question: Is grape juice, unfermented or in only initially fermented condition, "wine"? they answer with an unqualified Yes, and proceed to render it thirty-six times out of the thirty-eight by the term οἶνος, "wine," making this word cover the unfermented, as well as the fermented state. And this is in full accord with a note in earlier usage, from the days of Jewish contact with Egyptian life. In the narrative of the butler's dream the wine to be drunk was expressed directly from the cluster into Pharaoh's cup, clearly implying that grape juice fresh from the bunch was used as "wine." This corresponds, too, with the New Testament *usus loquendi* in which "new wine" is called "wine" (γελεῦκος, ὄνος νέος), (Matt. 9:17; Mark 2:22; Luke 5:37; Acts 2:13). In harmony with all this, moreover, is the fact that in the Vulgate translation of the Old Testament, Jerome, famous for his scholarly attainments, translates the Hebrew *Tirosh* with the Latin *vinum* thirty-two times.

2. *The words of its institution* (Matt. 26:26–28; Mark 14:22–24; Luke 22:19–20; 1 Cor. 11:23–26). The use of these is the true and only "consecration" of the elements—the continuing power of the first ordinance, a consecration in which by the force of divine appointment "the Word is added to the elements and they become a Sacrament." The consecratory efficacy is not of human will, or prayer of minister, but of the divine Word appropriating the offered material actually used in administration. The consecration effects no change in the essence or nature of the elements, and parts that may remain after communion are the same as before.

3. *The distribution and partaking* of the elements, thus set apart for the present need. Both these are essential to it; for it is not a Sacrament apart from communication and reception.

These three things, therefore, constitute the full form of the Lord's Supper. If any of these be wanting, say, when the "cup" is withheld from the laity, it is a mutilation of the ordinance—a mutilation not justified by the explanation offered for it by the Council of Trent. The question, however, of the distribution and reception of the wine, whether through one common cup or by a different cup, does not seem to affect the integrity of the Sacrament. For in either case, the elements being distributed and received, the form is complete. It is not an identity of vessel that forms the reality administered and received, but "the fruit of the vine," which is divinely made "the communion of the blood of Christ."

Christian Theology

ITS DESIGN

In generic purpose, the Lord's Supper, manifestly, was to provide an auxiliary form of the means of grace, helpful for quickening faith and the life of holy love. But the generic aim includes a number of specific intentions concurrent and convergent for reaching that aim. These appear from the circumstances and terms of the institution, and from apostolic explanation.

1. It was evidently meant to supersede the Old Testament Passover rite. This purpose is suggested by the time, place, and surroundings of its institution, and made certain by 1 Cor. 5:7: "For Christ our Passover (τό πάσχα, paschal Lamb) is slain for us; wherefore let us keep the feast," etc. Freeing the Church from the ordinance of the Jewish dispensation, which was being then fulfilled in His atoning death, He appointed a grace-bearing Sacrament to supersede the old typical ceremony. The designation of it as "the new covenant" (ἡ καινὴ διαθήκη) has its explanation in the *actual* blood-shedding of Christ, this furnishing the active efficiency *(activa causa)*, turning the typical promise into complete provision and assurance of salvation.

2. It is intended to be *mnemonic* of Christ, particularly of His sacrificial and redeeming work. "Do this in remembrance of Me" is the command in connection with the reception of both the bread and the cup. There can be no question of the memorial purpose of the Supper. As a "visible Word," issued from a most impressive and appealing hour, it is meant to remind vividly of His self-offering to death for men, and of the treasures of love and prepared grace in Him.

3. It is meant to be *confessional and declarative*. Its reception is intended to be an act making confession of Him as Redeemer and Savior. "For as often as ye eat this bread and drink this cup, ye do show forth the Lord's death, till He come" (1 Cor. 11:26). The word is καταγγέλλετε: "Ye proclaim your acceptance of His death for you."

4. It is designed to be an *individualized assurance, pledge, and seal to believers of the remission of sin*. Of the "cup" as the new testament (covenant) in His blood, the blessing distinctly named is: "Shed for you for the remission of sins." In accordance with the characteristic of a Sacrament as a sacred act which God transacts with us, not one in which we make an offering to Him, the Supper is God's most assuring call or appeal to "believe in the forgiveness of sins."

5. It is also meant to be a *manifestation and bond of union* among all true believers. They are through it joined together in one fellowship, one communion, "one body," as the apostle says: "For we are all partakers of that one bread" (1 Cor. 10:17). It thus becomes a church fellowship.

6. It is designed, moreover, to be *a communion of the body and blood of Christ*. (1 Cor. 10:16): "The cup of blessing which we bless, is it not the communion of the blood of Christ? The bread which we break, is it not the communion of the body of Christ?" The word, κοινωνία, means "fellowship" or "participation"; and such the cup and bread can be only by being communicative, in some true sense, of that in which the κοινωνία or communion is declared. In what sense we are to understand the "body" and the "blood," and the communion or participation of them through the bread and cup, belongs to the special doctrine of the Supper.

No one of these clearly marked features of the ordinance can properly be left out of view, nor any one pushed into an exclusive prominence. Here has come the bane in different dogmatic tendencies. Zwinglianism has resolved this means of grace almost entirely into a mere mnemonic, a decorous commemoration. Romanism has resolved it into a literal communication of the body and blood of Christ, counted as an ever-fresh atonement for sin. Some in our own Church, under their antagonism to Zwinglianism, have seemed to underrate all parts of its intention but the mystery of the communion of "the body and blood," exhibiting a one-sidedness untrue to the doctrine in its symmetrical integrity and power. As a means of grace, *all* elements of its aim and adaptations must be fully recognized and held convergent in spiritual efficacy.

It is hardly needful to add that we do not include in the design the suggestion of some speculative theologians who, on the basis of a distinction between food for "the body," and for "the spirit," have viewed the sacramental reception of Christ's body as providing the necessary germ for the believer's resurrection body. There is no word of Scripture teaching such a relation. On the contrary, the quickening of the mortal body is distinctly connected by St. Paul (Rom. 8:11) with the power and working of the Holy Spirit in men, giving again the true, holy life of the soul (Christ in believers) through the means of grace generically, and thus preparing for Christ's special resurrection action for the body.

The principle is fundamental that the Gospel first of all aims at the spirit-side of man, and only through it at transforming also the

Christian Theology

physical side into conformity with Christ's holy human nature. This accords, too, with the fact that the primary means of grace, namely, the Word preached or read, as truly as the secondary or sacramental, comes to man in a sensuous form, audible or visible. It would not be either Scriptural or commendable to create an impression that the Sacraments, in distinction from the Word, act directly, either only or peculiarly, for the redemption of the physical nature. This would lead back to the *opus operatum*, a process not requiring spiritual faith.

SPECIFIC DOCTRINE OF THE COMMUNION

The crucial point of this inquiry is: How we are to understand the declarations of Christ: "This is My body," "This is My blood." The differing interpretations of these words began to appear in the early Church, and have been specially divisive for Christendom almost from its beginning. For the progress and conflicts of thought, the student must be referred to the Histories of Doctrine. It will suffice for the present inquiry to recall the four distinct views in the modern and present Church as to the words of the institution and the presence of Christ in the Holy Supper.

1. *The Roman Catholic doctrine of transubstantiation.* This is that by the act of priestly consecration, the whole substance of the bread and wine is changed into the very body and blood of Jesus Christ, only the sensible qualities remaining; the whole Christ—body, soul, and Divinity—being contained under each species [*i. e.*, bread and wine], and under every part of each species, when separated. The transubstantiation is affirmed at the very moment of the consecration, and the "Sacrament" is held as being the body and blood, or the whole Christ, not only in the act of its reception, but also before and in parts that may remain. This view underlies the "worship" (*latria*) claimed and given to the consecrated elements in the elevation of the "host" and processional adoration.

This doctrine found germinal suggestion in several writers of the early Church, appeared in Radbertus of the ninth century, Lanfranc of the eleventh, and was adopted by the Lateran Council under Innocent III., in 1215, and set forth in full as the doctrine of the Roman Church by the Council of Trent. Protestantism found in this and its abuses some of the compelling necessities of the Reformation. But, unanimous in renouncing the error, minor differences arose in interpreting the Scripture teaching on the subject.

2. *The Zwinglian interpretation.* This makes the bread and wine mere *memorials* of the redemptive love and sufferings of Christ. There is no peculiar presence of Christ, nor any influence exerted by the Sacrament except by and through the truths thus symbolically expressed. The emphasis thus placed upon the symbolical import and value of the Sacrament, while excluding this interpretation from large confessional adoption, has nevertheless widely influenced individual views in many Churches.

3. *The Calvinistic view* holds, under some modifications, the symbolical conception of Zwingli, but unites with it elements which form the Sacrament into a means whereby "worthy believers do inwardly by faith, really and indeed, yet not carnally or corporeally, but spiritually receive and feed upon Christ crucified, and all the benefits of His death." It teaches that the glorified Christ remains in heaven, but becomes *efficaciously* present through the Holy Spirit, who communicates to the true believer the benefits of the atoning sacrifice. It includes these points: (*a*) That Christ's human nature is in heaven only, (*b*) His presence, or the presence of His body and blood, is purely spiritual, through the Holy Spirit's elevating the soul to an apprehension of Him. (*c*) That what the believer feeds on in the Supper is not the body and blood of Christ, but the virtue of them as given and shed for sin. (*d*) This feeding is by faith alone. (*e*) That the efficacy is *mediated*, not by the "body and blood," as in any way *present*, but by the Holy Ghost. (*f*) That the feeding, as upon the body and blood, is not confined to the Sacrament, but takes place whenever faith in Christ is exercised. This doctrine is the substance of the *Consensus Tigurinus*, drawn up by Calvin in 1549, to unite the Zwinglian and Calvinistic views, and was accepted as the consensus of the Reformed Churches.

4. *The Lutheran view*, in general statement, teaches that while the elements, bread and wine, remain unchanged, they really and without figure become the communion of the body and blood of Christ glorified after a supernatural, divine, and heavenly mode of presence, union, and communication to the communicants. It regards the *mode* of the presence as an inscrutable mystery, and only insists on recognition of the supernatural, divine fact, as a fact for our faith. Somewhat different theoretical explications appear from the first, a more thorough literalism of expression marking Luther's tendency, and less that of Melanchthon, and their

respective personal following. Divergencies increased among the dogmaticians. After accepting the truth of a real presence, as over against Zwingli's purely memorialistic interpretation on the one hand and Rome's teaching of transubstantiation on the other, it is not necessary to take all the many, and not always consistent, conceptions and definitions developed by the dogmaticians, as essential parts of the Lutheran doctrine. They are but human attempts to explain and defend the divine mystery; and not unfrequently they have drawn pictures in which the divine reality would, probably, not be able to recognize its true self. Yet the long discussion and exegetical endeavor have been serviceable in the interest of a real understanding.

The *primary norm* for the doctrine, it is rightly maintained, is to be found in the words of the institution, and such other Scriptural declarations as stand in express connection with this Sacrament, rather than in passages in which only verbal similarities may be found, which may be supposed to contain elucidation. This rule allows only secondary and indirect use of Christ's Capernaum discourse (John 6:26-63). Yet in this auxiliary way it seems entitled to be of force. But exegesis must find, if possible, the actual sense or thought of Christ, as it stood in His view and meaning in instituting the ordinance. His thought, unquestionably, was definite and distinct; yet the emotional glow of conception and picturesque brevity of expression have given a total of truth difficult for exact explication. Of course, concurrently with it, the necessary relations and bearing of other redemptory and vital truths, from Christ's own and apostolic teaching, must be collated and the "analogy of the faith" be given proper weight. Peculiarly close to the true explication are the great doctrines of justification by faith alone and the divine-human Person of Christ. From the one, the true nature of a "means of grace" sheds guiding and determining light; from the other, the possibilities of the administrative presence of the glorified Christ at His will may be conceived and trusted. By the former—from the side of the application of the redemptive provision—the Romish misconstructions of the Eucharist are excluded. By the latter—from the side of the divine making of the provision—the redeeming Christ who, by giving Himself through broken "body" and shed "blood," completed a full propitiation once for all and for the whole world, is seen to be, in His glorified state, forever the God-man, whose possession and exercise of the properties of both the divine and human natures enables Him, at His will, to be present with His people in the wholeness of His divine-human Person. Though in the way of a visible, tangible, localized presence, perceptible to the senses, He has, in His glorification, ascended and left the world, and is not here in that mode; yet in another mode, glorified, supernatural, and divine, by virtue of His eternal Deity, He is, or can be, present with believers everywhere in the completeness of His theanthropic Person. "Lo, I am with you always" (Matt 28:20). "Where two or three are gathered together in My name, there am I in the midst of them" (Matt 18:20). Christ's ascension to "the right hand of God" does not mean absence, but a rising above the limitations of restrictive space—"far above all heavens," declares St Paul, "that He might fill all things" (Eph. 4:10). Yet, by reason of the "indivisible union" of the divine and human natures in the unity of His person, He cannot be thought of as giving His "body and blood," *i. e.*, His Humanity, separate from His Divinity, in the Supper, as some dogmaticians have defined it. Such restriction to the "body and blood"—or even the whole humanity—would introduce a Nestorian separableness between the two natures—a divisive action inconsistent with the permanent union of them in the glorified Christ. It seems hardly consistent to begin with the fundamental doctrine of the *communicatio idiomatum*, in a form approaching the Eutychian confusion, and then, when the Divine Nature has carried the human into omnipresence, to assert a separation which imparts body and blood alone, as by Quenstedt and Hollaz. Moreover, Christ's own language allows no such division of Himself; for, speaking to the Father concerning His disciples, He says: "*I* in them, and Thou in Me" (John 17:23), and even when using the particularistic forms of expression in John 6:57, He adds the comprehensive declaration: "He that eateth *Me* shall live by Me."

Hence our logically consistent dogmaticians have represented the supernatural "presence" in the eucharist as the presence of Christ in His whole theanthropic Person, in Self-Presence and Self-communication to His people. Luther himself maintained the real presence of Christ Himself. Our modern theologians are rightly calling attention to the necessary bearing of this upon the self-consistent structure of the eucharistic conception. Martensen says: "He is present wholly and entirely *(totus et integer)* in His Supper, where. He in an especial manner *wills* to be. The sacramental communion is not a partaking of the corporeal nature of Christ apart from His spiritual nature; no more is it a mere partaking of His spiritual nature apart from His corporeity." "We believe that the whole and undivided Christ gives Himself as the aliment of the new man in the Lord's Supper." And he adds: "In His gifts, He gives Himself. Take, eat, drink, this is I; in this I give you what is *the innermost power of life in Myself.*" So Sartorius: "For bread and wine truly communicate and appropriate to us the *Christ* who was sacrificed for us." Also Luthardt, of Leipzig, recognized leader in confessional theology, says: "He who gave His body to death for us, who died upon the cross for us, now lives in heaven, in glorified human nature. He is risen, He is gone to heaven, and has promised, 'Lo, I am with you alway, even to the end of the world.' He does not merely send His Spirit; He will Himself also be present with us. He, the same Jesus who once walked upon earth, who once died upon the cross, and now sits at the right hand of God and is ever near His people,—He, the Son of Man, the exalted Savior, will be with us and *impart Himself* to us in the way of communion. We do not stand in merely spiritual, but in complete communion with Him." This impartation is His own act, not the minister's; and is co-incident with the reception of the elements.

Further evidence that this truth presents the correct guidance into the true conception of the "real presence" in the Supper appears from the concession by the dogmaticians that the literal eating and drinking of the literal "body and blood" in and through the bread and cup, apart from a 'spiritual reception by act of *faith*,' is, in itself, not only of *no saving value and without benefit, but "injurious,"* drawing *"judgment."* The Form of Concord says: "The *spiritual* manducation is useful and salutary in itself, and necessary to the salvation of all Christians in all ages, without which spiritual participation the sacramental manducation, that which occurs with the mouth only, is not only not salutary, but prejudicial also, and is a cause of condemnation." The spiritual eating by faith is thus represented as receiving all the benefits which Christ procured for us by His body and blood given to death for us—"the grace and mercy of God, the forgiveness of sins, and eternal life." Hollaz, among other things, thus explains the difference between the eating by faith and the sacramental manducation: "The former always contributes to our salvation; the latter sometimes may be done to our condemnation; the former apprehends the whole Christ, with all His benefits; the latter apprehends only the body of Christ in and under the bread." Does not this concession show the urgency for the oral or corporeal reception to be at least a misplaced emphasis in ideating the realities of the Sacrament? The strenuous insistence on it as the chief essential reality is hardly justified, in face of the admitted fact that there is no real necessity for it *per se;* that in itself, *without the spiritual reception at the same time*, it is inefficacious and damaging. The vital need in the sacramental doctrine is to lay the controlling stress on the spiritual reception of Christ through faith. *No grace* is received through either Word or Sacrament except through this. And he who thus receives Christ realizes in Him *all* grace.

This recognition of the truth that Christ in His whole Divine-human Person is present in the Supper, where He specially wills to be, thus suggests the possibility that there may have been no real necessity for the various *expedients to explain and assure* a literal or oral reception. We are reminded of the efforts to prove or show it in varied ways—from the literal force of the copula "is" (ἔστι) connecting subject and predicate in the words of institution; by claiming "this" (τοῦτο) to be synecdochical, the 'container for the thing contained'; by use of "in, with, and under" as locating the "illocal presence," and yet as meaning no one or all of these prepositions to be really definitive of the presence, but only asserting its reality; and by acute distinctions between an "absolute" and "relative," or "voli" or "multivoli" ubiquity. These methods of support or elucidation, which have been, or some of them, increasingly abandoned among our most prominent confessional theologians, have been, perhaps, more successful in continuing the controversy than settling it. But when the eucharistic Presence is clearly recognized as that of the glorified Christ Himself, it is at once divested of the incongruities and troubles connected with effort to think it under the materialistic and limiting terms of natural "flesh" and "blood," and the equally limiting acts of "oral" eating and drinking. By such recognition both the "presence" and "reception "are at once lifted above the naturalistic modes, and transferred to the generic and acknowledged reality of the mystery of the exalted Redeemer's omnipresence and bestowal of the gifts of His grace.

At this point, therefore, the positive evidence results in establishing a *definitive* or *special* presence under the generic *omnipresence of Christ according to both natures*. As orthodox Christology has always maintained, His human nature is not separated from the Divine, and the human is present according to the mode and power in which it is *made* present by its union with His Divinity. Such "special" presence is conceivable. For example, the omnipresent Spirit descended on Christ (Matt 3:16); came as a special breathing on the disciples (John 20:22); on the apostles as tongues of fire (Acts 2:3); and dwells peculiarly in believers as temples (1 Cor. 3:16). So the Omnipresent Savior may give a special sacramental presence. Through His omnipresence wherever He wills, the bread and wine are made the appointed media to His people of a special real "communion" with Himself, not as an *absent*, but *present* Christ and Savior. He fills these elements with His pervasive presence, with His glorified human nature as well as with the divine, making them the vehicles for His self-impartation in the fullness of His atoning self-sacrifice. This truth becomes *explanatory* and *defining* for the mode of communication and reception in the Supper.

But this recognition of the truth that the eucharistic Presence is that of the glorified Christ, together with the inferior necessity and value of the "oral" reception already noticed, makes it proper to give attention to another truth which modern theologians recognize as entitled to a very influential bearing. This is the Divine teleology of the redemptive aim and plan. The redemptive plan embraces the use of means for ends. This relation of means and ends must be fully recognized, and its bearing interpreted into the doctrine of the Supper. The doctrine must be explained in the light and order of the redemptive love. The incarnation itself, the Father's gift of the Son to the world, Christ's ministry of teaching, and peculiarly the specific work of giving His "body and blood" as a sin-offering, were not for their own sakes, or themselves the goal of God's seeking, but for human salvation (John 3:16). In giving His life a "ransom," it was for the sake of the "many" to be restored to God, "that they might have life and have it more abundantly" (Matt 20:28; John 10:10). He came to make Himself a bloody sin-offering to open the possibility of forgiveness of sin and all the grace of a spiritual and eternal salvation. The redemptive teleology is sublime in its loving, self-sacrificing purpose—to provide forgiveness and the powers of holy life. This principle is supreme, and reveals the "final cause" of the whole redemptive work and the ordained means of its application or bestowal. The "final cause" is often justly recognized as being, at the same time, the "efficient" cause, by being in reality the point whence moves the power which works out the intended end. The teleology of the Lord's Supper is unmistakable, and its bearing must not be neglected or refused full force in the theoretical doctrine. The institution of the Supper as a means for application of the redemptive provision wrought once for all through the body and

Milton Valentine

blood of Christ, cannot justly be held as having its *ruling* aim in anything short of the very essence of blessing to which the finished provision looked, *i. e.*, the forgiveness of sin, the inspiration of faith and love, and the new life of obedience. The standpoint of view in the Sacrament is that the provision of gracious salvation has been completed in the very gift of the Redeemer's "body and blood" to which the words of institution pointed. That gift has been made once for all on the cross. As a means of grace the Sacrament could aim supremely at nothing short of the spiritual realities which actualize the final aim of the accomplished redemptive provision. To the conferring of these spiritual blessings, as the gifts to which all the gifts of God's atoning provision looked, this Sacrament is, acknowledgedly, consecrated. This aim is, confessedly, so controlling for the divine constitution of the ordinance, that it is conceded that the communicant who does not possess the spiritual faith to apprehend and make it his own, receives the Sacrament in vain. It, therefore, subordinates everything else in the sacramental purpose and constitution. So it should help to determine the place of emphasis in its doctrinal formulation. Between holding the bread and wine to be carriers of the "true natural body and blood of Christ" in literal sense for the communicant's literal eating; and holding them as "signs" also to bring to remembrance Christ's atoning offering of Himself on the cross for faith's inspiration and acceptance, the latter takes superior importance. For while the former kind of reception alone is really non-recipient of saving grace, the latter, by spiritual faith through the Word—whether through Word heard or visible, or both—receives all the grace of salvation. The teleology, therefore, of the whole redemptive work of preparing salvation for the acceptance of man, to which the Sacrament as a means of grace is divinely adjusted, requires that the making of its doctrinal formulation, abating stress upon reception of the natural body and blood, should show not only the ruling importance of the presence of the glorified Lord Himself and reception of Him through spiritual faith, but distinctly define the gift or gifts of grace conferred as the very blessings of the actual and actualizing salvation for which He gave His body and blood to crucifixion.

As example of the tendency among our recent theologians in this direction, to which reference has already been made, we quote the conclusion reached by a most prominent confessional Lutheran, Dr. Kahnis. In an earlier discussion of the Supper (1851) he had

Christian Theology

drawn the doctrine in strong type of the earlier dogmatics. In his "Dogmatik," ten years later, he says: "The Supper is the medium of imparting to the believing communicant, in bread and wine, *the atoning efficacy of the body and blood of Christ that have been sacrificed for us*, which atoning efficacy places him to whom it is imparted in mysterious fellowship with the body of Christ." And a little more fully on a later page: "The Lord's Supper is the Sacrament of the altar which, in the form of bread and wine, the symbols of the body and blood of Christ which have been sacrificed for us, imparts to the believing communicant the *sin-forgiving efficacy* of Christ's death." This presentation not only holds the Sacrament adjusted to the divine teleology of the finished atonement, but spiritual faith as essential for its true reception, while the "grace" fulfills the supreme aim for which God gave His Son to redeem the world.

Dr. Luthardt, another representative of our confessional theology, teaches much in the same strain. Discarding, as Dr. Kahnis did, the old arguments drawn from an asserted synecdoche in "this," and from the force of the word "is" in the words of institution, he finds, indeed, a "real presence" in the sacramental administration, but it is the presence of the glorified Christ Himself dealing with us through the Church's administration. The stress for the communicant's reception of grace is rested upon its being a "believing reception," and the grace itself is the forgiveness of sins and strength for the spiritual life. The emphasis is not upon the corporeal manducation or literal eating of the "body." Dr. Luthardt, moreover, admits an anticipatory reference to both Baptism and the Supper in the teaching of Christ, recorded by St. John's Gospel, respectively in 3:3–5, and 6:47–63.

In the light of these facts and guiding principles we are prepared to sum up the essence of the Lutheran doctrine of the Supper.

1. The confessional statement is: "The true body and blood of Christ are truly present in the Sacrament under the forms of bread and wine, and are there distributed and received."

2. This is best understood when approached through a recollection of the two views which it was meant to oppose, viz.: on the one side, the Roman Catholic teaching of transubstantiation, which asserted and still asserts an actual conversion of the substance of the bread and wine into the body and blood of Christ; and on the other, the view of Zwingli and his followers, who interpreted the bread and wine as simply signs and memorials of the body and blood. While thus thoroughly rejecting the dogma of

transubstantiation, and admitting with the Zwinglians that the bread and wine in the Sacrament remain bread and wine, the Lutherans held that a proper regard for the literal force of the words of institution required recognition of the real presence of the body and blood and their reception by the communicants.

3. Acknowledging the mystery involved, the theoretical view is based on the orthodox doctrine of the Person of Christ, as formulated in the Ecumenical Creeds. That doctrine represents that through the union of the Divine and human natures, Christ in His state of glorification and exaltation is omnipresent, not according to one nature alone, but according to both natures. Wherever He is in His divine nature He is in the human. Though in the manner of a visible, tangible, and circumscribed presence, Christ in His glorified state has ascended and left the world and is no longer present in that way, yet in another mode *glorified, supernatural, supersensuous, and heavenly*, He is present in the unity and entirety of His theanthropic Person—and *especially* present when and where He wills to be, peculiarly in His own appointed means for bringing His redemptive work into spiritual effect. He is present in the Word, offering Himself to faith and for faith—whether the Word be audible or visible. And the "grace" He offers with Himself is the *same*. The terms body and blood stand for the humanity in which Christ gave Himself to death for sin; and since His exaltation, He is present in the mode of existence which His Deity gives or can give to His whole Person: "Lo, I am with you always, even to the end of the world"; "Where two or three are gathered together in My name, there am I in the midst of them."

4. It is of the body and blood of Christ as He possesses them since His glorification, and not of them in naturalistic sense or condition, that the Lutheran doctrine makes affirmation. It distinctly repudiates everything like a presence or reception after a gross, natural, or physical manner. Though it has sometimes been called "corporeal," this word is used, not at all with respect to the mode of it, but only adjectively to include the human or bodily reality in the presence. The mode is marked as "sacramental," "supernatural," "incomprehensible," and "spiritual." Though the terms *in, with*, and *under* are sometimes employed to state the doctrine, yet neither are these words used as specifications of any definite mode, but simply as assertive of presence itself. Hence, impanation, consubstantiation, and sub-panation are all repudiated as descriptive of the manner of it. "Oral manducation" of the gift in the Sacrament has figured

Christian Theology

largely in representations of the doctrine. But besides the fact already noted, that the reception "by the mouth" "cannot be demonstrated to be an essential part of Lutheran confessional statement"; and besides, also, the inherent tendency of such representation to materialize the content and significance of the Supper, the great truth, scripturally and theologically assured, that the "Presence" in the Supper is of the glorified and exalted Christ Himself, in the indivisible unity of His Divine-human Person, must surely countervail the force of that dogmatic characterization. This presence of the personal Savior leaves no place for it. The dogmaticians concede this, asserting, indeed, that the whole glorified Christ can be received only by spiritual apprehension and appropriation. Oral manducation is inapplicable to acceptance of His Divine Nature, and His human nature does not exist apart, to be separately given or received. And should the oral reception, except in its truth with respect to the eating of the sacramental elements, be displaced from emphasis or even lost from view, there would be no loss to the richness and value of the redemptive gifts offered and bestowed through the Sacrament to the appropriation of faith. For he whose faith receives the present self-giving Christ, receives in and with Him all the fullness of grace and salvation.

5. When the various definitions and explanations are brought together and correlated, they result in establishing for the Lutheran doctrine of the Lord's Supper, in its essential content and significance, a divinely-instituted Sacrament for perpetual use in His Church, which, while constituting a memorial of His redemptive suffering, is made also, through a *real, special definitive Presence*, under His generic omnipresence, a means by which He gives Himself to believers as the ever-living Savior, in the fullness of His provided grace and saving power. This grace and saving power are, particularly, "forgiveness of sin" ("justification by faith"), and, through enabled faith, the grace of regeneration and sanctification. This doctrine of the Sacrament recognizes the ruling force of the divine teleology which marks the whole redemptive work, and cannot justly be disregarded in the means of grace. It accords, too, with the recognized order of salvation, in which justification through faith is the precondition for the possible upspringing of love to God and the life of loving obedience marking the work of regeneration. And it corresponds with the great *principle*, unquestionably fixed by Christ (John 6:35–40, 47, 62–64), that it is to the spiritual eating by "*faith*" He has assured the grace of eternal

life. "Oral manducation" alone, confessedly, is only to condemnation. It is to a *believing* reception of the soul that the actual assurance stands: "He that eateth ME shall live by Me." This believing sacramental reception becomes a real "communion" (κοινωνια, fellowship) not only with Christ, but of believers with one another, as forming the Church, the spiritual "body of Christ" (1 Cor. 10:17; Col. 1:18–24; Eph. 1:22–23)—"one body, partakers of that one bread"—this latter aspect of the divinely-established principle of fellowship explaining the sacrilege when "close communion" sects take the very Sacrament of the Church's unity to repudiate fellowship with all other believers.

6. As to the oft-asserted reception of the grace of the Sacrament by unbelievers as well as believers, this is simply an associated feature of the oral manducation which cannot be proved an essential part of our confessional theology, and must be modified into accord with the ruling principles and order of grace. Of course, the formal Sacrament is received by unbelievers as well as by believers. The recipient's faith does not constitute it or determine what is present or offered. Its office is simply recipiency for what is offered. A real faith of the heart, however, is necessary to receive what is divinely present for reception. And the Form of Concord itself makes easy the necessary adjustment to the real truth when it declares that unbelieving communicants "repel Christ as the Savior from themselves" (*Christum ut Salvatorem a se repellunt*). They do *not* receive Him—either as to His Divine or human nature, or His offered grace. But He whose faith accepts Christ receives all grace in and with Him.

7. With respect to its practical bearing, it may be well to inquire whether the usual presentation of the doctrine, while rightly and necessarily putting leading and strong emphasis on "forgiveness of sins" as the gift of grace through this Sacrament, has given corresponding emphasis to that for the *new life* of love and holiness, to which the forgiveness looks and into which the life of faith is to move. The grace of the Sacrament is certainly meant to contribute to and pass into the realization of the whole salvation. Man is not saved, as in Divine intention, in mere forgiveness of sin. It must be also "from sin." And although the forgiveness of sin is divinely and sublimely adapted to issuance into holy obedience to God and conformity to His righteousness—into the regenerate and truly sanctified life and character—does it not seem that the stress laid upon the first, as the beginning, has left its relation to the second, as

Christian Theology

consummating, without proper accent? He who has furnished forgiveness of sin declares Himself to be *"the Bread of life."* While the Sacrament has been rightly regarded as calling to "believe in the forgiveness of sin," has not the doctrinal emphasis failed to carry the mind of believers to corresponding emphasis upon the onward and completing action of grace provided in both the Word and Sacramental Administration? Sometimes it looks as if some communicants believed in little else of the Christian provision but forgiveness of sin.

8. A similar suggestion is in place with respect to "communion" (κοινωνία) in the sacrament. In the needed insistence of a real fellowship as between Christ and the believer, that of believers with fellow-believers is often left without its true valuation and practical force. The Sacrament, though not the primary Church-forming rite, is yet a sign and expression of the Church reality as a communion of saints, a recognition and manifestation of the unity of all believers in Christ. The Church as His spiritual body, is one "communion" with a common Savior, and the brotherhood of all believers is to be confessed, made impressive, and developed into genuine fraternity before the world. Through Christ man is to be truly restored not only to God, but to his fellow-man. The Sacrament has been clearly adjusted to quicken and bring into ruling force the unifying life of Christ in His Church. Has this meaning of the Sacrament been brought into right prominence and practical exhibition? The history and present aspect of the Church do not seem to say so. And does it not appear to approach the character of a sacrilege when denominational Churches take this very Sacrament of unity to exclude from their Christian fellowship all dissidents from their peculiar holdings on some non-fundamental speculative doctrine?

9. It enriches the value of the Sacrament, as well as of the means of grace in general, to remember that it is a *continuance of Christ's high-priestly*, as also a part of His kingly, *administration*. Having given His body and blood in His atoning self-sacrifice, being both Priest and sin-offering, and having in His ascension entered into the heavens, He is both Priest and King forever, with all power to carry into effect the "propitiation" of the cross. Not absent from the earth, but present, this continuance of His priestly work, in union with the Holy Spirit's showing the ready redemption, becomes most impressively expressive of His desire and power to save to the uttermost them that consent in faith to come to God through Him.

Milton Valentine

The means of grace are not empty or only ceremonial, but saving to the receptive soul, according to "eternal purpose."

Christian Theology

Milton Valentine

CHAPTER III
THE CHURCH
(*Ecclesiology*)

The Church, with its ministry as an agency of service, has been mentioned as a means of grace. A fuller view of it is necessary. Its nature, in essential character and significance, must here be brought into distinct view. It is so multiplex and many-sided in its reality as to be difficult of description. It is a product of God's redemptive grace through His supernatural self-revelation as recorded in the biblical Scriptures. Its existence and import lie very close to the central Providential aim and outcome of human history.

1. DEFINITION OF THE CHURCH

That of Article VII. of the Augsburg Confession is sufficiently full and precise to begin with. "The one holy Church, to continue forever, is the congregation of saints (the assembly of all believers), in which the Gospel is rightly taught (purely preached), and the Sacraments are rightly administered (according to the gospel)." This is the more suitable for our purpose, as it gives the essentials of the standard Protestant definition.

Its New Testament designation is ἐκκλησία (from ἐκ and καλέω) to call out, an assembly, congregation called forth. Though sometimes applied to secular popular assemblies (Acts 19:32–39), it is appropriated to denote an assembly or congregation of believers, as associated in Christian fellowship. It is more than doubtful, however, whether the etymological signification "called-out, elect," in the Calvinistic sense, ought to be pressed. The word agrees with the Hebrew עֵדָה, an assembly in general, and קָהָל, one for worship; the former is translated in the Septuagint by συναγωγή, and the latter by ἐκκλησία. In the New Testament it has two distinct applications: *First*, to local congregations in particular cities or provinces, as the Church in Jerusalem, the Churches at Antioch, Corinth, in the house of Aquila and Priscilla, and of Nymphas, "the

Christian Theology

Church throughout all Judea and Galilee and Samaria." *Secondly*, it is used as the designation for the whole or universal body of those who profess the Lord Jesus Christ on earth, in Matt. 16:18, "Upon this rock I will build My Church"; Eph. 1:22, "And gave Him to be the Head over all things to the Church"; Eph. 5:25, "Christ loved the Church and gave Himself for it"; Col. 1:18, "He is the Head of the body, the Church"; 1 Tim. 3:15, "The Church of the living God, the pillar and ground of the truth." In this universalistic and comprehensive sense its application may include the redeemed in heaven (Heb. 12:23; Rev. 7:9–17). This last inclusion is the occasion for the theological distinction between the "Church militant" (*militaris*) and the "Church triumphant," *i. e.*, believers still in this life as in warfare against sin and contending for truth under Christ (*milites Christi*), and those who have overcome and entered into the heavenly rest.

Protestant theology, both from the teaching of Scripture and the facts of experience, has marked a further distinction between the Church as "*visible*" and as "*invisible.*" This does not mean two Churches existing alongside of each other, but expresses a difference as to the real spiritual relation which members of the organized body may sustain to Christ and the new life in Him. More specifically, it is called the visible Church when it is considered as an external organization with its ministry of Word and Sacraments—the body of professing Christians, among whom may be some hypocrites or wicked persons, with no true faith or real union with Christ. It is called invisible when it is considered as the body of *real believers* within this outward fellowship, who constitute the true spiritual "body" or congregation of Christ. Though the Church, whether visible or invisible, is one, its members are viewed as sustaining a diverse relation to Christ, some as true, others as false members. The latter are in the Church, but not of it. See the Parable of the Tares (Matt. 13:27–30); of the Net and Fishes (Matt. 13:47–48); the case of Simon Magus (Acts 8:13–21; 1 Cor. 5:4–5; 2 Tim. 3:5). A Church as an organization, with no ungodly in it, seems never to have been looked for in the divine foresight; and the attempts in history, as of the Cathari and others, to realize it, come from an empty dream. It is always a mixed body, though seeking, both for itself and for its members, the saving grace of Christ. This distinction, thus made in theology, was recognized by Augustine in early Christianity in his contest with Donatism. In the mixed visible body, he maintained, the Lord knew His own who formed the

Milton Valentine

Church in its inner spiritual sense. Yet some of his teaching contributed to the development of the tendencies then already shaping toward the long movement which formed the Roman Catholic Church into an external official organism, as a vicarious custodian and dispenser of all the grace provided in Christ to those who make themselves passive subjects of the hierarchical organization's ministrations—a Church consisting, not of the personal believers who through faith have come into conscious spiritual fellowship with Christ and one another in and through the Word and Sacraments, but of the outward organization itself, to which all divine authority, both priestly and kingly, has been deputized—a visible Church outside of which there is declared to be no salvation (*ex eccleasiam nan salus*) and *in* which salvation is guaranteed to all, however wicked. This official hierarchy, assuming autocratic rights as in itself the Church, and claiming to be identical with "the kingdom of God" on earth, took up the role of the supreme world-power over men and nations. From this extreme perversion of the doctrine the Reformation restored to Protestant Christendom the true biblical and evangelical conception. The definition, quoted from the Confession, is that of the Church visible—externally marked by right use of the means of grace for faith and the new life. This *contains* the true believers, in whom God sees the spiritual salvation for which the Church stands passing into real effect, though some hypocrites or unconverted persons may be associated with it. Luther and Melanchthon at once emphasized this distinction over against Rome's falsifications and abuses. Our later dogmaticians developed it clearly as a truth of profound import and practical bearings. Its *basis* is the indubitable fact, portrayed in Scripture and evermore clear in ecclesiastical experience, that the visible organization, though divinely holding and employing the means for the true faith and regeneration of its members, yet in its comprehension embraces many who do not belong to the true spiritual body of Christ. The fact is a loud and perpetual warning against the danger of mistaking the outward and formal connection for the reality of the provided salvation. It must be constantly held in the clear.

Another and allied distinction is between the *true* Church and *false* or *corrupt* churches. This is seen when a local or denominational church becomes heretical through departure from the *fundamental or essential* teachings of the gospel, or adds doctrines that nullify the practical force of these teachings. This phenomenon has appeared often in history, with its misdirection

Christian Theology

and blight. The falsifications of Romanism pressed this distinction into view in the Reformation period. Illustrations are never out of sight. Such organizations are incompetent for the function of teaching the way of salvation as prepared in Jesus Christ or guiding souls into true faith and the regenerate life. Our own day is marked by examples of this—organizing communions taught to reject the gospel of supernatural redemption, reducing Christianity into a mere naturalism or paganism, or relying on the competence of simple self-culture and morality, or upon some socialistic view of life which drops reconciliation with God into the background—to say nothing of such inventions as the Mormon and "Christian Science" churches. The perils of heresy are not past.

The metaphorical designations of the Church, as "The Body of Christ" (Eph. 1:22-23; v. 20; 1 Cor. 12:13), "The House of God" (1 Tim. 3:15; 1 Pet. 4:17), "The Bride of Christ" (Eph. 5:31-32; Rev. 21:9), and "The Pillar and Ground of the Truth" (1 Tim. 3:15), are profoundly instructive as to the composition, essential life, spiritual communion, relations of love, and offices of obedient service, that are its spiritual essence and form its necessary predicates.

II. DISTINCTION BETWEEN THE CHURCH AND THE KINGDOM OF GOD

This has already been mentioned, but reminder of it is necessary for clearness here. Of the one hundred and eleven instances of the designations, "The kingdom of God," "of heaven," "of Christ," in the New Testament, referring virtually to the same reality, probably not in a single case is any one of them exactly synonymous, equivalent, or coterminous with the term Church (ἐκκλησία). However closely related "the kingdom" (βασίλεια) and "the Church" may be, they are not the same and must be clearly distinguished. The kingdom of God which developed out of the Old Testament dispensation, preparations, and promises, and was established in the mission, work, and enthronement of Christ, stands for the new order of things in the world under redeeming provision, saving grace, and mediatorial sovereignty. Its establishment and progress is a spiritual reality, consisting in the power and sway of the redemptive order or grace in the minds and hearts of men, and the principles of love, righteousness, and service in the world. It is the increasing dominion of gospel truth and its saving influence, passing into control of human life and sanctifying it to God and the aims of His holy administration through the exalted Savior and King. It stands for and expresses the total spiritual reality and outcome of the redemptive work and its provisions. Unlike the Church, the kingdom is not visibly organized—though its divine powers are organic. The Church is, indeed, its great product on earth—the visible body of believers in organized fellowship, in the use of the means for personal salvation, the spread of the gospel, and the conversion of the world. The organization of the Church is one, and the chief, of its historical manifestations. Dr. Franz Delitzsch is unquestionably justified when he writes: "We acknowledge the distinction of Church and kingdom of God. The idea of the kingdom is of a larger extent. The final aim of history, according to God's eternal design, is not the accomplishment of the Church, but the divine kingdom. However, these two have neither a different center nor a different focus. Christ is the center of both, for it pleased the Father that in Him should all fullness dwell." It was Rome's terrible mistake when it identified its own hierarchical organization as the "kingdom of God" upon the earth.

A peculiar telic relation is assigned to the Church. As the collective body of believers, in the fellowship of the means of grace, it is the appointed agency for the progressive sway of the kingdom and the salvation of men. It is taught to pray: "Thy kingdom come," and employ its new life and resources for the conversion of the world. But while thus an instrumentality, it is more, and will blend at last with all the blessedness of the consummated kingdom of God. "Christ loved the Church, and gave Himself for it, that He might sanctify and cleanse it with the washing of water by the word, that He might present it to Himself a glorious Church" (Eph. 5:25).

III. THE ORIGIN OF THE CHURCH

The question here divides into three branches, viz.: as to authorship, time, and mode.

1. As to *authorship*, the Church is divine. Some, while recognizing Christianity as truly divine, have held the Church to be merely a natural human product consequent from Christianity. But the proof of its being a divine institution, as truly as the gospel itself is of God, is made fully clear: (*a*) Prom the divine grounding in man's religious nature of a necessity for fellowship in the worship of God—a necessity to be divinely provided for, as well as for forgiveness and the development of a new life. (*b*) From the necessity of a divine adjustment of the means of grace to re-uniting

Christian Theology

man with his fellow-men as well as with God. The communion of the Church is needed for healing all the alienations of sin. (*c*) From the express declaration of Christ Himself: "I will build My Church, and the gates of hell shall not prevail against it" (Matt. 16:18). (*d*) From all the Scriptures which recognize the Church as the "Church of God," "the body of Christ," "God's building." (*e*) From Christ's own appointment of a ministry and sacraments, together with authority for discipline and order (Matt. 18:17; 1 Cor. 12:28).

2. With respect to *time*, note must be made of both the Church's preparatory stages and completed form. In the first sense the Church existed under the Old Testament dispensation. As a body of believers and worshipers of God it has existed from the race's beginning. In all the stages of the long movement which created it, the Church is the one and same divine institution, passing through successive steps of unfolding to its complete endowment and organization in the New Testament. Three distinct forms are properly noted: (*a*) The *patriarchal*—which divides itself into two stages, viz.: *First, the pre-Abrahamic.* From historical allusions, as Gen. 4:26; 6:2, in connection with probably already instituted sacrificial offerings (Gen. 4:3–5), it is fair to infer not only private but united worship, a distinction between believing children of God and others. The Sabbath from creation looked to worship. While wickedness increased, so as to leave as the people of God only a few families, finally only one (Gen. 6:8–9), yet the germ of the Church continued to the flood and survived it. Noah's first act after the deluge was to build an altar. *Secondly, the Abrahamic.* With Abraham God distinctly and formally established His covenant of grace, redemption, and the Church (Gen. 12:1–3), calling him with his seed to separation from idolatry, sequestering them at once for both national and religious life under sealing of sacramental rite and assurance, a Church of faith, which was to open out at last into that Church which should carry redemptive grace to all nations. For the developmental continuity of the Church from the Abrahamic covenant see Acts 2:39; Gal. 3:7–17, 29; Rom. 4:11–16; Col. 2:11–12; Rom. 11:17–26; Luke 1:32–33; Matt 22:43–45. (*b*) *The Hebraic* or *Mosaic*—from the exodus to the times of Christ. This was marked by the gift and possession of the Law, the establishment of a ritual of sacrifices and worship, with Tabernacle, Temple, and priests, and fuller knowledge of God's will and plan through the teaching of the Prophets. The Hebraic form was in close connection with the State or civil administration. The Church and State were organized as

coterminous, a Church of the Jewish people or nationality—
theocratic at first, but afterward in kingly administration of the State
subordinate to the constitution of the Church. (*c*) Its completion as
the *Church of the New Testament* marked the beginning of the
present divine dispensation in which the reality and mission of the
Church and consequent kingdom of God on earth, are the supreme
characteristics. From its earlier development it came to full birthday
on the pentecost first after the Redeemer's ascension and
enthronement.

3. The *mode* of its origin has been in part indicated in the
historic progress of grace and Providence thus far traced. But the
completing divine action requires further specifications. These are
reflected from the birthday. The Church as the congregation of
believers was created through the word of the gospel and the Holy
Spirit (Is. 55:10–11; 44:3; Joel 2:28; Zech. 4:6; Acts 2:2–4, 16–17, 37–
42). A small number of believers had been gathered under the
ministry of Christ. The pentecostal union of the truth and Spirit
added, through baptism, a fellowship of thousands, with still
increasing thousands (Acts 2:41–47). Thus upon the completed
provisions for forgiveness of sin, and the presence of the Holy Spirit
using "the things of Christ," the Church appears as a divine product
through the means of grace.

But the truth on this point needs to be more distinctly marked,
and the principles involved clearly fixed. (*a*) The Church is a *product*
of God's grace through means of the Word and Sacrament. This fact
is basal. (*b*) Then it is made a *depository* of the means and an *agency*
of God's grace. The Sacraments had indeed been instituted, and
discipleship connected with a teaching to the ends of the earth, but
the disciples were directed to tarry at Jerusalem for full endowment
from on high. The word of the Gospel is given to the Church at its
very birth for use and administration, as the means by which it is to
carry on and fulfill its work for God in the world. And the apostle
explains: "God hath set some in the *Church*, first apostles, secondly
prophets, thirdly teachers," etc. (1 Cor. 12:28). The Holy Spirit that
created the Church also forever abides in it and in the truth
administered. (*c*) *The relation between these two truths.* Two extremes
have appeared, marked by different mottoes which were at first one.
The motto of one extreme has been: "Where the Spirit of God is,
there is the Church"; of the other: "Where the Church is, there is the
Spirit of God." Both are true. The extreme comes by unduly and one-
sidedly pressing one or the other. One rests only on and in the truth

Christian Theology

that where the Holy Spirit is, there He is perpetually quickening and gathering believers into the fellowship of saints. The Spirit is primary and originant, the Church secondary and dependent Were the whole organization to perish, the Spirit could originate it again. Through the printed gospel in heathen lands the Church might arise without being organized by the agents of the organization elsewhere. Sometimes this is pressed so as to leave the Church divine only in the sense of being incidental to the on working independent power of the Spirit. It has sometimes tended to a fanaticism which dissolves the objective Church. The other extreme is that the Church stands primary and originate, and the Spirit and life are secondary, dependent, and consequential. The Church organization perpetuates itself, and stands between the individual and Christ as the actual and only conveyancer of God's saving grace to him. In its full form, this is Romanism—viewing the Church as the provided and essential organism of dispensation of Christ's grace, apart from which the Holy Spirit does not do His saving work. The High-Church Episcopal view is allied to this. But the correct view avoids both extremes, and embraces the essential truth of both mottoes, as Irenæus himself did. The Holy Spirit, through the Word and Sacraments organizes the Church in the fellowship of the means of grace, and thus it becomes, by the Spirit's unfailing presence in these means, endowed for its appointed agency for human salvation.

IV. CHARACTERISTICS OF THE CHURCH

These are well named in the Apostles' and Nicene Creeds.

1. *Unity.* "I believe in *one* holy catholic and apostolic Church." The distinction noticed between the 'Church visible' and 'invisible' is no assertion of two Churches, but marks two aspects of the *one* Church in which we "believe." This one covers both the realities which the distinction describes. And the unity does not consist in being organized under *one visible Head* or supreme spiritual authority, as Pope or Pontifex Maximus, nor in any unbroken succession of *episcopally-ordained clergy,* nor, indeed, in any special feature of *external organization, polity, continuity, or uniformity of ceremonies.* These things, one and all, do not reach the fundamental and central essence of the body, in which Christ sees the reality of the Church of His founding. The oneness is far deeper and more spiritual, and unaffected by these outward features except so far as some of them may either promote or hinder the Church's spiritual

character and mission. But the true unity is, first, in the Headship of Christ Himself, in whom the whole body's life comes and abides; "in whom we have redemption through His blood, the forgiveness of sins according to the riches of His grace"; He is Head, not only of "the Church, which is His body," but "over *all things to* the Church"; "in whom all the building fitly framed together groweth unto a holy temple in the Lord" (Eph. 1:7, 19–23; 2:19–22; 4:15–16). Further elemental constituents of its unity we are to see in the oneness of the *faith and knowledge* of the one "gospel" which disallows "another" (Eph. 4:13; Gal. 1:6–8); *under one Spirit* (Eph. 4:3); and in *one fellowship, communion* (Eph. 4:8–13). Summing these up, in the harmony of the New Testament teaching, the essentials of the Church's true unity are, as the generic Protestant consensus claims, "that the community of believers, holding Jesus Christ as Head, abide in the true doctrine of the gospel, and fellowship, under the Holy Spirit, in the use of the Word and Sacraments."

The question arises as to the actual divisions now existing in the Church and their relations to this unity. It is a large question, which the Christianity of our day has to face. The Savior prayed for the unity of His Church (John 17:21). Paul warned against schisms (1 Cor. 3:3; 12:25–26). Only a few truths bearing on the problem can be introduced here. (*a*) *Local* Churches, in cities, country, or territorial districts, are not *per se* inconsistent with the required and true unity. The numerous churches gathered and organized under apostolic labors were not in breach of it, but an extension and illustration. (*b*) *National* Churches, in fellowship with other national organizations, are not inconsistent with the principle of unity. The principle of fellowship is no bar to the Church's extension and adaptation to different peoples, language, and conditions. If the fellowship crosses the lines of national reach, it reveals its largeness and divinity, (*c*) *Denominational* Churches which fully retain and build on the fundamental and essential saving doctrines of Christ and His redemptory work and requirements, are not necessarily a rupture of the unity. The infirmities of the human understanding of the gospel, and the impulsiveness of exegetical dogmatism make absolute unanimity very difficult, if not impossible; and a closer fellowship of types on speculative views and convictions may be conceived as consistent with the oneness of the Church, provided recognition of their common Christian status and communion is openly and cordially maintained. Of course, if the denominational fellowship rejects the fundamental and constitutive truths of the redemptive

Christian Theology

gospel, it ceases to be a Church of Christ and teaches "another gospel." The question of denominationalism and unity is apart from such case, and respects the numerous orthodox Churches of Protestantism. As these hold and preach the saving truths of the gospel and administer the sacraments according to God's word, they are real constituents in the unity of the faith and the Church of Christ. This fact has great practical corollaries in the obligations and responsibilities of these Churches to keep their interdenominational relations consistently fraternal and co-operative with each other as members of the same and only true body of Christ. It is a sign of the increasing life of Christ and of enlarging submission to the grace of His Spirit, that these Churches now, without diminution of devotion to sound doctrine, are losing the separatistic spirit of bigotry and cultivating a wider fellowship and more co-operative endeavor in the objects of our common Christianity.

But a remnant of practice still remains, already referred to, which is peculiarly at variance with this truth of the Church's unity, and for correction of which both sound doctrine and practical Christianity are loudly calling—the unseemly anomaly of an exclusive Lord's Supper. For the usual mate of this—exclusion from pulpit across denominational lines—some show of reason may appear in the supposed necessity and duty of safeguarding the flock against teaching that might contravene the peculiar tenets which the organization emphasizes as necessary for best spiritual welfare. While this reason implies a low estimate of the ability of these peculiar views to vindicate their truth under open discussion, and the courtesies of the situation are usually a guarantee of non-introduction of contrary views, it may be allowed to have some weight. Let that pass. But such plea is wholly inapplicable to the order of an exclusive communion table, which has been so widely practiced that few of the denominational Churches have been entirely free from it or able to place the blame of it wholly on others, if found erroneous. That the order is indefensible, and thoroughly inconsistent with the truth of the unity of the Church, becomes apparent when closely considered in its relation to the doctrine of both the Church and the Sacrament as confessed in the consensus of Christendom in the past and present.

As to the *Church*, all these orthodox denominations agree that it is Christ's own institution, constituted through the working of His saving redemption through His truth and Spirit, the fellowship of believers for the whole earth and all time. Its inclusions are as extensive as the action of His grace through His appointed means establishes a spiritual union with Himself as the Head of the Church, and as men may voluntarily associate themselves with the visible body through profession of faith in Him. The inclusions and boundaries of the Church are fixed as an *objective* reality or divine institution, independent of human theories and unchangeable by them. They exist to be recognized and conformed to—not to be disregarded, or obscured in party uses. The believer's union with the Church ecumenical, regularly formed and certified in one branch, entitles him to its fellowship and privileges wherever he may go, and, upon evidence of it, to fraternal reception. The reality is not that of a man-made organization, with rights and privileges of human determining and limitations, but of divine establishment and order, a Church that is *one everywhere*, in all its denominational branches or local fellowship. Believers have no right, in the name of Christ, to organize their Church fellowship on a different and more contracted principle than that which Christ Himself has established, who is the only and universal Head and Lord. The Creed of this Church says: "We believe in the communion of saints," not in the communion of sects. Such procedure is a sin against the Church, and the only Lord of the Church. The organization that adopts it, breaking away from the communion of the other denominational Churches, or parts of the Church, thereby proclaims itself as a sect or schism, or logically implies that the others are not true branches of Christ's Church. Such renunciation of the ecumenical spirit which should truly dwell in each of the denominational Churches has seriously impressed and confused the non-Christian and even the Christian mind of past and present times, to the hindrance of the progress of Christ's kingdom.

Even stronger force against the error comes in considering the acknowledged doctrine of the *Sacrament itself.* Unquestionably Christ meant it for perpetual repetition, and adapted it to the unity of the Church. Like Baptism, through which faith, in uniting with Christ, unites also with the body of believers, this, too, is undoubtedly of unifying, not divisive, import. Much more clearly than the word of preaching, or the administration of the first sacrament, the Lord's Supper was set in the midst of the Church of believers as an ordained expression of their union with Him, and with the household of faith. "We being many," explains St. Paul, "are one bread and one body; for we are all partakers of that one bread" (1 Cor. 10:17). In a most eminent degree, being the memorial of that

Christian Theology

death by which Christ has reconciled all alienations and divisions, between believers and God and between believers themselves, it is the Sacrament of unification and love, a bond and witness of unity. In a most distinct sense Christ has centralized the fellowship for His whole Church and for all time in this communion. A very climax of inconsistency and misappropriation appears when the Sacrament of the Church's ecumenical unity is, through "close communion," converted into an instrument for witnessing against other evangelical Churches. It is a crime against the communion, in that it usurps the right to make new and human conditions of its enjoyment, divisive instead of unifying the Church. It is to be borne in mind that Christ Himself is the Lord of this table, and, in its own realities and terms, it is what it is by His own, not by human creation. In the interest of the absolute *objectivity* of the Sacrament, the truth must not be lost sight of that its intrinsic content is not made by the administering Church, or even by the communicant's faith, which is only *recipient* of the blessing Christ has provided and bestows in it. This truth makes clear the point of the Church's right care in its administration, viz.: that no unworthy guests be admitted. The wrong of the rule of the exclusive communion is that *a priori* it holds *all* unworthy that do not belong to a particular denominational organization. It rests admission upon an external relation instead of upon true spiritual faith. Herein is the implication thrown before the world that the unity of the Church has been in fact overthrown, and that what is the real essential Christianity is indeterminable.

And the practice is inconsistent when the grounds on which it is urged and defended are viewed. These, generically, are found to be the duty and necessity of testifying against error and on behalf of the pure gospel. But when analyzed the basis of this plea is found to consist merely of two unfounded assumptions: *First,* that the peculiar teachings marking the exclusive Churches are surely the teachings of the word of God. But when examined they are far from being shown to be such. In the sincere and intelligent judgment of most of the Church universal they are not so settled. They are at best open questions, as the divisions themselves imply. The exclusion from the Lord's table can have no possible warrant short of substantial settlement in favor of the excluding party. *Secondly,* that these special doctrines are *fundamental and essential to Christian faith and salvation.* The untenableness of this proposition becomes apparent by the bare mention of some of the distinctive doctrines for whose sake denominational Churches have been organized and the exclusive witness has been borne. For instance: the immersion form of baptism and the rejection of infant baptism; the construction of a Church polity on the basis of a graded ministry through episcopal ordination; the exclusion of all human compositions in the Church's psalmody; or the speculative view of an absolute eternal predestination of all men. These and similar types of teaching about which Christian believers have organized denominational Churches neither place them outside the ecumenical Church of Christ, nor present the fundamental and essential doctrines of the Redeemer's truth and grace. Thus, while these Churches, holding also the fundamental doctrines, are parts of the one true Church of God, their differing special views cannot justly be regarded as making it their duty to pervert the Sacrament of the Church's real unity in exploitation and enforcement of their non-fundamental peculiarities. It is indeed difficult to conceive how this divisive communion can be viewed as presenting the exact and supreme adaptation of the ordinance to the Redeemer's saving aims and the Church's mission.

For the close communion in the Lutheran Church—nothing underlies its origin and continuance but the clash of controversy and strife of the Protestant Reformation, giving dissociated organizations. The separatistic temper exceeded the demands of truth and the confessional formularies of doctrine. The Lutheran Confession, both as to the Church and the Sacrament, neither calls for it nor logically justifies it. It points rather the other way. The Augsburg Confession declares that "One holy Christian Church shall ever continue to exist, which is *the congregation* of *believers* in which the Gospel is rightly preached and the Sacraments administered according to the word of God." In "The Apology," Melanchthon explains this article as concerning the *universal* ("catholic") *Church, which is gathered from every nation under the sun.* This makes the Church in which Lutherans believe as broad as Christianity. It is formed by all believers, all Christians—nothing less. What thus becomes the relation of the Sacraments in this Church? Art. xiii. answers: "Concerning the use of the Sacraments, it is taught that the Sacraments have been instituted, not only as tokens by which CHRISTIANS *may be known externally, but as signs and evidences of the divine will towards us, for the purpose of exciting and strengthening our faith.* Hence they also require faith, and are properly received only when received in faith, and faith is

Christian Theology

strengthened by them." Here the Lord's Supper is declared to be a divinely-instituted sign of the *union* of *Christians*. There is no restriction short of *all* the believers or Christians that form the universal Church. The Church is made to mean the sum total of believers, and these are to be, by the Supper, known externally from the world—not from each other. The position taken by the confessors, on the use of the Sacraments, seems to be almost a *protest* against a narrower or less generic conception of them. Is not the evidence thus even on the surface that in saying in Art. x., "Therefore the opposite doctrine is rejected," they meant only to reject the "doctrine," and not other *Christians* who form parts of "the Church universal," and who are to be "marked" or known externally by the use of the Supper? To reject them would defeat what the confessors declare to be, in part, the very purpose of its institution. Our Lutheran Church also joins in confessing: "We believe in the communion of saints." Whether this be a distinct item of the creed or epexegetical of the Church, its force is in the same direction. "The Apology" adds: "We say that this Church exists, viz., the truly believing and righteous men scattered throughout the whole world;" "We affirm and know in truth that this Church, containing saints, truly is and continues to be on earth; that is, there are children of God in different places throughout the world, in various kingdoms, islands, countries, and cities, from the rising and setting of the sun, who truly know Christ and the gospel." Put these things together. The Church believed in is the congregation of all saints, and the use of the Sacrament, one of its chief purposes, is that these Christians may be known externally. This makes the use of the Lord's Supper as wide as the whole Church, presenting it as one, over against the world, and is therefore virtually a position against any restriction. The other confessions are in harmony with this position. The statements in the Smalcald Articles, the Small and Large Catechism, the Formula of Concord, concerning the proper qualifications for the Supper, make no sectarian exclusion. That this was meant to be understood as the teaching of the confessors is, indeed, involved in their very purpose, when they unequivocally declare: "That it might be clearly perceived that by us nothing is received contrary to the Holy Scriptures or *opposed to the universal Church*." So long, therefore, as the Lutheran Church acknowledges so distinctly that other Churches are integral portions of the one holy Christian Church, its position stands as a logical contradiction and overthrow of all grounds for an exclusive communion table.

Milton Valentine

2. The Church is marked also as "*holy.*" The full meaning of this is based in the fact that it 'belongs to God,' as gathered into its unity through the action of His redemptive means of grace. There is thus expressed (*a*) its "holy calling" (2 Tim. 1:9); (*b*) its professed self-consecration to righteousness (2 Tim. 2:19); (*c*) and that while its holiness is not yet fully attained, it is in actual process of being "cleansed from all sin," and is looking to the consummation when "Christ shall present it unto Himself a glorious Church, holy and without blemish" (Eph. 5:27). This characteristic of the Church thus faces in two directions—piety toward God and ethical duty toward fellow-men.

3. It is marked as *catholic* in the sense of *universal*, in order to designate, not any local or sectional fellowship, but the entire body of Christian believers of all lands and for all time, having Christ as its head and the one gospel as its faith.

4. It is *apostolic*, as identical with that founded through the labors of the apostles and as abiding in the gospel as preached by them. There is no necessity to make this include the linkage of an identical form of ministerial succession or ecclesiastical government, as urged by high-church episcopacy. For *first*, there is no apostolic charge specifying or requiring this, and the evidence is explicit that the term "bishops" (ἐπίσκοποι) was simply another designation to express the function of the "elders" (πρεσβυτέροι). There is no proof that the order of apostles was perpetuated, or that "bishop" expresses a different order or higher rank than that of the elders of the Churches. And, *secondly*, the claim would class a special feature of the external form of the Church with its fundamental essentials of great saving truths of the redemptive gospel and of spiritual union with Christ through them. And, *thirdly*, the testimony of Christendom's experience is that there are true Churches of Christ which are not of that type of organization. The Nicene Symbol simply links the holy, universal Church in which we believe with that in which the apostles labored and taught.

V. THE DESIGN OF THE CHURCH

Its aggregate end is, of course, the salvation of men and the glory of God. In this it becomes identical with God's all-embracing eternal purpose which is supreme in His providential administration of the world. Indeed, since, according to both revelation and science, God's creational action for this earth looked to Man and his possibilities of blessedness as its aim, and the incarnation and redemptory

Christian Theology

provision look to his recovery from sin and the re-enfranchisement of his nature with divine fellowship and immortal life, God's intention in the Church coincides with His design in both His creative and saving love. But there are special and contributory purposes included in this design:

1. United worship, in associated or common use of the means of grace. Man's social nature, as well as the twofold bearing of righteousness, Godward and toward fellow-men, forbids the right and full movement of salvation through individual isolation. The law of the holy life is in the action of love to God and to our fellowmen. Hence the Church of redemption and salvation is organized in a twofold fellowship. Our worship of God—whatever the duty and blessing of secret devotion—must bring men together and overthrow all the alienations of sin. Christ has thus constituted His Church for associated worship, real communion, upon a principle inherent in man's nature and requisite for the double movement of the provided salvation.

2. Edification in Christian faith and life. Though believers are at once forgiven and accepted in Christ, this beginning is not the full consummation of saving grace. For the necessary growth and completion of the new life, its triumph over temptation and advance into the likeness of Christ, the needful provision has been made by endowment of His Church with the means of grace and their administration, effectual through the Holy Spirit for growth in knowledge, quickening of faith, and ever-increasing sanctification of life (2 Pet 3:18; Heb. 10:25; 2 Cor. 3:18). The believer needs the Church for the normal and best 'working out of his salvation' (Phil. 2:12).

3. Co-operation, unified and organized, for the extension of the kingdom of God in the world. The revelation of this design resounds in the Savior's commission to His original disciples: "Go ye, make disciples of all nations" (Matt 28:19). Reminder of it reaches us in the petition taught us: "Thy kingdom come." The law of its coming rests upon the evangelizing work committed to the body of believers. And this order expresses God's peculiar love for His Church. It is grace added to grace. For, to have exempted it from this agency would have been a deprivation of the spiritual training essential to the life of love and goodness. To have used the ministry of angels or proclaimed the gospel from the sky would have been the impoverishment of the Church, a withholding of the completing benediction of saving grace. Alas! that the Church, in its general

membership, especially in periods of doctrinal corruption and official maladministration, has so largely failed to measure up to this principle of duty and love, to the obscuring of its best ethical possibilities and the delay of the full sway of Christ's kingdom.

4. The specific purpose of reconciling inter-human alienations and harmonizing redeemed humanity into unity, brotherhood, and communion, already mentioned, must not be forgotten or minimized (John 13:34–35; 17:20–21; Acts 4:32; Eph. 5:2; 1 John 4:11, 21). "I believe in one holy catholic Church," is a faith in the power of the gospel to unite men again in genuine love. Hence the sectarian spirit of separation and non-recognition of brotherhood is in direct conflict with the very end and aim of the Church.

Christian Theology

Milton Valentine

DIVISION IV
THE LAST THINGS
(Eschatology)

We have seen that Christianity is supremely teleological, in whole and in its parts. This fact has been a guiding light for the understanding and correlation of its doctrines. In the light of the same great fact must the Biblical teachings concerning its consummating realities especially receive their correct interpretation. For these must trace the ultimate divine working and human experiences throngh which the aims of redemptional love and providence reach their saving goal. This introduces a distinction to be observed in the use, in this relation, of the Scriptures of the Old and New Testaments. While the Old Testament revelation guided personal piety into spiritual salvation, its great historic aim was specially shaped to foretell and prepare for the redemptive provision yet to be wrought in Christ, leaving the eschatology which closes the Christian revelation to be read in the teachings of Christ and His apostles. These eschatological teachings are parts of the gospel message itself, unified in the person and work of the Redeemer, but belonging distinctively to His enthroned redemptive administration in kingly grace and judgment, and marking its outcome. Moreover, since the aim of redemption from the beginning looked both to personal recovery from sin and its effects, and also to the salvation of social life from its disorganization and emptiness, eschatology must necessarily exhibit a consummation in reference to both individual character and the collective life of the Church as the completed kingdom of God—a twofold consummation. Its chief topics are *Death, the State of the Soul After Death, the Second Coming of Christ, the Resurrection of the Dead, the General Judgment, Heaven and Hell*, and the *Final Restitution of all Things*. These subjects involve questions of profound interest, attracting at present an increasing discussion.

1. DEATH

Christian Theology

1.To the first question: What is death? our answer must be: The dissolution of the personal union between the soul and body and the consequent resolution of the body into its physical elements. It is thus the termination of the present bodily life. This marked its conception already in Old Testament expression: "Then shall the dust return to the earth as it was, and the spirit shall return unto God who gave it" (Eccl. 12:7). It is continued in the New: A 'dissolving of the earthly house of our tabernacle' (2 Cor. 5:1); "The time of my departure is at hand" (2 Tim. 4:6); A 'giving up the spirit' (Acts 5:10); A being "absent from the body and present with the Lord" (2 Cor. 5:8). Often the term spirit (πνεῦμα), is used as a synonym for soul (ψυχή), though sometimes with distinctive meaning. While the word "soul" means "life," it also denotes the *essence* or *living entity* by whose presence and action physical substance becomes or remains *alive*, not dead. But when matter has been thus vitalized and organized into a living body, that body, on its material side, is open to the intrusion of foreign matter, either in a mechanical or chemical way, introducing disease or dissolving the physical organism. Or the physical forces may be measured to a certain continuance of time, when the material component fails. In either case, that conjunction or union presented in the living person as between the functions of physical vitality and those of the "soul," "spirit," "mind" (animus), whose essence forms the personal *ego* that thinks, knows, and is self-determining in free-will, and self-identical in consciousness from first to last, is in death dissolved, and the body returns to material atoms. We are necessitated to view man in this dualistic realism, not simply by Biblical representation, but by the demands of science. The long and earnest investigations of the latter have failed to show that mind and matter are one and the same essence, or that "life," even in its lowest forms, may arise from non-life, either by spontaneous generation or through possible mechanical or chemical movement. The life-entity and force must precede even the lowest known forms of animated existence in nature. And as to the lofty product of human personality, with endowments of intellect, sensibility, and moral consciousness akin to God's, the suggestion of its origin in the natural evolution of inanimate matter is utterly without any supporting evidence.

2. Its relation to sin. The Scripture teaching making it a consequence of the fall of our first parents and the sinful state of human nature, has lost, as we have seen, none of its reasonableness under the light of modern science and philosophy. The discovery of

Milton Valentine

death among pre-Adamite animals does not touch the question. The Scriptures make no assertion as to the cause or occasion of death among them, or impersonal organizations. Human death is a separate problem. Man has not yet been proven to be of animal parentage, or even a graft upon it. He is the only rational and personal being created on earth with endowments which lift him up into fellowship with his Creator's mind, reading God's thoughts in nature's language, a being of moral consciousness and responsibility, made for self-rulership and dominion over the realm of lower nature. Gifted with free-will, a complex of powers of knowledge, love, and righteousness, in balance of positive adjustment to holiness and duty, he was set forth into a life that was at once to reflect God's character and will, and to realize a continuous and ever-enriching blessedness. Such is the picture of him in Biblical drawing. In his freedom were posited at once his duty, his opportunity, and his responsibility. By his will he was not simply a cause in general, but a *free* cause. He was morally obligated to the right. No *necessity* for his falling away from the normal moral order of his being has ever been shown or ever can be. On the contrary, it is reasonable to believe that in the *spirit* side of his personality, by which he was endowed with Godlikeness, he was provided with an energy whose unlowered powers would have carried his bodily organism into unbroken and continuous vigor. The self-rupture of his spiritual life from God, it may well be thought, became the loss of the provided vital energies for the teleology of the physical embodiment. Whatever may have been its philosophy, there has been no disproof of this source of the racial fall.

Redemption has not been meant to annul, for the forgiven and justified, this experience of physical death, through which the redeeming Lord passed on human behalf (Rom. 5:12; Heb. 9:27; Jas. 4:14; Luke 16:22; 2 Cor. 5:1–8; Phil. 1:21–23; 3:20). The complete redemption from the death brought by sin is by following Him into His triumph over it. Nevertheless, the relation of death has been changed to believers. It is not to them an unforgiven penalty, but is transmuted into an experience in the progress of salvation—in three particulars: (*a*) They are lifted above its sting and fear (2 Cor. 5:8; 1 Cor 15:55–57; Heb. 2:14–15). (*b*) It is made the gateway to the "presence of the Lord" and the "rest that remaineth" (Rev. 14:13). (*c*) Death is ultimately wholly destroyed to them in the resurrection of the dead (1 Cor. 15:16–54). To the rejecters of salvation death remains the unrepealed penalty of persistent sin.

II. THE INTERMEDIATE STATE

This designation has been thus shaped because of its reference to realities lying between death and the resurrection, between entrance into disembodied condition and the "redemption of the body" (Rom. 8:23). It presents questions of surpassing interest. Though the Scripture outlines of truth are sufficient for our faith, their transcendent character and relations of necessity open to speculative theology many problems to which diverse answers are given. Our aim here is to mark and define the chief points of truth assured.

1. The fact all along assumed, as in anthropology, the *natural immortality of the soul*. This is fundamental in the Christian view of man. Though in death the physical life ceases, the soul (ψυχή), or spirit (πνεῦμα), lives on, with all the essential attributes and powers that belong to its nature. The evidence of this truth is multiform:

(*a*) As a Christian doctrine we accept it on the teaching of *revelation*. It is organically included in the Scriptures of both the Old and the New Testaments. In the Old it is primarily grounded in the creational representation. This puts man, for whom the earth was made, in a category by himself, lifted above all other ranks, "in the image and likeness of God," a moral and spiritual personality, a being of intelligence, affection, and free-will, capable of thinking God's own thoughts after Him, and holding ethical fellowship with His will; and as thus constituted placed in dominion over the powers of nature and its utilities (Gen. 1:26–30; 2:7; Ps. 8:5–8; Heb. 2:7–8). The personal essence of man, though embodied, is "spirit" (נֶפֶשׁ), a gift of God's special creative action—thus not necessarily subject to the dissolution of bodily organization or *physical nature*. We know not by what processes of thought those ancient writers counted the soul as surviving the dying body. But their *usus loquendi* shows that they did so hold. It may have been an inspiration of God. Whether so or not, their conception may be justified by such facts as these: "Death," as the body's ceasing to exist through disorganization, the dust returning to dust, is distinctly attributed to "*sin*," the lapse of the soul from moral likeness to God. It is consequent on the changed ethical character. The soul, however, is not a physical compound, but a spirit-unit. It is not dissoluble by decomposition. The *spirit* or *soul* of man may continue to *exist in sin*—not in its *true* ethical life, indeed, but in a fallen, unethical life, surviving the body. This, indeed, is *spiritual* death, yet continued existence. The reality may be conceived in this way: The created "spirit," or "soul," being in itself *life*, and also vitalizing the body, may, having no elements of dissolution in itself, live on in sin, having failed in its offered and possible dominion of holding its natural body above the action of the physical forces that dissolve the organisms which belong to mere nature's realm. But whatever was the logic of the view, beyond all fair doubt, the Old Testament conception reveals belief in the soul's continuance after death. It is variously, but distinctly, woven into the representations in numerous places:—in the way death is spoken of (Gen. 15:15; 25:8); in the frequent use of the term Sheol (Hades, *under-world*), to denote the realm of the departed (Gen. 37:35; Deut 32:22; Num. 16:30; Ps. 55:15; Hosea 13:14; Ps. 49:15); in the declared results of death (Eccl. 12:7); in the prophecy concerning the king of Babylon (Isa. 14:9–17); in hopes expressed (Ps. 17:15; 73:24). The preparatory and national character of the Israelite dispensation, laying special emphasis on the law of righteousness and upon the blessings of piety in this life, included relatively small appeal to the future. Thus we find only this generic recognition of it in terms that are applicable to all men alike. For we find as yet no doctrine formally separating Sheol into divisions according to character. Only the truth of continued existence is held before the view. And yet, as has been clearly traced by Dr. Salmond, the view taught appears in so unique and self-harmonious a type as to show it to have been developed and held separate from alliance with any of the peculiar notions which surrounding pagan nations had made part of their *post mortem* idea, and thereby adapted to open out consistently in the completed conception of immortality as unfolded in the gospel. As a recognition of the continued life of all men after death, the view stands apart from all pantheistic conceptions of the soul, from all the oriental notions of metempsychosis, or of its pre-existence and transmigratory experience, as well as from the exaggerated notions of either the value or worthlessness of the human body found in Grecian and Egyptian thought. It was not a conception borrowed from adjacent or associated peoples.

In the New Testament the soul's natural immortality is at once made the underlying view of man's nature, involved in the question of his redemption and salvation. Christ taught it in His pictured experience of the rich man and Lazarus (Luke 16:22–31). He emphasized it in asserting His divine mission: "Marvel not at this;

Christian Theology

for the hour cometh in which all that are in the tombs shall hear His voice and shall come forth; they that have done good to the resurrection of life, and they that have done evil unto the resurrection of judgment" (John 5:28-29). He made it stand out from His affirmation of the judgment day (Matt 25:31-46). He charged men not to fear "them that kill the body, but are not able to kill the soul, but fear him who is able to destroy both soul and body in hell" (Matt 10:28). It abides as the constantly accented view of the soul, exhibiting the significance of Christ's redemptory work and the supreme moment of the interests involved.

(b) But though accepted as a truth of revelation, and thus adequately attested to our faith, it is one that, like all the other leading doctrines of the Scriptures, vindicates itself before the court of reason, and fortifies its claims to confidence. Indeed, it furnishes an illustrative instance of the completely rational character of the doctrines of the Christian revelation and their basal harmony with the universal truth of things. We can but glance at the points of reason's support in this connection:

(1) From the world-wide and ceaseless impression naturally carried in the soul itself. Out of all nations and tribes, from earliest historic twilight to the present, has come witness to human hopes and fears as to conditions after death. The prevalence of it has been looked upon as a *consensus gentium.* An idea that has been so normal to human thought as to force itself into some recognition everywhere and forever, must have some measure of validity.

(2) From the immateriality, simplicity, and individuality of the soul. Every effort to show, or make credible, the suggestion that the soul is material has broken down and refutes itself in its own absurdities. The soul, being immaterial, a simple self-conscious spirit, an absolute unit of consciousness, presents no elements of dissolution. We know, indeed, of no termination of the existence of a single atom of matter; yet material bodies, being compound or organized, perish. They come and go, through discernible processes of organization and dissolution. But the spirit essence or oneness does not come under any such law of ending. It is true that we may not take this argument as a full *demonstration,* since it is conceivable that a created being, of absolute simplicity of essence, might be endowed with only a temporary measure of persistence. God alone has absolute immortality—eternal self-existence (1 Tim. 6:16). The argument, however, remains of great rational force. For in creature being all depends on the will and endowment of God. It is normal to

think of a spirit personally created by God in His own image as in itself superior to physical potencies and beyond their dissolving reach.

(3) From the prophecy of the future in the human faculties. There is a wonderful educability in man. His psychological powers never reach a limit in this life. The soul's capacities for increasing knowledge and progressive development are still open and eager for more to the last. Sometimes, out of the body's weakness and torpor, the active mind has exhibited a vigor flashing forth the most penetrative and brilliant thinking of the lifetime. If man be not immortal, the destiny legible in his adaptations must be delusive, the seeming promise not meant to be fulfilled.

(4) From man's moral constitution. This has been known as the "moral argument." It involves such points as these: First, *conscience*, in its perceptions of obligation and sense of responsibility, impresses men everywhere with a conviction that their account is not wholly settled in this life. It points premonitorily to the future. Secondly, in fact, the rewards and penalties experienced in this life do not seem to be measured to men's righteousness or wrong-doing. An equalizing, or adjustment in another life, seems to be called for by the universal sense of justice. Thirdly, the two great ends for which, necessarily, our nature is conceived as meant, *i. e.*, character and happiness, are not found brought into unity or real coincidence in this life. The situation implies a future existence as needed to reconcile and accomplish the here unaccomplished ends of man's moral constitution.

Possibly, some persons may think that present-day science has, through "Spiritualism," brought scientific verification to continued soul-life after death. However worthy of investigation the problem of spirit-communication may be, through that means or a more general telepathic communication apart from physical presence, the results do not seem to justify much confidence or expectation.

The doctrine, however, has its supreme verification in the teaching of revelation. This represents it as a fact that God, in making man in His own likeness, constituted an order of personal beings whose value He places so high in His purpose for and with the earth as to be worth preserving through endowment with immortality. This lofty rank of created beings, lifted to blessed fellowship with Himself, forever stood for much with God—in His plan for the world. It was the ideal of Love's creative aim. And when sin came into the race, a contradiction and impairment of the value

Christian Theology

of immortality, the entire divine redemptional dispensation intervened for recovery to the true endless life for which the soul was meant. Thus the greatest phenomenon of the world's history, the incarnation, the redeeming self-offering of the Son in the heart of Christianity, reflects God's estimate of the work of maintaining this sublime endowment in the creature life made capable of knowing Him and sharing communion with Him forever. In such view we are beginning to get at the significance of the mystery of both creation and redemption, and catch stronger and better view of what constitutes true values. Christianity allows no place for the thought that man was made like the impersonal animal creatures below him, to live a period of sensuous enjoyment, and then, like them, cease forever to be. The earth cannot be conceived as fulfilling its divine intent simply as the theatre of this short-lived humanity, without Godward vision or fellowship, in material pleasures or in carnal aims, personal and national, the gains of wealth or wrestlings of poverty, the ambitions and clashings of tribes and kingdoms, battle and victory, or even as possessing and using its fullest powers of mind and sensibility, in science and literature—each one and all sinking in short time into the darkness of non-existence. A reason for building this wondrous world appears only when we get vision of man as a lofty being akin to God, with endowments and possibilities which have sublime value in His plan—of even supreme and eternal import in its aim, and worth preserving. And, as I have said, the unspeakable mystery of redeeming love repeats and forever echoes the reality of immortal souls in these mortal bodies.

III. STATE OF THE SOUL AFTER DEATH

Concerning this human fancy and invention have run riot. We are safe only in keeping close to the Scriptures, which assure us simply of what is needful for us to know, viz.:—

1. That the souls of believers at once enter into rest and happiness with the Lord. St. Paul makes absence from the body equivalent to presence with the Lord (2 Cor. 5:1–8; Phil. 1:21, 23). Lazarus was carried into Abraham's bosom (Luke 16:22). The penitent thief on the cross was to be with Christ in Paradise the day of his death (Luke 23:43). The souls of martyrs slain for the word of God are apocalyptically seen as present in the worship of heaven (Rev. 6:9). St. John tells of a voice from heaven, declaring blessed "the dead who die in the Lord," as resting from their labors and

followed by their works (Rev. 14:13). It is this blessing, in its all-comprehensive sense, to which Christ referred in assuring His disciples: "I go to prepare a place for you" (John 14:2, 3, 6), and in His prayer (John 17:24). These representations necessarily imply that these souls there, though without their physical bodies, possess their true personal consciousness, faculties of knowledge and enjoyment.

2. That the souls of the wicked and unbelieving at once pass into a state in which they suffer the penal consequences of unchecked sin. The rich man of the parable finds the fruitage of his life to be immediate misery. "He that believeth on the Son hath eternal life, but he that obeyeth not the Son shall not see life, but the wrath of God abideth upon him" (John 3:36)—*i. e.*, abides under the retributive action in which sin works misery. St. Peter speaks of it as a keeping "of the unrighteous under *punishment* unto the day of judgment" (2 Pet 2:9). Of Judas it is said, "He went to his own place" (Acts 1:25).

3. That the intermediate state differs from the ultimate in that it still waits "the full redemption of the body" through the resurrection (1 Cor. 15:53–54). Thus, though believers are truly saved, re-established in the principle of obedience and in spiritual holiness, there is yet a crowning benediction of redeeming love. And though the wicked are actually lost, there is a stage of advance through resurrection to condemnation.

Besides these essential truths some speculative theories claim notice.

First, the theory, which appeared as early as the third century, viewing the intermediate state as a state of sleep or unconsciousness, called psychopannichia, and opposed by Origen. It was revived in the twelfth and thirteenth centuries, but condemned by Pope Benedict XII., and the University of Paris. It appeared again among the Swiss Anabaptists, and was opposed by Calvin. Luther favored it, at least for awhile, as we find in his comments on "Abraham's Bosom," in Church Postel on the Rich Man and Lazarus, and also in letters to Amdorf, 1522. It has found supporters in modern times, in Wetstein, Reinhard, Archbishop Whately, Isaac Taylor. The article on *Hades*, in McClintock and Strong's Encyclopedia, approximates it closely. But the theory is in clear conflict with the almost essential activity of the soul, and its gloomy cheerlessness contrasts strongly with the Scripture statements of the gain of the Christian's dying. Moreover, the passages already quoted effectually confute it.

Christian Theology

Secondly. The theory of Purgatory, adjusted by Romanism in full topographical scheme, in which the whole realm of souls is divided into various receptacula. (*a*) On the opposite extremes it locates heaven and hell distinctly so called, the abodes respectively of saints and the damned. Christians who have reached perfect sanctification in this life enter at once into heaven. Unbaptized adults or those outside the Church are consigned to hell. (*b*) Intermediate between these two regions lie others, viz.: (1) The *limbus patrum*, where went the Old Testament saints, till Christ at the time of His descent into Hades went and delivered them, taking them to heaven and vacating the place; (2) The *limbus infantum* or *puerorum*, next to the former, for reception of all infants that die unbaptized, a place without positive suffering, but with no vision of God; (3) *Purgatory*, lying next to hell, where the great mass of but partially saved Christians, dying in the Church, go, and where by sufferings their sins are atoned for, and they are purified for heaven, and where, too, the prayers and money of their friends on earth, and masses said, may aid them.

The structure of the scheme is purely ecclesiastical, the Scriptures quoted for it (Matt. 3:2; 12:32; 1 Cor. 3:15; 1 Pet. 3:19–20, etc,) affording no warrant for it. Because of hierarchical abuse of it, to the dishonor of the redeeming Savior, and its falsifying of the way of salvation by grace, Protestant theology is compelled to continue protest against it.

IV. THE INTERMEDIATE STATE IN RELATION TO OPPORTUNITY OF GRACE
Progressive theology has for some time been contending for an advance in this direction. Natural, and much more, Christian interest in the countless multitudes of mankind dying without any knowledge of the gospel has impelled the inquiry whether their fate is closed with the earthly probation. Under the leadership of such devout and scholarly theologians as Bishop Martensen and Dr. Dorner, on the continent, Archdeacon Farrar in England, and the Andover faculty in America, the movement developed large prominence. It is urged that the theory of a *post-mortem* probation is tenable at least as expressive of the "larger hope" for those dying in ignorance. It takes the double ground: First, that the redemptive provision which God has made for all the race in Jesus Christ implies that the offer should be made to all. Secondly, that it would not be consistent to condemn hopelessly such as were never

informed of the saving love. Hence, it is alleged, no man will be judged finally until he has had a chance to accept salvation through a fair knowledge of the Savior. Concerning this middle-state probation, note:

1. It is made to apply, at most, only to such as have not had an opportunity through acquaintance with Christ to accept Him in this life, viz.: the heathen and such in Christian lands as have been excluded from a fair knowledge of the gospel. It has no place with respect to those who hear the call to salvation. It does not mean a *second* chance. It is not the doctrine of an *endless* probation, whether of ancient or modern universalism.

2. At best the supposed opportunity is an *unknown one*. The Scriptures have not made it explicit. No open affirmation of it is asserted by those who maintain it. It is simply claimed as a justifiable inference or corollary from the general love and consistency of God—while effort is made to show favorable light from special texts. The main passages used thus to support the view are:

(*a*) 1 Pet. 3:18-19. This statement is one of the most enigmatical in the New Testament. There are three difficulties in building confidently on it. *First*, the *time* of Christ's preaching to the "spirits in prison" is not clearly stated. From the days of Augustine, exegesis has shown a divided judgment as to whether it is to be understood as done between His death and resurrection, or in His divine nature, by His Spirit through "Noah, a preacher of righteousness," on the earth. It may be that Peter meant simply to identify the divine risen Christ with the same divine Being who had long been revealing Himself in grace in the Old Testament dispensation. To the question when Christ preached to them the answer may be: "When the long-suffering of God waited in the days of Noah as a preacher of righteousness"; see 2 Pet. 2:5; Heb. 11:7. *Secondly*, even if the passage refers to Christ as personally preaching in Hades before He arose (this being the most generally defended interpretation), it yet fails for logical proof by its being, not an offer of grace to those who never here had a call, but to those who proved disobedient under the call. *Thirdly*, there is no hint of its acceptance. If, therefore, there be such middle state opportunity, it is not commended to us for dependence, or for preaching, as the truth of gospel concern for direction of the living. "Behold, now is the accepted time; behold, now is the day of salvation." "Go, ye, make disciples of all nations" (Matt. 28:19).

Christian Theology

(*b*) 1 Pet. 4:6, "For unto this end was the gospel preached even to the dead, that they might be judged indeed according to men in the flesh, but live according to God in the spirit." But this, too, is at best of very doubtful reference, and probably "the dead," to whom the gospel was preached, were simply the believers who had already suffered martyrdom, or in other ways passed into the spirit realm.

(*c*) Subsidiary texts: Eph. 4:8-9; Matt. 12:31-32; Phil. 2:9-11; Col. 1:19-20. But no one, nor all of these passages together, give certainty to this inference of a future probation in Hades, or authorize the holding of it as an article of faith. It is surely not the message of the gospel as to the present duty of mankind.

3. Many Scriptures clearly point to death as the closing of human probation. Some of them represent the state of the wicked after death as *fixed*, as the parable of the rich man and Lazarus (Luke 16:19-26); the word to the penitent thief (Luke 23:43); the parables of the ten virgins (Matt. 25:1-12); the unjust steward (Luke 16:1-9); the pounds (Luke 19:11-27). Some of them mark out this earthly life as the time of probation (Matt. 7:13-14, 21-23; 16:25-26; Mark 9:43-48; Luke 12:4-5; 13:23-24; Rom. 2:5-10; Gal. 6:7-8; Heb. 4:1; 1 Pet. 4:17; 2 Cor. 5:1-8; Rev. 14:13). Some passages connect it with a "judgment" decision (Heb. 9:27; 2 Cor. 5:10; Rom. 2:5-16; Rev. 20:12; 2 Pet. 3:7; Luke 13:24-30). Over against such incessant affirmation of the present life as the period of human probation, there is not found a single explicit assurance of its extension to the intermediate state, or of a restoration beyond it.

4. A further check to over-confidence in the theory is the fact that the Scriptures seem to teach that the heathen, as well as others, will be judged according to the religious light they have had; so that on the basis of an actual atonement in Christ for the sins of the whole world, there will be not only a just but a merciful judgment which may accept even such as know Him not according to the gospel, if they have lived according to the light afforded them. Indications pointing to the salvation of some heathen may be traced as follows:

(*a*) We start with a concession of advantage in the possession of the gospel—"much every way" (Rom. 3:1-2). The Jews had much light; the Gentiles little. But advantage as to salvation has no logic for utter exclusion of all without it. (*b*) Such little light puts the heathen under moral responsibility and opens possibilities of *some* obedience to God. (*c*) Obedience to given light may show the obedient receptivity, under the Spirit of truth, ready to move into the higher obedience of faith, as and when truth comes. Such recipiency has thus, in a measure, the nature of implicit, though not explicit, faith. It seems to stand for the reality recognized by Augustine, "O God, my heart was made for Thee, and cannot rest without Thee"; therefore responsive to the light as God gives to see it. (*d*) God's acceptance of such seems to be clearly asserted, e. g., Acts 10:34–35. In these words of Peter a general principle is clearly drawn from a particular case, the heathen centurion, Cornelius. St. Paul elaborates the logic of the situation (Rom. 2:6–26), and opens to view a vision of the universal judgment which exhibits divine recognition of the sincere endeavor of pagan piety. (*e*) And linked with this view, illustrative examples are on divine record: e.g., Abraham himself, as reaching a divine acceptance of faith while yet in his uncircumcision (Rom. 4:9–11); Job (Ezek. 14:14; Jas. 5:11); Melchizedek (Heb. 7:1–4). These were without the gospel and the Bible, but not without God, even in their gentile privation. (*f*) The atoning value of Christ's humiliation and cross extends to "the whole world." "He tasted death for every man." The world is under a mediatorial probation, and all humanity sustains a different, and it may be open, relation to forgiveness and healing grace. Let it be distinctly understood that such heathen are not to be thought of as saved on the ground of their own virtue, merit, or righteousness; but because Christ is the propitiation for the sins of the world, such as have not heard of Him, yet "feel after Him that they may find Him," are counted as His. Dr. Christlieb says: "Scripture nowhere teaches that all who die without knowledge of the revelation of God in Christ are irretrievably lost It is one thing innocently not to *know*; it is quite another thing willfully to *reject.* The express doctrine of Scripture is that men will be judged hereafter 'according to their works,' and that the measure of such judgment will be the degree of revelation, supernatural and natural, vouchsafed to them in the present life." This basis and order of judgment, as appointed for the heathen, still further invalidates the theory of a probation in the intermediate state.

V. THE SECOND COMING OF CHRIST

The first of the great events that are to mark alike the close of the present dispensation of probation on earth and of the intermediate condition of the dead, is the Second Coming of Christ. We will find

Christian Theology

the essential truths on this subject by considering in order the *Fact* of this second advent, the *Time* of it, and its *Objects*.

1. The Fact is assured by manifold Scripture declarations. Our knowledge of it is only and purely of supernatural revelation. Announcement was variously made by Christ Himself (Matt. 24:30-31; 25:31; Mark 13:26; Luke 12:40; 18:8; John 21:22); and continuously repeated in apostolic testimony (Acts 1:11; 3:20; 1 Thess. 4:16; 2 Thess. 1:7-10; Heb. 9:28; Jas. 5:8; Tit. 2:13; Rev. 1:7; 20:1-15). This second coming must be clearly distinguished, as it is plainly different, from the subordinate and ordinary coming asserted of Christ in various Scriptures and leading on to that, *e. g.*, Matt. 24:3-21; 16:28; John 14:23; Rev. 2:5. "I will come again" stands prefatory to His appearance with His disciples visibly after His resurrection, as assurance of His redemptory work and saving power (John 14:18-21; Acts 1:11). The term *parousia* (παρουσία) or παρών (present) has different meanings and applications; and in Christ's mind answered not simply to a visible manifestation, but to that unseen approach or nearness in which He has promised to be always with His people, and comes to them in the working of their salvation and the progress of His kingdom. This invisible part is not less real than the visible. It is referred to when He says: "I will not leave you desolate; I will come to you;" "He that loveth Me shall be loved of My Father, and I will love him, and will manifest Myself to him"; "Where two or three are met together in My name, there am I in the midst of them"; "I am with you always, even to the end of the world." In the deepest and most essential sense the ascended Savior is an ever-coming and present Savior. Indeed, the entire doctrine of the means of grace and their personal and Churchly use, as outward media, rests on this truth—an ever-present Christ as well as a present Holy Spirit, working forward the redemptional purpose. There is not only a gracious, but a judgment coming of Christ, in which He is evermore appearing for judgment on sin and the salvation of believers. Sometimes these comings mark crises and epochs in the progression toward the consummation. But the second coming, distinctively so-called, marks the conclusion of the ordinary manifestations in a literal personal appearing of the Son of man. So the orthodox Church has always understood the Scripture teaching.

2. The Time of His coming. (*a*) *Relatively*, at the end of the world (αἰών, age, dispensation) (Matt. 24:3, 14, 30-31). His session at the right hand of God, as designative of His relation to His heavenly work of saving mankind, continues till the redemptory purpose

comes to the day of consummation (Acts 3:21; Heb. 10:12–14). The gospel must be preached to all nations (Matt. 24:14). His coming thus signals the general resurrection of the dead, the transformation of the living, and the day of judgment (1 Thess. 4:16; 1 Cor. 15:23; John 6:39–44). We are justified in accepting Dr. Julius Müller's statement: "It is the plain doctrine of the Scripture that the general resurrection of the dead, contemporaneous with the transfiguration of the living, is to occur at the appearance of Christ (the παρουσία) at the end of the world." (*b*) Of the time *absolutely*—how far in the future we are not permitted to know. "Of that day and that hour knoweth no man, no, not the angels which are in heaven, neither the Son, but the Father" (Matt. 24:37; Mark 13:32; Acts 1:7; 1 Thess. 5:2).

The only question to detain us here is whether the apostles expected the second coming of Christ in their day. Among German commentators the affirmative has been the prevalent view, followed by not a few in England and America. But as this representation amounts to an assertion that the apostles were in error on a great point of Christian truth, misleading to others, it ought not to be made unless required. A close view of the facts seems hardly to justify it. For (*a*) no one of them makes any positive or direct statement that Christ would return in their day. They everywhere assume the time unknown. See the texts last indicated. (*b*) Both Peter and Paul speak of their expectation of actually dying (2 Pet. 1:14; 2 Tim. 4:6; Acts 21:13; Phil. 1:21–23: 2 Cor. 5:1–9). (*c*) John, too, seems to have expected to *die*, and not to "abide" till Christ should come (John 21:21–23). (*d*) In 2 Thess. 2:1–5 (Revised Version) Paul corrects the error of those who expected an immediate coming of Christ, and puts the great apostasy of the "man of sin" as something that would take place before that coming. (*e*) The passage quoted for it, "*We* shall all be changed," in 1 Cor. 15:51, is not decisive. For in the same Epistle (6:14) Paul includes himself among those who should be "raised up." So also in 2 Cor. 4:14. The whole argument for the notion rests, indeed, upon this use of "we," speaking as if, with others, he would be living at the second coming. But the use of "we" on the other side, in connection with those to be "raised up," is just as strong in favor of the idea that Paul expected to die. And John, who lived the longest, seems specially careful to disclaim expectation of living to the *parousia* in verses 18–23 of the last chapter of his Gospel. The attitude of their minds seems rather to have been one of high and intense valuation of the given assurance of a divine Redeemer who had conquered death and was enthroned

Christian Theology

in heaven, but would come again for the full consummation of every believer. This truth was a living inspiration of their daily life. This accounts for their frequent reference to it.

3. The Objects of His Second Advent. These are fixed by its time. He comes to raise the dead and judge the world, and through these acts consummate the purposes and plan of redemption. Proofs are in texts already indicated. His coming looks, therefore, to the completion of the individual life of the believer, the fellowship of the Church and kingdom, and the transfiguration of the earth.

The only differing interpretation on this point is the Pre-millenarian, or Chiliastic explanation, founded on Rev. 20. Though indefinitely varied by different writers, from the early Church to the present day, this is marked generally by the following features:—(*a*) The immediate object of Christ's Second Advent is the establishment of a visible reign or kingdom on earth for a thousand years—the *millennium* (v. 4). (*b*) At His appearance He will raise the sainted dead, and only those, forming "the first resurrection" (v. 6). (*c*) With them and living believers He will establish a visible rulership, with Jerusalem as the capital. (*d*) During this thousand years both the Jews and the Gentiles will be converted. (*e*) At the close of this millennium, and probably after a final apostasy, the rest of the dead will be raised, and the final judgment take place. But this whole scheme, in the manifold types in which it has been developed, stands widely apart from the general Scripture statements which represent how the work of the first coming of Christ is to effect its great redemptive and saving aims, and accomplish the conditions for the consummation designed in His second coming. About the nature, means, and character of this movement, there is no ambiguity. It is a spiritual process, through the gospel message and the sacraments, the agency of the Church with its ministry and service, under the reign of the ascended Savior and the presence of the Holy Spirit, giving saving effect to the truth. The history of Christianity is witness to this as the order of the Divine plan, the ideal of this gospel dispensation. The Redeemer *is* the enthroned King, *has set up* His kingdom on earth, has "sat down on the right hand of God, henceforth expecting till His enemies be made His footstool" (Heb. 1:1-14; 10:12-13; Rev. 3:7-12; 1 Cor. 15:24-28). Through this order of spiritual work, under the invisible Christ's kingly dominion from heaven, with real but unseen *presence* in His Church on the earth, through His gospel and Spirit, God has appointed this dispensation, to its end (συντέλεια αἰῶνος), for His gracious providence, for the

Milton Valentine

salvation of men and the vanquishing of hostile powers. And it is significant that the pre-millenarian impulse has always been very largely an idea of inadequacy in the provided means for the accomplishment of the result. An unbelieving despair of success through Christianity's present equipment for its mission is not a good reason for the Chiliastic interpretation. In Christ's hand is all spiritual power in heaven and earth. The gospel is forever young, and Christ is both "the power and wisdom of God" (1 Cor. 1:24). No necessity can be shown for a transfer of Christ's throne to the earth, or increase of victorious power by it. Moreover, the Scriptures teach that He remains "in heaven" to the time for restitution of all things (Acts 3:21); till the subjugation of all His enemies (Heb. 10:12-13); till the day of judgment (Matt. 25:31-45; Luke 19:12-27).

This pre-millennial theory, though held by many distinguished writers from early Christian times, has never received Church authority or recognition in its creeds. The Augsburg Confession rejects it.

In discarding it as unsustained, how are we to understand the Scripture teaching as to a millennium? The word, in frequent use, has still an applicable meaning in Eschatology. It is legitimate as expressing the following features of Christian longing and expectation suggested by various Scriptures: (1) That by the power of the Holy Spirit, through the established means of grace and their missionary use, a period will be reached marked by a very general and victorious power of the gospel over the earth. This is promised in both the Old and New Testaments (Isa. 49:6; Dan. 7:27; Hab. 2:14; Mal. 1:11; Matt. 24:14; 28:18-20; Rom. 10:18; Rev. 11:15; 20:1-3). The apostle Paul seems to have expected, before the end, a flowering and fruitful time of the Church's life (Rom. 11:15-25, in connection with Matt. 24:34). There is no hindrance to counting the prosperity of Rev. 20. as but a part of the happy triumphs forecast by Paul under the normal and inherent consummating possibilities of the gospel. (2) This triumphant success will include the conversion of the Jews (Rom. 11:26-29). The long separateness of the once chosen people appears to index a preservation for a recovery to the spiritual issue of their original calling. (3) This period will continue about a thousand years. (4) Its close will be marked by some apostasy and violent conflict (2 Pet 3:3-4; Rev. 20:7-8). (5) The consummating action of the history of redemption will include simultaneously, or, rather, in immediate succession, the second coming of Christ, the resurrection of the dead, with the change of the living, and the general judgment, followed by the eternal state of the righteous and the wicked, and the new heavens and the new earth.

VI. THE RESURRECTION OF THE DEAD
This belongs to the completing of salvation. For the salvation is of the whole man—of his total composite being (Rom. 8:23). As this is purely a truth of revelation, and the fact yet future, we must be guided in our conception of it simply by the Scriptures. The words ἀνάστασις, ἐξανάστασις, ἔγερσις, translated "resurrection," are of closely kindred import with others that express the raising or rising of men out of their spiritual death in sin (John 5:21-25; Eph. 5:14). They are specifically employed to express the restoration of the body to life.

The truth of the resurrection of the dead is clearly taught in the Old Testament. It was, indeed, involved in its fundamental principles as contained in its distinctive teaching concerning God and man, and the intent of man's creation. Supernatural revelation assumes from the first that the composite human personality was a reality of great value to God. Redemption would not be complete without recovery of the twofold constitution of the human being. Implication of the resurrection of the body is distinct in Ps. 16:10, and the *idea* appears in the recovery of life in Ezekiel's vision of the valley of dry bones (37:1-14). In Dan. 12:2, it is clearly asserted. In the Jewish apocryphal books it is frequently taught. Unquestionably, when Christ came the resurrection of the body had become the faith of the Jews. Not of all, indeed; for the Sadducees or Essenes made themselves conspicuous by their denial of it (Matt. 22:23; Luke 20:27; Acts 26:6-8). In the New Testament, the doctrine at once becomes both fundamental and explicit in the teaching of the Redeemer and His apostles (Matt. 22:24-32; Luke 14:14; Acts 23:6; John 5:28-29; 6:40, 44; 1 Cor. 15:1-58; 1 Thess. 4:16; Rev. 20:5, 13).

1. Its organic relation in the order of salvation. (*a*) It is a triumph of the grace of the divine love over the work of sin. It is, therefore, distinctly and directly redemptory. (*b*) It is based on Christ's own resurrection and involved in it. He is "the Resurrection and the Life" (John 11:25). Having vicariously for us gone down into death, He has, by His victorious rising, opened the way of triumph over it to all who, through reception of Him, share in His triumphant Life. "Christ in" the believer, as well as Christ "for him," is the twofold explanation of His turning the abstract reality of "resurrection" into

Milton Valentine

His self-designation, "*I am the Resurrection.*" The spiritual resurrection from the soul's deadness in sin thus becomes guarantee of what Christ will be for return to bodily immortality. This, however, only explains the true believer's relation to the resurrection. *(c)* But there is resurrection for the wicked also—"of the just and the unjust" (John 5:28–29; Dan. 12:2; Acts 24:15). It is of the bodily resurrection 1 Cor. 15:22 makes affirmation. This is one experience linking every man with Christ, not contingent on faith, which unbelief cannot break. The question arises: How may we explain to ourselves this reach upon persistent sinners of this effect of Christ's work? The proper answer seems to be twofold: *First*, it seems to be normally included in the full redemptory provision for the complete salvation of all mankind, 'tasting death for every man,' and furnishing the grace of true spiritual life for every believer. "All things are ready" for the full immortal resurrection-life, and thus also for the true and sincere appeal of the divine Love to every soul to accept it. It is teleologic for the redemptive aim and goal. *Secondly*, the alternative result, the resurrection to condemnation, comes under the essential and necessary principle of moral responsibility for wrong-doing, and the rejection and abuse of the divine gifts of pure goodness. The soul that refuses the blessings of both creative and redeeming love fills itself with its own ways and eats the fruit of its doings—administrative justice allowing the reaping to go on in both the components of personality that have acted together on earth.

2. The Mode of the Resurrection. It is enough that our faith accept the truth or fact of it. But, as speculative theology has naturally formed different theoretic views of what it will consist in and how it will take place, it seems proper to safeguard the truth from misconception by most careful interpretative adherence to the Scripture delineations and suggestions. The mystery of the event is so profound, its presuppositions and effective force so supernatural as to make us docile to the divine teaching. St. Paul has himself raised the questions of perplexity: "Some will say, How are the dead raised up? and with what body do they come?"

(*a*) The power that shall effect it is God, in the Person of Christ (John 11:25; Matt. 28:18; 1 Cor. 15:22, 25, 26; Rev. 1:18).

(*b*) As to the body in which the dead will come forth, it certainly seems taught that the body raised up will be in some legitimate sense the body that died, the person's own body, not another with no connection whatever with his past, *e. g.*, Rom. 8:23, "Waiting for

Christian Theology

the redemption of *our* body"; 1 Cor. 15:53-54, "This corruptible must put on incorruption," etc. Our resurrection, we are taught, is prefigured in the resurrection of Christ, in which the body raised up was the body that died (John 20:20; Phil. 3:21). But what is essential to the identity meant—that an organ should be accounted the same to a person through such a transitional experience? There is given in natural science a suggestive principle—a reproductive reality moving through recreative forces. The body of the seed continues itself in the product. Two realities are involved—the same *life-principle* passes from seed to stalk—also the *same formative* principle, insuring to each its own body. These two being the same are enough to constitute the center of bodily identity. Not even a particle of matter that was constituent of the body buried may be used by the life-principle in the construction of the resurrection body. Yet the body may be our body. This conception is implied in the very illustration St. Paul gives of the matter in 1 Cor. 15:36-38, *i. e.*, the new grain out of the seed sown and dying. This gives a kind of identity, real and all-sufficient, yet far other than that of a recombination of all or even any of the particles of matter buried. The life-principle of the human person is in the immortal soul, and the Divine Omnipotent Power can work along that same principle to form for each again his own body. This relieves from the difficulty supposed to lie in the scattering of the particles of bodies to the four winds, or their incorporation into thousands of the dead, and also removes the necessity of thinking of the resurrection body as a gross materiality or in the form of literal "flesh."

(c) The resurrection body of the saved will not be a "natural" (ψυχῖκὸς), but a "spiritual" (πνευματῖκὸς) body, *i. e.*, not adapted to the natural life in the flesh, or the present mode of existence, but to the uses of the spirit in the higher mode of the heavenly world. Calling it "spiritual" or pneumatic does not imply that the new body's substance is "spirit," but expresses its elevation above the carnalized state in which it was a body of sin and death here.

(d) It will be like Christ's glorified body: "Who shall fashion anew the body of our humiliation, that it may be conformed to the body of His glory, according to the working whereby He is able even to subdue all things unto Himself" (Phil. 3:21; 1 Cor. 15:43; 1 John 3:2). Christ's resurrection body was the same that was crucified; yet how changed, spiritualized, etherealized. The attributes of matter seem to have disappeared in other exalted attributes in which His body became a perfect organ of the spirit.

Milton Valentine

(e) It will be immortal. "This mortal must put on immortality." The forces of death which sin put into the body the power of Christ's grace will put out of believers in the victory of the "power of an endless life."

The difficulties of thinking of a purely bodiless condition of the soul in the intermediate state and the seeming impossibility of intercommunication and fellowship in such condition, it is well known, have led many modern writers to seek modification of the Church's interpretation as generally framed. Recourse is had by such mainly to Swedenborg's suggestion of a spiritual body as already in existence in the present life, an inner enswathement of the soul, in which, at death of the outer visible body, the soul rises to immortality. It makes death and the resurrection essentially simultaneous. This theory breaks too thoroughly from the Scripture order and affirmations for acceptance as the Biblical doctrine. While the supposition of such a present dual embodiment of the soul may furnish some help for conception of conditions in the intermediate state, it is too remote from Biblical portrayal to be substituted for the great redemptive doctrine of the final resurrection.

In view of the difficulty of fixing the exact sense of the term "body," and the condition in which it is to be raised in the full actualization of redemption, and especially in view of Paul's declaration (1 Cor. 15:50), "This I say, brethren, that flesh and blood cannot inherit the kingdom of God," it is surprising that in the Apostles' Creed the word "flesh" (σάρξ, caro) should be found as expressing the faith of the Church as to the resurrection. For it is just the flesh that the apostle declares the resurrection shall *not* carry into the immortality of God's kingdom, *i. e.*, the gross material body as at present constituted. It is just in this extreme realistic way, we are taught, we are not to think of the mystery of the resurrection. It is "the body" (τὸ σῶμα) that is declared to be the subject of the divine revivification. The apostle stripped off all the materialistic grossness which the creed-makers put on. They probably were actuated in doing so by desire to safeguard against the gnostic efforts of their day to spiritualize the whole doctrine. But their well-meant aim brought them in contradiction with the apostle. To get the right idea, we must interpret the term σάρξ in the sense of σῶμα. The old English translation had the literal rendering "flesh." In 1543, in "The Necessary Doctrine and Erudition for Any Christian Man," set forth by Henry VIII., it was changed to "body." In the Interrogatory Creed, however, used at Baptism and Visitation of the Sick, "flesh" is still retained.

* 3. Modern rationalism discredits the doctrine of a real resurrection of the body by explaining the Scripture statements either as accommodations to the Jewish notions, or by resolving them into representations of a continued and extended or ascending existence after death. But such exegesis would explain away all the great truths of the Bible.

VII. THE GENERAL, JUDGMENT

As the second coming of Christ stands in immediate connection with the resurrection, so the resurrection does with the General Judgment. The following points are to be noted:

1. The *Fact* of it. It is a doctrine of the Scriptures, and rests only on their declarations. There clear and positive (Matt. 11:24; 16:27; 25:31-36; Acts 17:31; 2 Thess. 1:7-10; 2 Pet 3:7-13; Rev. 20:12; 2 Cor. 5:10).

2. The *Subjects* of it. All men without exception, together with evil angels (Matt. 25:32; Rom. 2:6; Acts 17:31; 2 Pet. 2:4; Jude 6).

3. The *Judge.* The Lord Jesus Christ All judgment has been committed to the Son. His theanthropic person and His position as Redeemer, one with us and one with God, fit Him for this office (John 5:22, 27; Acts 17:31).

4. The *Mode* or *Form* of it. We need to guard against taking in too literal a sense the symbolic and pictorial language in which it is stated. This is often highly anthropomorphic, drawn from the modes of human tribunals, with books opened and investigation conducted. The great fact set forth is that of an assigned recompense according to the deeds done in the body. But how far the drapery of such scenes as are used to set it forth may accompany the judgment, we cannot say; *e. g.*, the words, "shall give an account of himself to God," may mean simply 'shall be formally and actually held responsible before Him.'

5. The Judgment is *conclusive of all judgment for man and the world* (Rev. 22:11). It sums up and completes all judgment. It constitutes not the first passing of judgment, but the summation and manifestation of it. It ends the mediatorial dispensation, and exhibits its results. In a large sense, judgment is ever going on all through this dispensation, and at death particularly (Heb. 9:27). The whole movement is in harmony with the Scripture doctrine of sin and the

Milton Valentine

penalty of death as already an incipient and progressive action upon men; and the doctrine of grace, according to which believers already begin to enter into the joy of the Lord. The general judgment completes and exhibits it all.

The need or propriety of such final summation and manifestation is apparent from the fact that not at death, but often only after long years, or even centuries, do the full results of men's good or evil life ripen or close.

VIII. HEAVEN AND HELL

These two words express the issues or consummation of the dispensation of redemption. One expresses the positive side, the other the negative. They exhibit the results of the scheme and ages of grace with respect to the race. Note these two issues:

1. Hell expresses the negative side of the consummation. It seems that not all will be saved. With those who have not believed the present death in sin becomes eternal. The judgment according to the deeds done in the body exhibits the doom of those who neglected or rejected the great salvation. The term Hell (Gehenna) expresses:

(1) A *state; i. e.*, a state of endless suffering, which is sin's eternal punishment. At the basis of what constitutes Hell is eternal sin—a bottomless pit—the soul's being lost in sin, in bondage to sin's action and control forever. The beginnings of Hell are in the sinfulness and miseries of sin here. The deepest element in the wretched condition of the lost will be the confirmed, hopeless, ever-growing sinfulness of the lost soul itself—the wreck of all good powers from its constitution.

(2) A *place*. The Scriptures so speak of it. It is called γέενναν τοῦ πυρός and γέενναν (Matt. 5:22, 29, 30). Once included in ᾅδης (Luke 16:23); also, the "place of torment" (Luke 16:28); "lake of fire" (Rev. 21:8). Much of the Scripture language is highly figurative in describing its sufferings, and is not to be taken literally. See Mark 9:43–48; Matt. 8:12; Rev. 14:11, etc. To this *place* the wicked are banished by the decisions of the judgment day. The whole manner of the Scripture representations leaves no doubt that these sufferings as the punishment *from* and *on* sin will be unspeakably dreadful, though varied in degree proportionately to the guilt of each (Matt 11:22; Luke 12:47), and *endless in duration*.

Christian Theology

Hell is to be avoided not so much as a place as a state. To be *sinful*, lost in sinfulness, is the core of all the lost condition. It would be better to be holy, though in Hell, if that were possible, than to be wicked and in Heaven.

The doctrine of eternal punishment is denied, and its overthrow sought, in our day, by three distinct theories or modes of teaching:

(1) That *of universal salvation immediately at death.* It denies Hell entirely—all future punishment. The "death and glory" theory. This gross universalism, by its insult to the moral sense, is losing all hold on men. See Townsend's "Lost Forever," p. 391.

(2) The *annihilation*, or extinction of the wicked. This general theory varied:

(*a*) The *conditional immortality* view. This teaches that man is not naturally immortal, but that immortality is a special gift of God through participation in the life of Christ. To all out of Christ death is annihilation.

(*b*) The view which teaches punishment until the sentence of "second death"; *i. e.*, annihilation at the judgment day. A. A. Hodge's "Outlines of Theology," P. 583.

(*c*) The view that punishment for the sins of this life takes place in the intermediate state till the resurrection, the resurrection coming then to the wicked as a redemptive act, restoring them to a new probation, the failure of which, if there be any failure, must issue in the "second death" as annihilation. This is the theory of Rev. L. C. Baker, in "The Fire of God's Anger." See pp. 107, 112, 121, 131, 136, 142, 146, 149, 154.

(3) The theory of *Restoration*—a restoration of all at last after an indefinite purifying by punishment either before the resurrection or afterward. Origen seems to have taught this, "De Principiis," I. 6. Quoted for this: Acts 3:21; Rom. 5:18; 8:19–24; Eph. 1:10; Col. 1:19–20; Phil. 2:9–11. While these passages might be consistent with such a view if elsewhere clearly taught, they do not require it. Henry Constable sets forth this view in "Nature and Duration of Future Punishment." See New Englander, October, 1871.

Of the idea of annihilation, whether at death or subsequently, the Scripture teaching is clear disproof, viz.:

(*a*) All the clear passages which declare punishment eternal, everlasting, etc. (Luke 3:17; Mark 9:45–46, 48; Rev. 14:10–11; Matt. 12:32, etc.) Some say that extinction *is* eternal punishment. But extinction would make an ended, not an endless, punishment. Bibliotheca Sacra, January, 1889, pp. 126–132.

Milton Valentine

(b) The views current when the Savior and His apostles used such language make it certain that the terms they employed were understood, and intended to be, as meaning "eternal" punishment. For the doctrine of eternal punishment was held among the Jews, some disputing. See Bibliotheca Sacra, January, 1889, pp. 133-136.

(c) The Scriptures represent future punishment as a *continuous process* (Matt. 12:31-32; John 3:36; Jude 7; Rev. 20:10). The idea of annihilation is in open conflict with this presentation.

(d) The Scriptures describe the future punishment as *suffering*, which it would not be in extinct beings.

(e) The Scriptures describe the punishment as marked by *degrees*. Annihilation, unless after the future punishment, would make this an impossible characteristic of it. See Dr. S. C. Bartlett, in New Englander, October, 1871; Rev. E. P. Gould, Bibliotheca Sacra, April, 1880, p. 22; Prof. H. Cowles, Bibliotheca Sacra, July, 1878.

2. Heaven expresses the positive issue. This, too, stands for two things:

(a) A *state* of the soul. This state called "life," "eternal life," "salvation," etc. It is a condition of restored holiness and harmony with God. The beginnings of it are realized in renewed character, purity, and joy here. After death and the resurrection this holiness will be completed in the perfect recovery of our whole nature from sin and its positive conformity to God. This state is the everlasting "kingdom of heaven" to the redeemed. It will consist, negatively, in the absence of all sin, and, positively, in the perfection of our nature and the beatific vision. "Saints made perfect in light."

(b) A place (ποῦ). The redeemed being finite beings with bodies, they must exist somewhere. That somewhere for the redeemed is called Heaven (Matt. 5:12; 6:20; Luke 6:23; 12:33; 2 Cor. 5:9; 1 Peter 1:4; Rev. 5:6). This place, of course, in accordance with the divine order, must be adapted to the exalted and blessed state to which the ransomed have attained. Prom Rom. 8:19-23; 2 Peter 3:5-13; Rev. 21:1, some have supposed that this earth, when renovated, will be the place of the heavenly state.

In our conception of the heavenly state and place two extremes are to be avoided: *First*, that which holds it too much after the analogy of the present life. *Secondly*, that which disconnects it too broadly from this analogy. The tendency of the first extreme is to degrade its character and joys after material and carnal associations. Mohammedanism does this. That of the second is to break the normal relation of the present life with that to come as the true beginning and preparation for the future.

Safeguard against error in this connection may be found in recalling, as far as may be possible, what features will be changed in the heavenly condition and what will be continued. Thus the following changes will be involved:

(*a*) Sin and its consequences will be removed.

(*b*) Our carnal and corruptible bodies will be changed into "spiritual" bodies, with consequent changes in means and modes of subsistence.

(*c*) The new heavens and the new earth will take the place of the present heavens and earth.

The following elements are essential, and therefore permanent:

(*a*) Man's personality, as body and soul.

(*b*) His capacity for growth and knowledge—ever attaining fuller insight into God's works and ways.

(*c*) His memory, which will afford him everlasting possession of the past and enrich the treasures of his joys as a consciously-redeemed soul.

(*d*) The essential activity of his powers, by which he will continue to work and forever serve God's will.

(*e*) His social nature, which will make the heavenly work, service, and joy a real fellowship.

(*f*) Various degrees in capacity and attainment of joy.

IX. FINAL RESTITUTION

Together with the final judgment and consummation of the salvation of believers in heaven, while the persistently wicked are consigned to hell, must be noted the further attendant and involved events designated by this phrase (Acts 3:21). This is to be taken as expressing the entire change and renewal which the present earth and heavens shall undergo when the whole earth shall be made to share in the renovation, according to Rom. 8:21; 2 Peter 3:10–13; Rev. 21:1–14.

This restitution of all things in the new heavens and new earth wherein dwelleth righteousness, is not to be held as including the actual recovery of all moral agents to holiness, as that would be in conflict with the clear declarations of Scripture concerning the condition of lost men and angels, as already noted.

Milton Valentine

The question whether the renovated earth, after passing through the fires of judgment, whatever form that judgment may take (2 Peter 3:7, 10), with new heavens, shall form the abode of the saved, as the Church triumphant, must be left in doubt. Some so argue from the Christian "expectation" as to this "new" earth, as in verses 13 and 14, and from the fitness of things in making the triumph of grace and righteousness complete where sin so long held anarchic sway. But as this point belongs to unfulfilled prophecy, it is incapable of dogmatic proof.

www.ingramcontent.com/pod-product-compliance
Lightning Source LLC
LaVergne TN
LVHW051111080426
835510LV00018B/2002